From BREAD to WINE

CREATION, WORSHIP, AND
CHRISTIAN MATURITY

JAMES B. JORDAN

Theopolis™
BOOKS
AN IMPRINT OF ATHANASIUS PRESS

From Bread to Wine
Creation, Worship, and Christian Maturity
Copyright © 2019 James B. Jordan

First published in Rite Reasons 62-77 (February 2000 - May 2001) by Biblical Horizons
P.O. Box 1096
Niceville, Florida 32588

Theopolis Books
An Imprint of Athanasius Press

Athanasius Press
715 Cypress Street
West Monroe, Louisiana 71291
www.athanasiuspress.org

ISBN: 978-1-7335356-6-3 (softcover)

All rights reserved. No part of this publication may be reproduced, stored in a retrieval system, or transmitted in any form or by any means—electronic, mechanical, photocopy, recording, or any other—except for brief quotations in printed reviews, without the prior permission of the publisher.

Contents

INTRODUCTION: A Work in Progress — v
CHAPTER ONE: The Ritual of the Lord's Supper — 1
CHAPTER TWO: Priest, King, and Prophet — 11
CHAPTER THREE: From Bread to Wine — 23
   Bread and Cup — 31
CHAPTER FOUR: God's Life and Our Lives — 45
   How God Lives Within Himself — 45
   Human Life — 53
CHAPTER FIVE: From Three to Five — 61
   Three, Five, and Seven — 62
   A Double Sequence — 66
CHAPTER SIX: The Ritual Offerings — 75
   The Lord's Supper — 87
CHAPTER SEVEN: Death and New Life — 97
CHAPTER EIGHT: Repeating the Ritual — 107
   David, Adam, and Jacob — 108
   Jesus — 112
CHAPTER NINE: The Places of Trial and Suffering — 115
   The Patriarchs — 115
   Jesus' Three Testings and the Lord's Supper — 116
   Bible History — 118
   Our Lives — 119
   Suffering With Those We Love — 120
   Conclusion — 122
CHAPTER TEN: Journey to Maturity,
Part One: Leaving Home — 125
   Leaving Home — 126
   Rejecting All Change — 129

Ritual Applications	131
CHAPTER ELEVEN: Journey to Maturity, Part Two: Midlife Crisis	133
Biographies	136
Ritual Applications	140
CHAPTER TWELVE: Journey to Maturity, Part Three: Becoming Prophets	145
Biographies	146
Ritual Applications	151
Conclusion: The Three Crises	153
CHAPTER THIRTEEN: Genesis One:	
History and Biography	155
Sevenfold Covenant History	163
Sevenfold World History	167
God and Genesis One	168
CHAPTER FOURTEEN: Genesis One and Ritual	171
History and Ritual	172
Calendar	176
Biography	179
Christian Liturgy	180
APPENDIX A	
Christian Piety: Deformed and Reformed	185
Primeval Piety: Its Corruption and Restoration	187
The Deformation of Piety	197
The Reformation of Piety	206
APPENDIX B	
Twelve Fundamental Avenues of Revelation	99
Trinitarian Revelation	213
Three Modes in Four Spheres	214

Introduction
A Work in Progress

Liturgical Theology is virtually non-existent in Calvinistic circles in the United States. While work has been done by Reformed thinkers in France, such as Jean-Jacques von Allmen and Richard Paquier, for the most part theological reflection on liturgics is found only in Anglican, Lutheran, Roman, and Orthodox circles. Reformed liturgists, such as they are, seem content with repeating lists of dos and don'ts or with making historical studies. The works of von Allmen and Paquier have been made available in English, but from Lutheran and other non-Reformed publishing houses!

At this point in my life, I have neither the time nor the resources to write a comprehensive Liturgical Theology to present to the Reformed and Presbyterian world. (And how many would read it?) I have put out material piecemeal over the years. Peter Leithart, Jeffrey J. Meyers, and others, are also thinking and working in this area. Perhaps at some point a comprehensive study can be written and made available.

But I'd like to make a start now. Heretofore my publications have focused mainly on the traditional evangelical and Reformed questions, such as whether we may sing hymns, whether musical instruments are fit for divine worship, whether or not a church calendar is a wise pastoral device, the matter of icons and images, whether "ritual" is useful or bad, and what the rite, elements, and meaning of the Lord's Supper are. Here I'd like to move into something "larger," which is the whole question of the nature of liturgical action.

What I can bring to the table at this point in my own studies and development, are theological reflections on the interrelationship of God's inner life, human life, and ritual. I have done this once before, in my study "Christian Piety: Deformed and Reformed,"[1] where I show that the rite of the Supper is the same as every human action done by God's images. In the present endeavor I shall try to develop a bit more the beginnings of a Biblical Theology of liturgy.

Patterns of historical movement are of tremendous importance in the Bible. These sequences correspond, in various ways, to the order of the sacrifices, the sequence of the sacrifices, the ritual of covenant renewal, the biographies of individuals, and the course of human history. This series of essays reflects on aspects of some of the fundamental ways this basic contour of history is set forth in the Bible and how it is encapsulated in biblical rituals.

In short, what I am seeking to develop is a unified theological understanding of history, biography, and ritual.

The fundamental thesis that underlies these studies is that biblical rituals are not something strange or different from the pattern of human life, but that those rituals move through the same steps as human life and thus are designed to key us in to God's ways, His paths in this world. Sin has distorted the rhythm of human life, but the rituals in the Bible help restore our rhythm by duplicating human life in a small, short, compact, and stylized way. Just as the Tabernacle is a small, or microcosmic, replica of the whole cosmos, so biblical rituals are short,

---

1   Included here as Appendix A.

or *microchronic*, replicas of (macrochronic) human history and of human biography. Comparing biblical rituals with biblical history and biblical biographies should provide us with a better vision of how we can live our lives under God's guiding hand.

1.

The Ritual of the Lord's Supper

We must begin with some preliminary meditations on the ritual Jesus has left for us to perform, the Lord's Supper. This is necessary because unless we pay close attention to the details of this, the one prescribed New Covenant rite of covenant renewal, we shall not be able to understand its wider meanings—and as we shall see, those details are very often overlooked or ignored.

Baptism is not so much a rite as an act. One thing is done: Applying water while speaking certain words. Nothing more is part of the act. The Supper, however, consists of a series of actions performed in time, in a ritual sequence.[2] The ritual consists of two halves, two rites within the one larger rite. Taking everything into consideration, we find that

---

2 The two other "sacramental acts" prescribed in the Bible for use in the New Covenant time are unction, the anointing with oil for the sick, and ordination, the laying of hands (manual imposition) upon those being set aside for special service. While the

A. 1. Jesus took bread.
    2. He gave thanks.
    3. He broke it.
    4. He gave it to them.
    5. He commanded them.
    6. He identified the bread with His body.
    7. They ate it.
    8. They rested in it.
B. 9. Jesus took the cup, after supper.
    10. He gave thanks.
    11. He gave it to them.
    12. He commanded them.
    13. He identified the wine with His blood.
    14. They drank it.
    15. They rested in it, singing a psalm before
    they went out.

It is the progression of the two halves that are of interest to us at this point. But before we move to a consideration of that movement, we need to be very clear about precisely what the prescribed ritual is.[3]

The ritual is found described and prescribed in four places in the Bible. I shall translate these literally, using the numbering already provided.

In Matt. 26:26–28,
  1. And while they were eating, Jesus, having taken bread,
  2. And having said a blessing,
  3. Broke;
  4. And having given to the disciples,
  5. Said, "Take. Eat.

Spirit does move and act in the course of these rites, they are not ordinarily termed "sacraments" because they do not apply to every believer simply as a believer.

3   I should also point out that the fifteen numbered steps here are for the sake of this discussion only. If we cast our net wider in the text, we might begin with their reclining for supper, and end with their singing a psalm and going out, which would expand our list.

The Ritual of the Lord's Supper

6. "This is My body."

7. And having taken a cup,

8. And having given thanks,

9. He gave to them,

10. Saying, "Drink from it, all of you;

11. For this is My blood of the covenant, which on behalf of many is shed for forgiveness of sins."

In Mark 14:22–24,

1. And while they were eating, having taken bread,

2. Having said a blessing,

3. He broke;

4. And having given to them,

5. Said, "Take.

6. This is My body."

7. And having taken a cup,

8. Having given thanks,

9. He gave to them,

10. And they drank from it, all of them.

11. And He said to them, "This is My blood of the covenant, which is shed on behalf of many."

In Luke 22:19–20,

1. And having taken bread,

2. Having given thanks,

3. He broke,

4. And gave to them,

6. Saying, "This is My body,[4] which is given for you; do this unto a memorial of Me."

7. And the cup, in the same way,

9. After they had eaten,

10. Saying, "This cup is the new covenant in My blood,

---

4 A few manuscripts break off at this point and do not include the (second) cup or its words of explanation. For a full discussion and defense of the longer version, see Joachim Jeremias, *The Eucharistic Words of Jesus*, 3rd ed (Philadelphia: Fortress Press, 1977), 139ff.

which is poured out for you."

In 1 Cor. 11:23–25,

1. The Lord Jesus in the night He was betrayed, took bread,
2. And having given thanks,
3. He broke,
4. And said, "This is My body, which is for you; do this unto a memorial of Me."
5. In the same way also, the cup,
6. After supper,
7. Saying, "This cup is the new covenant in My blood; do this, as often as you drink, unto a memorial of Me."

Several comments on the rite are in order, since there are many errors in how it is usually done in most churches.

First of all, we notice that it is only after they had finished eating the bread that Jesus took the cup.[5] This is clear not only in the Gospels, but also in the rite as prescribed by Paul for the churches in his letter to the Corinthian church. This means that any mixing of the bread and wine, whether by dipping a wafer of bread into a cup of wine (as some Anglican churches do), or stuffing part of a loaf of bread into a cup of wine and spooning it into the mouths of the recipients (as some Eastern churches do), is a departure from the apostolic command and tradition (tradition, because Paul says that this is what he had received and was passing on; 1 Cor. 11:23a). Moreover, it implies that all present should eat the bread before all are given the cup, which strikes against the practice of serving both elements, in sequence, to small groups one after another (as is the custom in most Anglican and Lutheran churches, for instance). This is important because part of the meaning of the rite is that the entire congregation is knit together into one loaf

---

5   Perhaps it would be well to note at this point also that though the Bible speaks of the "cup" and not of "wine," the contents of such cups in the Bible is always alcoholic wine, fermented fruit juice. Preservation of non-fermented fruit juice was impossible until modern times. Moreover, the peace-inducing effects of alcohol are inseparable from the meaning of the cup. For more on this, see the essay by Jeffrey J. Meyers, "Concerning Wine and Beer," *Rite Reasons* (November 1996; January 1997), 48–49.

by eating the body of Christ, for the "body" is not only Jesus but also the Church (1 Cor. 10:17; 11:29), and then the congregation as a whole is sacrificed by drinking the blood of Christ.

Second, it is clear that Jesus did not identify the bread with His body or the wine with His blood until after He had passed the elements out of His hands into the hands of the disciples. Indeed, according to Mark, it was only after the disciples had finished drinking the wine, or at least while they were drinking it, that Jesus so identified it. Mark thus implies that there was a brief span of time between steps 12 and 13 as found in the Matthean account. What this means is that the bread provides Jesus' body and the wine His blood in the act of consumption. There is no hint of "consecrating" bread and wine before they are passed out, and this eliminates any kind of adoration of bread and wine as they sit on table or altar. It also means that any leftover bread and wine are nothing more than bread and wine. They function to transmit Jesus' body and blood only during the course of their actual consumption. The Bible clearly teaches what is called a "receptionist" view of the Lord's Supper.

Third, the Greek words translated "having said a blessing" (English: eulogy) and "having given thanks" (English: eucharist) do not imply any kind of consecration of the bread and wine. Both terms refer to prayers of thanksgiving offered to God, the former a blessing to God for His gift and the latter a thanks to God for His gift. There is no hint of calling down some kind of blessing upon the bread and wine, as if they are somehow to be changed into something else (whether by addition or transformation).

Fourth, the phrase "do this unto a memorial of Me," does not mean "do this in memory of Me." The rite is not, first and foremost, a symbolic sermon to remind the participants. Rather, in the Bible a memorial is an object or ritual displayed or performed to call God to remembrance. In Genesis 9, for instance, the covenant sign of the rainbow is established for God to see, so that God remembers the covenant, not primarily for man to see and remember (Gen. 9:15–16).[6] Similarly, in Acts 10:4, Cornelius is told that his prayers have "ascended as a memorial before God." The reader is invited to consult Greek and Hebrew concordances and trace down the usage of the relevant terms for memorials. He will find that they almost invariably are used with reference to bringing something before the face of God, especially when it is the covenant that is in view, as it is here.[7]

Fifth, this Godward emphasis is obscured not only when "do this as My memorial" is mistranslated "do this in memory of Me," but also when the eucharistic eulogy is viewed as some kind of blessing upon the bread and wine, some kind of consecration of them, rather than as a prayer to God. Both the prayers and the fact that the rite as a whole is a memorial show that the rite is not primarily a symbolic sermon, but a symbolic prayer. Now, as with all biblical prayers, it is also sermonic. We hear the words, do the action, and say the prayers, so that they are instructive for us also. The burden of the present studies is to explore the wider ramifications of the teaching contained in these rituals. But we must be clear that the rituals themselves are not primarily sermons, but prayers. In Christian worship, the Word and attendant sermon come to us from God, while the rite of the Supper is our response back to God.

Sixth, the fact, however obscured, that the ritual is a symbolic prayer has led some churches to serve the meal to recipients who are kneeling or in some other posture of prayer. Jesus, however, instituted this rite during a meal, and it is clearly a meal. It is a meal that is a symbolic prayer, and following the Lord's example, should be enjoyed in a posture appropriate for a meal. In our culture, this normally means sitting, in a posture of relaxation. The covenant is a sign of peace between us and God, and the meaning of God's giving us bread and wine is that we are seated with Him at His table. To receive the elements

---

6   In Revelation 4, the rainbow encircles God's throne, so that He always sees it, and only views the earth through its refraction. Compare Rev. 10:1.

7   Jeremias paraphrases Jesus' words, "do this that God may remember Me." For a full discussion of what a memorial is, see Jeremias, *Eucharistic Words*, 237ff.

in a posture of penitence is to obscure its meaning. In Christian worship, the time for kneeling and penitence is at the beginning of the service, when sins are confessed and absolution is received. Then we stand for praise and to hear the word of our King and are invited to "recline" at a meal.

Seventh, according to Paul, Jesus added the words "as often as you do it" to the drinking of the wine, but not to the eating of the bread. This does not mean that the second rite is purely optional, but it does imply that there are times when some congregations may be so impoverished that they cannot serve wine on a regular basis. On such occasions, it is proper to do the first rite, while leaving off the second.

Eighth, we can note that Jesus' explanation of the wine is more extensive than His explanation of the bread. It is the wine that is called the covenant, and Luke and Paul specify it as the new covenant. This is not said about the bread, nor is it said about the whole rite. As we shall see in the next chapter, this difference is accounted for by the distinction between priest and king, between the first and the final covenants. Bread is priestly, and priests live by commands. Wine is kingly,[8] and kings rule not only by hearing commands from God, but also by the wisdom of understanding. Thus, more explanation is given for the kingly part of the rite. And, since the kingly covenant follows the priestly, incorporating and superseding it, it is precisely the kingly rite that reveals the covenant, the new covenant, the final covenant.

The fact that the cup and the wine are associated with the new covenant raises the question of how this part of the rite can ever be omitted in new covenant worship. I suggest that the breaking of the bread is what "releases" the wine, as the centurion's slicing into Jesus' dead body released the blood and water from His side (see Chapter 2 below). Thus, when only the first rite is done, which by itself only carries us up to the new covenant and not fully into it, the new covenant is implied. Even if no wine is available on a particular occasion, the performance of the first rite carries the implication of the performance

---

8   As we shall see later on, the cup is kingly, and the wine is the prophetic advice given to the king. See chapter 3 below.

of the second.[9] This does not mean that the second rite is optional, but only that when it cannot be performed, God counts it as having been performed anyway.

We can compare this situation to that of Israel in the wilderness. During this time, the bread rite of the Tribute Offering (Leviticus 2) was the "memorial" of the bloody rite that preceded it. There was no wine rite until Israel entered the promised land, and that rite was prescribed in Numbers 15 as they approached their destination. Thus, to do only the first rite of the Supper implies that the church is, for that occasion, "in the wilderness." But if we are in the wilderness, we have already left Egypt, and our eventual entrance into the land is certain—even if it takes forty years for it to happen. Thus, while the new covenant is affirmed by the second, wine rite, it is contained by implication in the first, bread rite. Moreover, the addition of the wine rite in Numbers 15 points forward to the Kingdom era, which came about four centuries later. To reject the wine rite is to reject the promised land and the promised kingdom; but to be unable to do the wine rite on occasion is not to reject it. The believers will look forward to the time when they can again have both bread and wine, so that in such a case the temporary omission of the wine is in fact an affirmation of it.

Ninth, it should be observed that the command to eat occurs only in the Matthean account, while the statement that these two rites are memorials occurs only in Luke and Paul. The "words of institution" used in most churches are a mixture of the various accounts—even though many churches do not obey precisely what Jesus commanded to be done.

Finally, Luke's account of the Last Supper shows Jesus eating Passover and then sharing a first cup with the disciples, after which He institutes the Lord's Supper (Luke 22:13–20). The order, thus, is:

A. Passover Lamb
B. Cup
A' Bread

---

[9] If no bread is available, then the congregation is clearly about to starve to death.

B' Cup

We can see that the rite of the Lord's Supper duplicates and memorializes the events of the Last Supper. Luke shows Jesus taking the Nazirite vow not to drink wine again until His work is accomplished, after the first cup, before the institution of the Lord's Supper (Luke 22:18; Numbers 6). Matthew and Mark record this vow after the Lord's Supper, after the second cup (Matt. 26:29; Mark 14:25). Since Luke's narrative is fuller, we can assume he is providing fuller details, and that the other Gospels have condensed the events.

Since it is nowhere recorded that Jesus drank from the second cup, perhaps He did not do so, having already taken the vow. The "they" who ate and drank the Lord's Supper during the Last Supper are the disciples. Jesus had another cup to drink, given Him by His Father, before He would drink with them again; and the same seems to have been true regarding eating bread with them.

Now, this leads us to a fuller understanding of the sequence of events.

First Jesus recapitulates the Old Covenant rite, with lamb and wine. Then He takes the vow. He then gives the rite of the Lord's Supper, but does not share in it with them on this occasion. On the cross, He continues to reject wine until His work is finished, and then He drinks it again (Mark 15:23; John 19:28–29).

Thus, we have a threefold sequence, as follows:

    1. Summing up the old creation: Jesus partakes with the disciples:

        A. Passover Lamb at Last Supper.

        B. First cup. Then Jesus takes the vow, isolating Himself from the disciples so He can die for them.

    2. Fulfilling all prophecy: Jesus partakes alone, apart from disciples:

        A' Jesus as Lamb is offered ("broken") at the cross.

        B' Jesus drinks wine as a sign that the work has been accomplished.

3. New creation insertion into all of history, including the finished work of Jesus: Jesus partakes with all His new disciples:

        A" Bread as new lamb.

        B" Cup.

Such is the double rite that Jesus has left us, in all its details. With these detail firmly in mind, we are in a position to reflect on the wider meanings of the ritual, and that is the concern of the remainder of the chapters of this study.

2.

Priest, King, Prophet

Before we can begin to reflect on the biographical and historical meanings of the Christian ritual, we need to have an understanding of the roles of priest, king, and prophet, as these are set out in the Bible. This can be a problem, because various ecclesiastical traditions are bound to confessions and catechisms that give inadequate, and sometimes misleading or even erroneous, explanations of these terms.

We can begin with the phrase "prophet, priest, and king." This is the order normally heard from preachers and theologians. But it is not really the biblical order. The age of priests ran from Moses to Saul, the age of Kings from Saul to the end of the Kingdom, and the age of prophets from Elijah to Jesus. If we believe in any kind of development and maturation of the kingdom of God in history, we shall have to admit that king is more than priest, and prophet more than king. Since, however, the prophetic function is associated with predicting the future, it has often been abstracted from its historical context and placed at the beginning. At the same time, as we shall see below, the prophet does come at the beginning as well as at the end, so that the usual ordering of these terms is not so much erroneous as incomplete.

The Larger Catechism, produced by the Westminster Assembly in England in the 1640s and used by Presbyterian churches and some others, follows the order "prophet, priest, king." Let us look at what it says about them.

> **Question 43:** How doth Christ execute the office of a prophet?
> **Answer 43:** Christ executeth the office of a prophet, in his revealing to the Church, in all ages, by his Spirit and Word, in divers ways of administration, the whole will of God, in all things concerning their edification and salvation.

Now, as a matter of fact, these things are not unique to prophecy at all. According to Mal. 2:7,

> The lips of a priest should preserve knowledge;
> And they should seek the teaching from his mouth;
> For he is the messenger of Yahweh of armies.

This statement seems pretty definitive: What a priest is includes, by definition, bringing messages from God. As we shall see, that is not all that a priest does, but what is clear is that the catechism's definition of "prophet" does not go far enough. Moreover, the wisdom literature associated with King Solomon is also a revelation of the Word of God.

Jesus reveals the Word of God, thus, as priest, king, and prophet. So the catechism fails to tell us what is distinctive about Jesus' work as a prophet. As we shall see, what is distinctive about the prophet is that he is a member of God's privy council, and it is as such that he brings the decisions of the council to the people.

> **Question 44:** How doth Christ execute the office of a priest?
> **Answer 44:** Christ executeth the office of a priest, in his once offering himself a sacrifice without spot to God, to be a reconciliation for the sins of his people; and in making continual intercession for them.

There are two problems here. First of all, the answer seems to equate being a priest with being a sacrifice. There is much truth in this, but it is not enough. In Leviticus, there are three parties in every offering: the worshiper ("son of Israel"), the priest ("son of Aaron"), and the animal "(son of the herd").[10] Thus, priest and sacrifice are different, and Jesus' work as a priest is not precisely the same as His offering Himself as a sacrifice. According to Heb. 9:11–14, Jesus work as great high priest includes His self-offering for our sins, but being a priest is more than that, as we shall see.

It is correct to say that part of the calling of the priest is to die for others, to be a sacrifice. Israel as a nation of priests was under the laws of uncleanness (symbolic death), and thus was living under death so that the nations might live; and this calling is pointed in the Aaronic priesthood and ultimately focused in Jesus Christ, the great high priest. But it is also true, as we shall see in these essays, that the king is called to die.[11] Jesus died for us as priest and as king, so that we might become priests and kings. As the book of Hebrews makes clear, He dies as Melchizedekal priest-king, not as Aaronic priest only.

Second, intercession is not the peculiar duty of priests either, though it is one of his duties. In fact, Gen. 20:7, which is the first time in the Bible that the word prophet is used, defines a prophet as the intercessor: Abraham "is a prophet, and he will pray for you, and you will live." Certainly it is true that the men who are priests do offer prayers of intercession, but it seems that this function is more that of the prophet than of the priest. The prophet is not merely a servant, but a member of the Divine Council, and so bringing petitions before the Council is much more a prophetic than a priestly task. The catechism answer seems to transfer one of the special properties of the prophet

---

10 We take this up in detail in chapter 6 below.

11 We shall see that bread is priestly and wine is kingly. The breaking of the bread speaks of Jesus' death as priest, but when He says that the wine is His "poured out" blood, this speaks of His death as king. See chapter 3 below.

to the priest. Indeed, in 1 Kings 8 we see King Solomon offer a long intercessory prayer on behalf of the nation, as the nation's representative. Thus, intercession is not the unique quality of priesthood.

The priest is a servant, specially a palace servant. This is how he differs from king and prophet. We shall take this up more fully below.

The catechism's discussion of kingship is also problematic:

> **Question 45:** How doth Christ execute the office of a king?
> **Answer 45:** Christ executeth the office of a king, in calling out of the world a people to himself, and giving them officers, laws, and censures, by which he visibly governs them; in bestowing saving grace upon his elect, rewarding their obedience, and correcting them for their sins, preserving and supporting them under all their temptations and sufferings, restraining and overcoming all their enemies, and powerfully ordering all things for his own glory, and their good; and also in taking vengeance on the rest, who know not God, and obey not the gospel.

Since ruling or governing is a distinctive quality of kingship, the catechism's answer seems adequate. But there is an important aspect of kingship that is completely missing from this long list, and that is that the king must die. Jesus was crowned king, with thorns, and given a royal robe, and then He was executed with a sign over His head that said, "Jesus of Nazareth, the king of the Jews." Jesus did not die only as priest, but also as king, for as the greater Melchizedek He was and is both priest and king.

The fact that the king is called upon to give up his glory and "die" for others is overlooked in this set of answers, because of the notion that sacrificial death is associated only with priesthood. This is a significant error, which we must see if we are to begin to understand the biblical teachings regarding life and history.

My purpose here has been to deal with common and widespread misconceptions, not to interact with the more detailed and nuanced discussions of these matters found in the works of various theologians. Before we can discuss how the Lord's Supper relates to our lives, we have to understand how we grow from priesthood to kingship and then to prophethood, and in order to do that we must have a more accurate and fully biblical notion of what these three functions are.[12] To that task we now turn.

While we think usually of priest and king as two aspects of our lives or as working side-by-side in God's kingdom as officers of church and state, it is also true that priest comes before king in the Bible. At Mount Sinai, Aaron was made high priest, but we do not get a king (a "high judge") until we get to Saul. Thereafter, we have priest and king together over the Kingdom: ox and lion, Jachin and Boaz.[13]

What is a priest? Peter Leithart has shown that a priest is a palace servant.[14] Notice how Heb. 3:1–5 associates the Mosaic priesthood with being a servant of God's palace:

1. Therefore, holy brethren, partakers of a heavenly calling, consider Jesus, the Apostle and High Priest of our confession,
2. Who was faithful to Him who appointed Him, as Moses also was in all His house.

---

12 Readers who are still bothered by my objections to the catechism definitions can perhaps rest in the notion that the catechism provides stipulated definitions for use in Systematic Theology, while I am seeking definitions appropriate for the field of Biblical Theology. It is often the case that the use of such terms differs between these two fields. The words "election" and "regeneration," in Calvinistic Systematic Theology, have very particular definitions that pertain to the doctrine of predestination. But in Biblical Theology, we must remember that the Bible uses these two terms in a more general way: People who have been elected by God can reject their election and be lost; and people given new life, regenerated, can destroy that new life and be damned. Thus, we distinguish between the use of the terms "election" and "regeneration" in Decretal Theology, on the one hand, and in Covenant Theology, on the other.

13 See two of my monographs, "Thoughts on Jachin and Boaz," Biblical Horizons Occasional Paper 1 (Niceville, FL: Biblical Horizons, 1988) and "Chariots of Water: An Exploration of the Water-Stands of Solomon's Temple," Biblical Horizons Occasional Paper 12 (Niceville, FL: Biblical Horizons, 1991) for more discussion of priest and king in the Kingdom era.

14 Peter J. Leithart, *The Priesthood of the Plebs: A Theology of Baptism* (Eugene, OR: Wipf & Stock, 2003).

> 3. For He has been counted worthy of more glory than Moses, by just so much as the builder of the house has more honor than the house itself.
>
> 4. For every house is built by someone, but the builder of all things is God.
>
> 5. Now Moses was faithful in all His house as a servant, for a testimony of those things that were to be spoken later. . . .

Leithart shows that to define "priest" as president of sacrificial worship, or as mediator, or as sanctuary guard, does not do justice to the usage of the Hebrew word *kohen* (priest) in the Bible. Only the notion of housekeeping, of serving a king in his palace, is both broad enough and specific enough to account for the duties and characteristics of a priest. And, since the Tabernacle and Temple, as palaces of Yahweh, were symbols of the people-house of God's worshipers, the priest is a servant of God within that religious community. In fact, the biblical office of priest is virtually identical to that of pastor or minister in the New Covenant Church: He teaches God's Word, supervises religious meals, and organizes and disciplines the people for worship.

Servant is the key word here. The priest as such has very simple jobs: He inspects the animal brought for sacrifice; he helps the layman offer it; he inspects for leprosy; he does certain rituals in the palace of God; and so on. All of these are simple tasks and involve nothing but sheer obedience. The priest judges between right and wrong, between lawful and unlawful, between clean and unclean, between holy and common. Is the sheep blemished or not? It's a black and white issue. At the time the priesthood was set up, at Sinai, the Law was given, and again, when we think of law, we think of obedience, of right and wrong. It is simple: You either obey or your don't.

Jesus is not only priest but king. He is Melchizedekal priest-king. Thus, He is not merely a servant in the house, but the Son-king over the house. He does not rule the house as priest, but as king. And He does not die as a priestly servant but as a house-ruling king.

A king has a different and far more mature task. When we get to the Kingdom era, we get wisdom literature. Wisdom concerns not simple questions of right and wrong, but questions of timing. The priest has his times set out for him in the Law: the times of the rituals, the calendar, and so forth. The wise man must determine when it is good to speak and when it is better to keep silent.

More than this, the king must usually decide not between right and wrong, but between two evils. He must choose the lesser of two evils. Think of a commander in the field. He may have to send one platoon of men to its death in order to draw fire from the enemy, so that another platoon can circle around and destroy the enemy. That is not an easy decision to make. It is kingly, not priestly. An example of such kingly wisdom is seen when Solomon must decide between the claims of the two harlots in 1 Kings 3.

The king is not going to have such wisdom unless he learns the Law first. Wisdom builds on law, and king builds on priest. There must be a "priestly phase" of our lives, during which we learn wisdom through obedience and struggle, before we enter a "kingly phase" and have wisdom to give to others. As should be obvious, this is very similar to the relationship between childhood and maturity. As children, we obey. As adults, we have to make hard decisions. Bread is for priests and for children, while wine is for kings and adults.[15]

If a priest is an obedient servant, and a king is a wise ruler, then a prophet is something beyond this. In the Bible, a prophet is one of God's chief counselors, whom God consults before He acts (Amos 3:7; 7:1–6; Gen. 20:7; 18:16–33). The prophet is the mature image of God, now woven into God's fellowship as a junior partner in His Council.

Becoming prophets is a third phase of our lives, our eldership, when we have not only acquired wisdom, but have tested our wisdom through years of being "kings" and now have acquired the ability to pass on both law and wisdom to others, those coming after us. This is because we are mature enough to know how to pray, how to advise God; and thus, we are mature enough to advise others also.

---

15   Leviticus 10 forbids the priests to drink while they carry out their tasks, and priests never sit during their tasks, but kings are repeatedly shown drinking wine while they rest enthroned. See Meyers, "Wine and Beer."

Thus, the distinctive quality of a priest is obedient service. The distinctive quality of a king is wise rule. And the distinctive quality of a prophet is mediation and instruction, carrying prayer-petitions to the Council and reporting back the decisions of the Council.

Each is associated with passing judgment. The priest passes judgment according to the rules of the law: supervising the killing of animals and distinguishing clean and unclean. The king passes judgment according to wisdom, in the wider sphere of national life. But judgment is preeminently associated with the prophet, who brings judgment upon the whole culture, thereby ending one period of history and initiating the next.

That the prophet is judge and advisor explains why the prophet is not only the culmination of one phase of life and history, but also the initiator of the next.[16] Moses comes as the great prophet to tear down old Egypt and to set up the history of Israel, which then runs through priestly, kingly, and prophetic phases. Jesus comes as the climax of the prophetic phase, tearing down the old Adamic world and instituting the next (and final) cycle of history. The first prophet was God Himself, who set up first three phases:

Adam – priestly
Cain – kingly
Sons of God – prophetic

The culmination of the third phase was Noah, who prophesied before the Flood, and then initiated the next phase of history:

Abraham – priestly
Jacob – kingly
Joseph – prophetic

Moses was the culmination of the third phase, prophesying against Egypt and initiating the next phase of history.

---

16   I have discussed this in more detail in *Crisis, Opportunity, and the Christian Future*, 2nd ed. (Monroe, LA: Athanasius Press, [1994] 2016).

We can see the same kind of pattern if we distinguish the youthful prophet from the aged prophet. We see this in the book of Daniel. In Daniel 2, Daniel is able to advise the king and to prophesy the future, because God explicitly reveals the future to him during a night of prayer. Daniel is a very young man at this time. In Daniel 5, however, the aged Daniel is able to prophesy out of his own lifetime of experiences, without any special explanatory revelation from God. Indeed, the following sequence can easily be observed in Daniel 2–5:

Daniel 2 – Daniel as youthful prophet
Daniel 3 – Daniel's friends as true priests, who reject false worship
Daniel 4 – Nebuchadnezzar as king
Daniel 5 – Daniel as aged prophet, revealing the end of the old Babylonian age and the beginning of the new Persian age.

The flow from childhood (being under an older prophetic initiator), to priestly service, to kingly rule, to prophetic "divinity" as a member of God's council,[17] is not only the course of human history as a whole, but also is found in smaller time sequences within history. We could look at each of the biblical covenantal periods and see in them a general movement from a time of priestly service to a time of kingly action and then to a time of prophetic judgment and reordering.

The same is true in our lives. Not only do we grow from childhood to eldership over the course of our lives, but we pass through this sequence many times in shorter ways. Let us take an example.

1. *Initial prophethood.* The home computer is invented. This is a new thing, superseding the old: The older typewriter is now dead. You purchase such a computer. You have now entered into this new phase of your own life and activity. The producer of the computer provides you a law-book that tells you how to use this new machine. This is the prophecy uttered by the prophet at the beginning of this new phase of your life. Compare it to the books of Moses.

---

17 The word *'elohim*, "gods," is used in the Bible for those who are older, who rule with wisdom, as in Psalm 82.

2. *Priesthood.* You must obey the book. You must learn how to use the computer. Probably others will help instruct you, and you will be asking them for advice. During this period of time, you are under such tutors and governors, as a "servant" learning how to use the computer.

3. *Kingship.* Gradually you become able to use the computer yourself. You begin to learn more, by trial and error rather than by consulting authorities. Of course, if you actually disobey the law found in the book, you will not be successful with your computer. Still, because you have internalized the law, you don't have to consult the book as often, nor do you have to ask advice as often. Also, you gradually become sensitive to what the computer can and cannot do. This is wisdom, the sensitivity to the situation that comes from experience.

4. *Prophethood.* After much time of using the computer, you become able to instruct others. You become one of the advisors, consulted by other people who have just bought their first computer. Moreover, you can also advise the "god" who made the computer. You can send the company email messages with advice on how to make the computer better. If they are wise, they will take your experience and advice into consideration.

Notice that you don't cease to be a priest when you become a king. The rule book is still there, and occasionally you have to go back and consult it. The rules still govern how you use the computer, and you'd better not depart from them. Similarly, you don't cease to be a priest and king when you become a prophet. You still use your own computer, even though you are also advising others how to use theirs and advising the maker how to make things better in the future.

We can go through the same sequence looking at the activity of baking a cake. The first time you make a bundt cake, you need to open the book and follow the rules very carefully. After a while, you become more kingly in how you make the cake: You begin to experiment a little, trying a bit more of this and a bit less of that, adding a certain spice, and so on. Through trial and error, you acquire wisdom about making a bundt cake. Then, when people praise your cake as especially good, you can write down the recipe for them and instruct them in how to make one. You can even write to the publisher of the cookbook with your new ideas.

From these two examples, which could be multiplied billions of times, we can see that the passage from priest to king to prophet is not something distinctively "religious," but is in fact the essence of human life and growth. We are moving through these phases all the time, not only in small ways, but also in the larger course of our entire lifespan.

This is part of what it means to be an image of God. The image of God passes through these three stages, and the three phases have much to do with the Trinity, as we shall see in later essays. And since all men and women are by definition images of God, all human beings move through these phases, for better or for worse.

Because of sin, human beings apart from grace are bad priests, bad kings, and bad prophets. As bad priests, they are disobedient and rebellious. As bad priests, they don't follow the rule book. They buy a computer, plug it in, and then start messing with it. They may learn a few things, but they resent having to obey the book. Also, as bad priests, they are not willing to be learners for a time. They move right away into the trial-and-error phase that should come later, and often blab away their opinions to others, trying to be prophets to them when they have little useful to impart.

As bad kings, they rule poorly. Because they refused to serve, they don't know how to rule well. Our computer analogy does not help us much here, but the reader need only think of the multitudes of bad kings, owners, and managers that have afflicted human history.

As bad prophets they give bad advice and set in motion evil trends that move history in the wrong direction. We need only think of the many older people who are not elders, but only bitter and self-centered old people.

The meaning of Jesus' perfect human life is not only that He came to die for our sins, but also that He gives to us His perfect life. He gives it to us not so much as a model, for we do not in fact do the same things Jesus did, but as a type. A type is a deep-pattern impressed into us by the Holy Spirit. We are placed in union with Jesus, and the deep-pattern of His life is given to us. By eating His body and drinking His blood, we are restored and renewed so that we can move properly through these three phases of life.

We are now ready to begin to consider how the Lord's Supper reveals this course of life for us.

3.

From Bread to Wine

We can now begin to consider the rite in its larger meaning as a display of history and biography. To begin with, in the Bible, bread (and beer, usually translated "strong drink," liquid bread made from grain) is priestly and wine is kingly and prophetic. Bread comes first and wine later. Bread is alpha food while wine is omega food. You eat bread in the morning and drink wine at night. Bread is suitable for children while wine is for adults. The grain harvest precedes the grape harvest; Pentecost comes before the Feast of Booths. The Tribute Offering uses bread in the wilderness, and has wine added once the promised land is reached. Bread is made quickly, but wine takes much longer to ferment and mature.[18]

---

18   These associations have been explored at length in Meyers, "Wine and Beer."

The entire Old Creation, the childhood of humanity (Galatians 4), is the time of bread, while the New Covenant, our maturity in Christ, is the time of bread and wine. Between the two comes the breaking of the bread, the death of Jesus Christ. Jesus comes as priest, not as king. He refuses to act as king and divide peoples' inheritances. Instead, He professes to be doing nothing more than obeying His Father. In this regard, it is as priest that He dies, and then ascends to be enthroned.

Thus, the sequence of our ritual recapitulates the whole of human history and reinserts us into God's historical plan as He renews the covenant with us sinners Lord's Day after Lord's Day. God's plan is done before His face, and thus our ritual is a memorial, a form of prayer, done before His eyes. It shows us not only the contour of life and history, but also that life and history are under Him.[19]

The Old Creation is a time during which the loaf of bread is formed. Humanity is formed up to a certain point, and then is broken, in Jesus. Biblical bread (that is, the symbolic bread of Leviticus 2) is made by adding together flour, water, oil, salt, and sometimes leaven. Various elements are combined together through the "salt of the covenant" (Lev. 2:13), and these elements can be seen to represent the human race: Israelite and Gentile, man and woman, with the Spirit.

If the "bread" consists only of oil mixed with flour and salt, it is not baked over fire; but as we shall see in a moment, the inclusion of salt speaks of fire and baking. Baking puts the formed loaf into the fire and completes the bread-making. All the elements are transformed by the heat into something new.

Now, what I have just described is a sequence: Form the loaf and then bake it. But in fact, salt represents fire in the Bible, and the inclusion of salt is the beginning of the baking process for that reason. Thus, the making and baking of the loaf should be seen as going on

---

[19] Romans 11 uses the analogy of the olive tree, which is the history of the covenant. We are plugged into that history, so that it becomes our history.

at the same time. This is made clear by the fact that the first form of "bread" discussed in Leviticus 2 consists only of flour, oil, and salt. The salt is the essential part of the baking; actual fire is optional.[20]

Moreover, every form of bread found in Leviticus 2 is broken, by being divided into the part burned up as a memorial to Yahweh and the part left for the priests.

Jesus is formed as The Loaf at His baptism, the climax of human development up to this point in history. Then He is broken. Though no bone of His personal body was broken, we see the breaking of the bread in the fact that as Jesus died the veil of the Temple was rent (Matt. 27:50–51). The removal of the veil means that there is now full access to God, but the veil might simply have fallen. Its being ripped in half signifies the first half of the curse of the covenant, which is to be ripped in half and devoured by the birds and beasts (Genesis 15). Ripping bread in half has the same meaning. Both rippings speak of Jesus' taking the curse on Himself for us—its first part, because He was not left to be eaten by birds. He died, but was not destroyed. His death is like that of believers, not like that of the wicked, who both die and are "destroyed" in hell.[21]

Perhaps more importantly, Jesus' "body" was the body-politic of Himself and His disciples, which was built up starting after His baptism. Their abandonment of Him in the garden of Gethsemane was

---

20 Mark 9:49 reads: "For everyone will be salted with fire, and every sacrifice is salted with salt." (The second half is not found in some manuscripts, but it has many witnesses in favor of it and there is no scholarly consensus.) The fiery taste of salt speaks for itself. Salt is not a symbol of preservation or of destruction as such, but is a symbol of the fire of the Spirit, baking God's people and destroying His enemies. The "salt of the covenant" speaks of the Spirit, who is the bond of our covenant with Jesus.

21 Medieval pictures of demons eating people in hell are not without symbolic foundation in the Bible. Not only did the dogs eat Ahab and Jezebel, and not only do the vultures gather to devour the wicked, but the primeval serpent is cursed in Genesis 3 to eat the dust, and we have to recall that in Genesis 2, man is made of dust. Unless sinful dusty man is made into something new by redemption, he will be eaten by Satan. Christian artists have not intended that their pictures of hell be taken literally, of course, but as displaying the biblical symbolism.

the rending of this body, the breaking of the loaf. Notice that after this "priestly death," Jesus is crowned and robed as a king by the soldiers and crucified as "the king of the Jews," so that the crucifixion is more His kingly than His priestly death.

Immediately after Jesus died, the centurion pierced His side so that blood and water flowed out (John 19). The blood and water are signified by the wine of the Supper, which is given to us after the bread is broken. The breaking of the bread, so to speak, releases the wine.

As mentioned, wine speaks of kingship and maturity, but in that the wine is also blood, it speaks also of suffering and death. As the book of Revelation shows us, we overcome by being ready to suffer for Jesus' sake. His blood enables us to be suffering kings, for he who would be great in the Kingdom must be least of all. Jesus' Kingdom will gradually cover and transform the world, but those glories will always be rooted in humility. The fact that we as kings must die points forward to the end of history, as predicted in Revelation 20, when there is a final attack by Satan upon the Church, a final tribulation.

As the course of history is encapsulated in our ritual, so is the course of human life. In the first part of our lives, God adds things into us, making us into a loaf. We learn things from our parents, teachers, and supervisors, and acquire a wife and children.

In our lives, however, there is always some kind of midlife crisis, when we are broken and our lives seem to fall apart. For women, this is focused in menopause. For men it often means a sense that one's life is not amounting to anything. The difficulty may be wholly internal, or it may be accompanied with outward affliction. Often people feel deserted by God as they go through this experience, as Jesus felt deserted on the cross. It is a real form of death, an experience of separation from God.

Those who have been through this experience, provided they don't leave their wives and reject the faith, become elders. Their lives become more influential than ever before, even though they often don't realize it. They move from the bread-time of life, the first phase, to the wine-time of life.

Finally, however, the wine is poured out. The Christian dies as a libation to God, and in that death our influence spreads one last time (Phil. 2:17 and 2 Tim. 4:6). Those left behind remember what we stood for and are moved to represent us and our concerns to others, since we are no longer present to do so.

We have set forth two simple sequences, in biography and history. In the first part of our lives we are like priests, obedient servants of our parents, teachers, and employers. Various things are added into our lives, and we become a loaf. Then we are broken, and we come out with wisdom, beginning the eldership or kingly phase of our lives. Similarly, the Old Covenant is a time of law and bread-forming, followed by the breaking of Jesus in the central crisis of history, and then by the enthronement of the Church with Jesus and a time of kingly sacrificial service.

With this simple structure in mind we must now modify this scheme just a bit.

Consider biography first of all. Long before we go through our midlife crisis, we have begun to have wisdom and to make hard decisions. We do start out as children, as priests, with bread alone, but the wine of wisdom begins to come into our lives before the crisis. In our 20s and 30s we begin to learn wisdom. After the crisis, we still have to obey, even though eldership means we are primarily manifesting wisdom.

History shows the same. Israel was a priestly/law/bread nation for 400 or so years before she became a kingly/wisdom/wine nation. But she did move into this preliminary kingly/wisdom/wine status before Jesus came and brought the great change in history.

Similarly, Jesus starts out simply as a priest. He is baptized and soon preaches the Sermon on the Mount, a very legal address. But as time moves along, we get more "wisdom" in the form of parables. And Jesus allows Himself to be proclaimed a king six days before His crucifixion.

Thus, though Jesus comes in the middle of history, His life encapsulates the whole of history, both its priestly and kingly phases. His death is not only a breaking of bread, but also an outpouring of wine, of His blood (Luke 22:20). He dies at the age of 33 or so, in the middle of His life, and so the breaking of bread may be seen as the more prominent aspect of His death. But by anticipation, He is also dying at the "end" of a full human life, at the age, so to speak, of seventy or eighty years (Ps. 90).

Our ritual applies both of these kinds of death to us, and in the same sequence. First the veil was ripped in half, and then the blood was poured out from Jesus' side. First the priestly community of the disciples with Jesus was ripped apart, and then Jesus died as king, pouring out His blood-wine. The first points backward over the first half of human history, summing up the Old Creation, while the second points forward to the second half of human history, summing up the New Creation.

Similarly, the Supper speaks of both halves of our lives. Whether we are one year old or one hundred, it points backward to our bread time and forward to our wine time. Each time we do it, we affirm that we are being broken, and that we will at the end be poured out. But more than this: Paul speaks of his being poured out before he actually dies (Phil. 2:17 and 2 Tim. 4:6). The full outpouring comes at the final end, at physical death; but the meaning of that outpouring is applied to and manifested in us before we reach the end, and that is what makes us prophets. The breaking of the bread speaks of our transition from priests to kings, and the outpouring of the wine speaks of our transition from kings to prophets.

Thus, the rite of the Supper also points to this third phase of our lives. In a sense, the third, prophetic phase of life and history is an amplification of the kingly phase, as the kingly phase of life is an amplification of the priestly phase. While serving as priests, we learn how to be kings; and then we are broken so that we can become kings. While serving as kings, we learn how to be prophets; and then we are poured out so that we can become prophets.

In the history of Israel, the transition from the priestly Mosaic time to the kingly Davidic time consisted of the Tabernacle's being ripped in half. Between Eli and Solomon, the Holy of Holies was located in one place and the Holy Place in another. The Tabernacle was a symbol of Israel as God's people-house, and its being rent in half is equivalent to the breaking in half of the body-politic, the bread, of Israel.

The transition from kingly times to prophetic times came when the Temple was completely torn down and taken into exile. The Temple was poured out. And as the Temple was, again, a symbol of the body-politic of Israel, its being poured out represented the people's move into exile. God's people became prophets, moving from ruling one nation to being involved in the rule of the entire "world" as that world was set up in Daniel 2 and 7. They became advisors to the emperors; and the first of these advisors was one of the very first men taken into exile: Daniel.

Now, both the period from Eli to Solomon and the period in Babylon are associated with the wilderness period between Egypt and the Promised Land. It is clear in Jeremiah that Judah and Jerusalem are Egypt, and that moving to the safety of Babylon (under Daniel's protection) is a move out of Egypt. With the coming of Cyrus seventy years later, the people left that wilderness and moved into the new Promised Land, which was not only the land of Canaan but the entire imperial oikumene. The period from Eli to Solomon, during which Israel was delivered from Philistia (Egypt: Gen. 10:13–14) is the same kind of wilderness passage.

The first of these "death" experiences consisted of the breaking of the body-politic that had been formed at Sinai. The second consisted of the pouring out of the new kingly body-politic into a wider world.

With this type in mind, we can see Jesus' death in two phases. To be sure, His death on the cross was total, involving priestly, kingly, and even prophetic aspects. But from the perspective we are discussing here, Jesus' priestly death came when He was cut off from His body-politic and left alone in Gethsemane. Then He was made king, and then He was poured out as King on the cross. This outpouring is the beginning of the prophetic phase of His life, and we who drink His blood are those sent forth into all the world as prophets.22

Thus, the ritual of the Supper, by making us priests and kings, also makes us prophets, since the prophet is a combination of the two in a more mature, larger way. We are made priests/kings/prophets in a world that is even larger than the empires set up in Daniel 2 and 7.

We can see the prophetic phase as part of the overall ritual if we consider that the ritual ends, and we are sent out. The rites make us priests and kings, through bread and wine, and then the rites kill us twice, through the broken body and outpoured blood of Jesus. Twice dead, we are now raised to the fullness of prophetic life and sent out to carry this with us, as prophets, into the wider world. It is the sending forth, the commissioning and dismissal with which the Supper and the whole worship service end, that speaks of our being prophets, for we are sent forth to "disciple the nations."

The prophet is not called to die, for he has already died twice and is now a mature image of God, a member of the Divine Council. Jesus died as priest to become king, and He died as king to be seated at God's right hand as His chief prophetic counselor, as well as king and great high priest.23 His double death is given to us, so that now all the people are prophets (Num. 11:29; Acts 2:17–18).

Much more could be written on this, but this is enough to illustrate the point that ritual, history, and biography follow the same pattern. As we proceed, we shall investigate the many rituals of the Old Creation as these provide many and varied instances of this general point. With these in mind, we shall be able to say much more about the infinite implications of the simple rite of the Lord's Supper.

---

22 The wilderness period is the time of the Apostolic Age, from Pentecost to the destruction of Jerusalem in AD 70.

23 Indeed, the ascension should be linked more with Jesus' assumption of prophetic office than with His assumption of kingly office. Jesus was king primarily on the cross.

BREAD AND CUP

We must now investigate the use of the word "cup" for the wine. I suggest that the cup itself corresponds to the firmament shell between heaven and earth and that the liquid in the cup corresponds to the waters above the firmament. The bread is earthly; the wine is heavenly; and the cup is between.

Before Jesus' ascension into heaven, no human being went into the highest heavens. Departed saints lived in "paradise" (Luke 23:43), "Abraham's bosom" (Luke 16:22–23), "under the altar" (Revelation 6). They were in the nice part of sheol, but not in heaven. Now the saints are positioned in the heavenlies, in the highest heavens, where Jesus is enthroned.

During the former time of history, the saints fought earthly enemies. But now we fight not only against flesh and blood, but also against principalities and powers in heavenly places. In the New Creation, the saints engage in warfare both on earth and in the heavens, through prayer. "Resist the devil, and he will flee from you," we are told (James 4:7).

We have looked at the progression from bread to wine as a progression from priest to king and prophet, from Old Creation to New Creation. It is also a progression from lower to higher, from earthly to heavenly, and this can be seen especially when we consider that now all the people are prophets (Acts 2) and that the prophet is a member of the heavenly Divine Council, which back in the days of Job consisted only of God and the angels.[24]

What of the cup, then? Jesus might have "taken wine" and given it, but He is said to have taken the cup. We find in 1 Kings 7:26 that the brim of the great Bronze Sea was "made like the brim of a cup" (compare 2 Chron. 4:5). Now the Bronze Sea, like its associated ten

---

24 Specifically, the ascension of the saints to thrones in heaven, as enthroned prophetic advisors to The Throne, came in AD 70. For a discussion, see my *The Vindication of Jesus Christ: A Brief Reader's Guide to Revelation* (Monroe, LA: Athanasius Press, [1999] 2009) and the discussion of Daniel 7 in my *The Handwriting on the Wall: A Commentary on the Book of Daniel* (Powder Springs, GA: American Vision, 2007).

Water Chariots and the earlier Tabernacle's Laver of Cleansing, represents the firmament, and its waters represent heavenly waters. In all three cases, the cup is held off the ground on a pedestal, on which it rests as a separate item. Water had to be taken up and dumped into it, and then the priests had to climb ladders again and get the water out of it and bring it back down. This seemingly pointless and tiresome activity recapitulates the work of the second day of creation. The water is taken up into a firmament and then "rains" back down as baptismal waters from above.[25]

The association of these laver-firmaments with cups is all we need understand to see that the cup of the Lord's Supper speaks of the firmament and its contents speak of heavenly contents. If eating the bread reunites us with the earth and with our priestly earthly calling, drinking the wine unites us with heaven and with our heavenly kingly and prophetic callings.

We can go further with this symbolic consideration. Jesus poured out His blood while He was held up off the ground on the cross. Jesus is the firmament mediator between heaven and earth. His body is the cup, and His blood is the wine in the cup, poured out as the new covenant, as the heavenly phase of the covenant.[26] In terms of this, we again consider the breaking of the bread as the abandonment of Jesus by His disciples, since the loaf represents the community as well as the individual body of Jesus. The bread is broken when Jesus is abandoned by the rest of His body. After this priestly death, He is crowned with thorns and given a royal robe as king by the soldiers and elevated to the cross-throne. Then the blood-wine is poured from the cup of His crucified body.

If we arrange these items spatially, the bread is of the earth, Jesus on the cross is of the firmament between heaven and earth, and Jesus' blood is of the highest heavens, the waters above the firmament.

---

25   See my monograph, "Chariots of Water."

26   The Bible speaks of men as vessels in such places as Acts 9:15; Romans 9:21–23; 1 Thessalonians 4:4; 2 Corinthians 4:6–7.

Thus, the bread of the Supper speaks of earthly priesthood; the cup itself speaks of kingly exaltation under heaven; and the wine in the cup, which is poured out into us, speaks of prophetic enthronement in heaven itself.

With these associations in mind, we can understand better why cups and cups of wine are associated with kings in the Bible, and not with priests. The priest does his work standing in the Tabernacle, with his unshod feet in contact with the soil of the earth.[27] The king, however, sits on a pedestal, a throne, elevated above the earth but under heaven. The king is in the firmament position. The cup containing wine is a symbol of the throne carrying the king. Notice also that the priestly Laver of Cleansing is not said to have had a lip like that of a cup, while the Solomonic Great Sea is associated with the cup.

Drinking wine, which is above the cup itself (above the shell of the cup), can be seen as the king's drinking the advice of the prophets.[28] Pharaoh's cupbearer was his chief "prophetic advisor." This is clear from the fact that Joseph becomes the chief cupbearer, and he speaks of his silver cup as that which he uses when he gives such prophetic advice to Pharaoh (Genesis 44). Nehemiah was such a prophetic advisor to the king called Artaxerxes in the Bible (Neh. 1:11). Repeatedly the Bible speaks of God's giving wicked men cups full of His blessing or wrath, and such language does not appear until we get to the Psalter, where David the king is given the contents of such cups, and in the prophets, where God gives various cups to various people. The content of the cup is God's prophetic blessing or curse, as administered not to a priest but to a king, and usually by a prophet.

---

27 There are no shoes among the garments of the priests (Exod. 28). Like Moses, he is unshod on holy ground.

28 Saul became an adopted son of Samuel when he prophesied and was thought of as one of the "sons" of the prophets. King Rehoboam refused to listen to the elders, and acted foolishly, splitting the kingdom. Elijah and Elisha advised kings, and in 2 Samuel the kings frequently call the prophets "father." King Zedekiah's quixotic responses to Jeremiah's advice pervade the book of Jeremiah.

It is no accident that alcoholic beverages are called "spirits." The prophet, as advisor to the king, is what the Spirit is to Jesus. And as Leviticus 17 tells us that life is in blood, so the Spirit of life is associated with blood as well as with alcoholic spirits. Jesus' outpoured blood is a symbol not only of His death, but also of the pouring out of the prophetic Spirit from His bodily cup.

Thus, to repeat what we wrote above, when Jesus gives us bread, He makes us priests. When He gives us a cup, He makes us kings. When He gives us the contents of the cup, He makes us prophets. The movement is from earth to firmament to heaven.

To repeat with more careful nuance: Jesus gives us broken bread, so that we become priests who are willing to die for others, as He did. Then He gives us wine, blood, Spirit. From His cup, His body, the wine moves into our cups, into our bodies. In this way, Jesus gives us the Spirit, coming to us as a prophet and treating us as kings. Just as we act like true priests when we eat the broken bread, so we act like true kings when we drink the outpoured wine. Then, as the wine permeates us, as the Spirit permeates us, we grow from being kings to being prophets ourselves, so that we also begin to pour out our own good spirits for others. Eventually the firm cup of our lives, of our bodies, of our kingly power, will begin to break down, and eventually it will crack and die; but our spirit will continue to flow to others in our eldership, and even after we are gone for a time as people remember us.

A final consideration. To this point, we have considered the breaking of the bread and the outpouring of the cup as marking the ends of the priestly and kingly periods of Israel. But in fact, they mark out the entire periods, from the beginning. To be a priest is to be someone who is willing to be cut off from others in order to do one's task. To be a king is to be someone willing to be poured out in death for others. Let us now explore this in a bit more detail.

Circumcision was an action that divided the human body into two parts, cutting it in half. It represented Abram's separation from all the other people of the earth as God's appointed priest to the nations. At Sinai, when the nation entered its priestly phase, Israel was cut off from all the other nations by the laws of diet and uncleanness, and by other such provisions. These established the "dividing wall" between Israel and the nations. Thus, being broken off from the rest of humanity, even from God-fearing Gentiles, for the sake of the rest of humanity, is an essential aspect of priestly service.

We must consider Jonathan, son of Saul, if we are to understand the relationship of death and being poured out to the establishment of the kingdom. Jonathan was crown prince, but he gave his armor and his sonship to David. Jonathan died, pouring out his blood fighting God's enemies, so that David could become king. This action on the part of this great saint established the pattern that all the kings were to follow. They were to risk their lives for the sake of their people. The king must be willing to pour out the cup of himself that others might receive the benefit of his shed blood.

4.

God's Life and Our Lives

History, biography, and ritual all come from the Triune God. Thus, the pattern or sequence of history, biography, and ritual arise from God's inner essence, His inner life. If we are going to develop a more biblical and Reformed theology of liturgy, we shall have to keep our eyes constantly focused on the intra-Trinitarian life of God as the model for human life.

How God Lives Within Himself

To begin with, consider that since God acts out of His own character and essence, the sequence of God's actions in history says something about God's actions within himself. And not only so, but since human beings are images of God, the sequence of human life also relates to how God lives in Himself and how He acts in history. There is a consistent pattern in how God acts, a pattern that arises from His inner life as the Three-Personed God, and a pattern that is replicated in the lives of His images.

The contours and patterns of life and history reveal the life of God. In the broadest sense, this is what is meant by "typology," the study of how God's existence is imprinted upon His creation. This imprint does not come directly from above or from outside the creation, but is worked from within by the Spirit, who has indwelt the creation from the moment of creation itself. Three things—individual items, patterns of spatial arrangement, and patterns of temporal sequence—are typologically related to God, the supreme Archetype and Prototype. These three aspects of typology relate respectively primarily to the Father, the Son, and the Spirit.

To get into this matter, we have to think a bit about time. Time is a tricky thing to define, but however we think of it—whether as a "flow," or as a "succession or moments," or in some other way—the time that we experience is part of the creation. We experience created time. Yet, everything that is in the creation is a reflection of some aspect or quality of the Creator. God exists in a kind of eternal super-time. As creatures, we cannot envision such a thing, because we would have to be God to imagine it. In some way God exists in an "eternal now," because He who is I AM WHO I AM does not change (Mal. 3:6; Exod. 3:14)—God's covenant faithfulness is rooted in His unchangeableness, His immutability.

On the other hand, God is not static like a stone. He is "eternally active." Moreover, His activity does not consist of something circular, going round and round as it were. Rather, His eternal activity is somehow progressive and transforming: God exists in a way that is always *new*.

How can this be? How can God be unchanging and also live in a Divine life that is always transforming, always new? We cannot ultimately understand the depths of this. But we must say that both the unchanging aspects of creation, and the aspects of creation that move from glory to glory, find their ultimate root in God, in aspects of His being.

Created time is a reflection of something that is a quality of the supra-temporal God, the God who is "beyond created time." The Spirit is the Motion of God, moving from Father to Son and back again. At the moment God created the world in Gen. 1:1, the Spirit embraced the world (Gen. 1:2) and since then He carries it along in His motion back and forth between the Father and the Son. The Spirit carries the creation from the Father to the Son, to Jesus, and then carries the creation from Jesus back to the Father. The creation is feminine, and so the Spirit carries the creation from the Father to the Son as mother of the incarnate Jesus, and then the Spirit carries the creation from the Son back to the Father as the bride of Christ. (Just to be clear, it is the creation, not the Spirit, that is daughter, bride, and mother.)[29]

This eternal supratemporal movement within the Godhead is also seen as each Person places His entire faith, hope, and love in the other two. Since God has made the creation and human life as reflections and images of Himself, we can look at human life to understand something of the relationship between faith, hope, and love—provided we let the Bible be our guide as we examine human life.

In the fullest sense, love is something that comes after we have become well acquainted with someone else, especially after we have gone through a trial with him or her. Often people fall in love as they go through a crisis together. In the crisis, they learn to trust each other, get to know each other, and come to love each other. Thus, love is primarily eschatological, coming at the climax of a process of time.

In the fullest sense, faith is something that comes at the beginning, before we know the other person well enough to love him or her. Faith is an expression of helplessness, and that is why Jesus calls attention to the faith of small children and babies. The baby does not really love his mother, because he does not know her well enough to do so, but he trusts her. He trusts that when he cries she will pick him up and comfort him.

---

29 For more on the Spirit as the Motion of God, and on the three kinds of typology, see my essay "Twelve Fundamental Avenues of Revelation," originally published in *Open Book* 30–34 (December 1996–August 1997) and included here as Appendix B.

Hope comes in the midst of life as we go through trials. Our initial trust is matured through experiences to become love, as we learn the ways in which our seemingly hidden God is really with us all along.

Faith, hope, and love are there all along, but faith is most prominent at the beginning, hope in the middle, and love at the end.

Notice how John puts it in 1 John 2:12ff. The children's sins are forgiven, and this is where the life of faith begins. The young men are involved in battle, and thus must persevere by hope. The old men know Him who has been from the beginning, and the word "know" in the Bible carries connotations of love, as in the loving and electing foreknowledge of God, or as in Adam's "knowing" his wife.

This is also how God lives, which it is why it is how we live. Each Person of God delights to humble Himself to glorify the other two, which is why we are to be humble. Each lives by faith in the other two, which is why we are to live by faith. The Father gives up His particular glory to the Son and the Spirit, confident in true hope (which is confidence, not mere wishfulness) that they will return their glory to Him, and this return of glory brings them into the full expression of their mutual love.

Thus the Spirit, the Motion of God, yields His motion to the Father and to the Son and lets Himself be sent by them, directed by them. The Son, the Word of God, yields His language to the Father and to the Spirit, letting the Father speak Him and letting the Spirit carry His Word. The Father, the root of identity, particularity, or personality in the Godhead, yields His personal presence to the Son and to the Spirit, remaining in the background while the Son and Spirit manifest His particularity.

Thus, while the Father's peculiar property is Personhood, He gives that property to the Son and Spirit also, so that they are also Persons. While the Son's peculiar property is Language (Word), He gives that property to the Father and Spirit also, so that they also speak. While the Spirit's peculiar property is Motion, He gives that property to the Father and Son, so that they also move. This is a way of expressing the traditional Christian doctrine of the intra-Trinitarian Divine relations. I'm simply focusing on one perspective of this, which is that each

Person dynamically gives Himself and His properties to the other two. I stress this because I'm interested in its implications for the flow of time as we experience it in this created world. The root of that temporal flow is not in the static conditions of the Godhead, but in their mutual interaction.

When we speak of the distinctive properties of each Person of God, we have to bear in mind that our understanding of God is always partial and incomplete and that, because we are creatures, the essence of God is something that is ultimately beyond our ability to comprehend. We will always learn more and become able to express things better and more precisely; and at the same time, there will always be a fullness of mystery about God that we cannot in the nature of things ever understand. Such mysteries are things that we don't even know about and so we won't miss knowing them, because all our knowledge is that of creatures and we shall increasingly, over googols of aeons, approach knowing everything a creature is able to know. In other words, to know the mysteries we would have to be God, and since we aren't and never will be, we will never know anything about these mysteries, or even what they might be.30

I've spoken of the three members of the Godhead as three Persons and also said that the Father is the source of Personhood or Separate Identity in the Godhead. I've balanced that by saying that each Person speaks to the other two, because you cannot be a person without language of some sort, yet the Word of God is the source of Language in the Godhead. Finally, clearly each Person is alive, has life, yet the Spirit is the source of Life in God. I've written of Motion, but immobility is death, and the Bible clearly associates the Spirit with life. Yet, you cannot be a person without being alive. In "Twelve Fundamental Avenues of

---

30 I have discussed this in much more detail in my *Creation in Six Days: A Defense of the Traditional Reading of Genesis One* (Moscow, ID: Canon Press, 1999), chapter 5.

Revelation"[31] I wrote of the Father as the root of thingness, of identity, of matter; the Son as the root of spatiality and of relationships between things in space; and the Spirit as the root of time and rhythm.

All of these things are true, but they are not necessarily true to the exclusion of other perspectives on God. I'm not comfortable saying that the Son and Spirit would not be persons apart from receiving personhood from the Father; that the Father and Son would not be alive apart from receiving life from the Spirit; or that the Father and Spirit would be silent and unable to communicate, or would be isolated and not face to face with each other, apart from receiving language and "spatial structure" from the Son. Yet, perhaps if we meditated long enough on the timelessness of God and the fact that He is fully and totally One and that the three persons indwell each other fully and exhaustively (theologians call this mutual indwelling perichoresis), we might become comfortable with such a formulation.

For the present, though, it is probably safer and wiser theologically to formulate the matter this way: While each Person of God is fully a Person, yet there is a primacy of Personhood in the Father, and in some way that Personhood is communicated to the other two. Similarly, while each Person communicates with the others and thus possesses the property of Language, yet there is a primacy of Language in the Son, and in some way that property of Language is provided to the other two. And finally, while each Person has life in Himself, and thus the eternal quality of Motion, yet there is a primacy or fullness of Life and Motion in the Spirit, which is in some way passed to the other two.[32]

Along these same lines, the properties of holiness, righteousness, and glory can be associated with the Father, the Son, and the Holy Spirit respectively. The word "holy" in the Bible does not mean

---

31 See Appendix B.

32 There may be, and doubtless are, better ways of expressing these realities. I've included this discussion to show that much more can be said about the subject than I'm saying in these essays. What I am setting forth here is adequate for the subject of these studies, but is not all that must be said about the intra-Trinitarian life of God.

righteousness, but is associated with separation: separation both from sin and also separateness in one's own person or one's own house. It is closest to the English word "integrity." Let me suggest that the peculiar property of the Father is holiness, in that the Father is associated with particularity, identity, and "personhood" in that sense. The word "righteous" is associated with covenant loyalty, faithfulness in marriage for instance.[33] Let me suggest that the peculiar property of the Son is righteousness. Finally the word "glory" is associated with manifestation and with bringing something that is good forward to something that is better. It has a temporal connotation, and thus I suggest that the peculiar property of the Spirit is glory.

Perhaps we can gain a bit more insight by looking at human life, which images the Divine life. A son receives his separate identity or personhood by being begotten by a father. This is analogous to the way I'm saying the Personhood of the Father is given to the Son and Spirit.

Also, the moment a son is born, or conceived, there is a second person for the father to interact with. Thus, spatial relationships and linguistic communication come into existence, between a father and son, only when the son actually has come into being as a separate person. In this way, it is the son who brings into being the phenomena of relationships and language, because as long as the father is alone, he has no relationship with his son and no son (or daughter as the case may be) to speak with. We can even notice that parents usually first speak consoling words to their babies after the baby utters his first cry, so that the baby speaks first and elicits language from the parent. Or, even if the baby is quiet, parents will speak to him to elicit a response. Either way, the infant provokes language from the parents.

---

33 "For a reader of the Septuagint, the Greek version of the Jewish scriptures, 'the righteousness of God' would have one obvious meaning: God's own faithfulness to his promises, to the covenant. God's 'righteousness,' especially in Isaiah 40–55, is that aspect of God's character because of which he saves Israel, despite Israel's perversity and lostness. God has made promises; Israel can trust those promises. God's righteousness is thus cognate with his trustworthiness on the one hand, and Israel's salvation on the other" (N. T. Wright, *What Saint Paul Really Said* [Grand Rapids: Eerdmans, 1997], 96).

Finally, what passes from the father to his son is life. Life, we may say, is the link that forms the bond between the two and that brings the son into existence. In human experience, this is the mother. The father initiates the son, the mother gives her life to him for nine months, and then the son comes forth as a separate being. The Spirit, thus, is the archetype of the mother. We have to say right away that the Creator as a whole is masculine as over against the feminine creation, but also that since the Spirit indwells the creation, it is He who makes the creation into mother, daughter, and bride. What the mother contributes to the process of childbirth is precisely time and development, consisting of nine months. And this is analogous to the gift of time, motion, and life that the Spirit, we have said, provides to the Father and to the Son.

Father, son, and mother are all persons; all use language; and all exist in time; but there is a certain primacy of person, language, and time associated with each. This reality might be discussed at great length, for it is a fact that women, especially mothers, are much more oriented to time, ritual, calendar events, and the like than are fathers and sons. Women never forget birthdates and anniversaries; men often do. Similarly, fathers provide the model of human life for their sons, and sons speak out of their experience with their fathers—consider that Jesus is the Word of the Father. There is a book here for someone to write, but not for me, or at least not for now.

Each Person of God yields Himself totally in trust-filled faith in the other two. That is the beginning point of their eternal, supratemporal action. Each is sustained in total confidence-filled hope in the other two. And each finds, in these motions of faith and hope, total love from and for the other two.

As each Person yields His glory to the other two, in humility, He "experiences" a kind of loss. Each Person joyfully dies to His own things that the other two may have them, and then the other two return that gift, transformed by Themselves, to the first Person. This humble "death" in the Godhead is the passage through hope, for hope is what sustains us when it appears that all has been lost.

Notice that what is returned is double what has been given up, since, for instance, the Father receives back from both the Son and the Spirit. What we see here is "eschatology" in the Godhead, a progression from something that is good to something that is better. This is the root of the phenomenon in human life that what we give up, we receive back in abundance, as we see in the doubling of Job's fortunes and in the Parable of the Talents.[34]

Thus, each Person trusts the other two in faith, "dies" to Himself for the other two in hope, and finds new joy and love as the other two return Themselves to Him. This "motion" is supratemporal in God, but it plays itself out in history, biography, and ritual as a sequence of events in time.[35]

HUMAN LIFE

For human beings and for history, the sequence of faith, hope, and love corresponds to creation, history, and eschatology. Considered this way, the order in history is Father, Spirit, Son: The Father sends the Spirit to bring us to the Son. At the end is the Marriage of the Lamb, the fullness of love. At the beginning is bare creation and the first assurances of trust: "Fear not! Fear not! Be not afraid! I am with you! Fear not! Fear not! Fear not!"—this is the command Jesus repeated over and over to His newborn children. At the beginning we cry out, "Abba! Father!" Then, building on this confidence in God, we are able to move through

---

[34] For a fuller discussion of this doubling and its theological roots, see my essay on the Talents, "Jesus' First Eschatological Discourse (2)," *Studies in the Revelation* 37 (May 1997).

[35] We shall have to return to this matter of humility and "dying" when we come to consider in detail the death of the animal in the rites of the Old Creation, for the ultimate root of this passage through death lies not in God's response to our sin—though that is factored in as a result of the fall of humanity—but in the awesome humility of each Person before the other two. Our experience of death is a curse-deformed version of God's yielding and humility. See chapter 7 below.

the middle of life with hope in His promises of eventual glory, moving through test, trial, division, suffering, fear, and ultimately physical death. It is the Spirit who moves us through this life.

Thus:

1. *Faith is associated with holiness.* Holy is what we are, who we are. We are holy because God is holy. We are to believe this and then act upon it. In our justification, God declares us holy. Then we are to live and move and act in terms of who we are, as holy people. Faith accepts God when He tell us that He has given us the same kind of integrity, the same kind of holiness, the same kind of uniqueness, the same kind of specialness, that He Himself possesses—because, after all, we are His images. Holiness, the gift of the Spirit, is the special property of priests. We begin as priests, holy servants of the holy God.

2. *Hope is associated with glory.* Glory comes to us in two phases. We are given some kind of glory, and then we must give it up, trusting through hope in the reception of a greater glory later on. Those who cling to their early glory will not come to receive the greater glory. (We shall explore this in great length as these essays proceed.) Glory comes to us from the Spirit, and we can associate our earlier glory with being the daughter of the Father, and our later glory with being the bride of Christ. Between the two, we must undergo the same kind of death and resurrection as our Husband went through, the same abandonment and renewal of glory. Glory, the gift of the Spirit, is the special property of kings; but the king must never cling to his glory, but must be ready to abandon it for the sake of his people.

3. *Love is associated with righteousness, with covenant loyalty.* Love, our covenant marriage to Jesus, is the climax of the sequence. The righteousness of God is His covenant loyalty to us, despite our waywardness; and our covenant loyalty, our righteousness, is our response to His. Such righteousness is the concern of the prophets, who call God's people back to Him on the basis of His covenant loyalty to them. We learn to be loyal, to be righteous, as a result of our passages through faith and hope.

Of course, throughout all our lives faith, hope, and love are present, and we are always to some degree priests, kings, and prophets. But there is also this sequence of emphasis.

Children are developing primarily as persons into maturity. This development in personal uniqueness is the special gift of the Father. This time is priestly, and such maturity comes from obedience.

In the middle of life we move into glory and then must give it up. This movement, this passage, is the work of the Spirit. This time is kingly, when we have responsibility to govern something and must do so by the trial and error of wisdom.

Finally, in old age our ability to speak, to pass on what we know, comes to the fore. This linguistic ability is the special provision of the Son. It is prophetic in character, not only in the sense that we know how to teach and exhort in terms of God's law, but also in that, from years of experience, we know something about time and can even understand what is coming in the future.

This progression is simply a fact of human life as the image of God. Children are beautiful, but not glorious. They lack skill with language. They lack full bodily strength. They are small. They cannot wear heavy clothing (the Hebrew word for glory means heaviness). It is in the middle of our lives that we become glorious in these ways. But toward the ends of our lives we begin to lose such glory. We lose strength. Our faces droop and acquire wrinkles. We lose hair. We begin to decay. People try to cover this up with makeup, hair dye, toupees, and plastic surgery, but eventually none of this avails. Sooner or later, God calls on us, and forces us, to lose our glory, and we have to come to look for the future glory of the resurrection and transfiguration.

This is the sequence of the sacrifices, and thus of the Christian ritual of covenant renewal. The killing of the animal and the offering of blood assures us of God's acceptance and calls us to faith. The blood makes us holy. The dividing and washing of the animal's parts, and their placement in the fire, shows us the need to move through our lives in hope amidst difficulty, because God's Spirit and Word are washing us all the while we endure it. The glistening water and the flaming fire make us glorious. The ascension of the animal into God's presence assures us that we shall be enfolded into His love at the end.

We can see, thus, that the rite of the Lord's Supper displays the sequence of faith, hope, and love. The bread-making phase corresponds to the time of faith, as we begin to learn to trust God. The crisis period, the breaking of the bread, is the time when hope comes into focus. After we have been through this and seen how God took care of us even when we did not think He was doing so, we begin to appreciate the love of God more than we did before. The warming and rest-inducing wine gives us "more" than the earlier bread did.[36]

We can summarize our associations this way:

Father	**Spirit**	**Son**
person	motion	language
things	time	space (relations)
faith	hope	love
holiness	glory	righteousness
priestly	kingly	prophetic

This triadic movement of human life and history is not the full picture. Many readers will have misgivings, noting that after all we usually associate kingship with the Son and prophecy with the Spirit. I remind the reader that we are discussing a sequence of emphases, not isolated periods of time or isolated kinds of people. All aspects are always present, but some are more important at a given time, in a given person, then others.

At the same time, while the triadic movement from Father to Spirit to Son is clearly taught in the Bible, as we have seen, there is also a movement from Father to Son to Spirit. Both the Son and the Spirit are equally highlighted in the second and third phases of the

---

36 A word of thanks to Jeffrey J. Meyers for some advice on the phrasing of the more technical parts of this chapter.

movement, but in different ways. In my book Crisis, Opportunity, and the Christian Future,[37] I pointed out that biblical history repeatedly moves through the following triadic cycle:

1. Father-Son relationships. The son is a priestly servant in the Father's house. Adam and Abraham are the examples in Genesis, and the whole period of the Mosaic era is focused here. Here the Father is highlighted, and the Son is manifest as archetype of various human sons. It is individuals, in their holiness, that are paramount in such times. The work of the Spirit is to keep us close to our Father.

2. Brother-brother relationships. The Son is manifest as Older Brother, and it is our relationship to Him that comes into focus. These are kingly times, when brother-brother strife is in focus: Cain and Abel, Jacob and Esau, the period of the Kingdom in Israel. The work of the Spirit is to keep us close to our Brother, and to our brothers.

3. Husband-wife relationships. The Son is manifest as Husband, and it is that relationship that comes into focus. The Spirit is the Divine Matchmaker, who seeks to keep the Sethite sons of God from marrying the Cainite daughters of men. Joseph is a patriarchal example, and the prophetic Restoration era of Israel's history focuses on this matter, for the marriage of priestly Israel to the nations is a type of the marriage of Jesus to humanity.[38]

Thus, the Son comes into focus as Older Brother and thus King during the second phase, while the Spirit comes into focus as Matchmaker during the third phase. And, the Spirit comes into focus as Glorifier and Death-bringer (hope) during the second phase, while the Son comes into focus as Husband (love) in the third phase.

We can refine this a bit by considering that the firstborn son is said to be the first of a father's strength (Gen. 49:3; Deut. 21:17; Ps. 78:51). Strength or power is an attribute of the Spirit. The Older Brother, the King, gives his strength, his Spirit, to the younger brothers. He gives his

---

37 James B. Jordan, Crisis, Opportunity, and the Christian Future, 2nd ed. (Monroe, LA: Athanasius, [1994] 2016).

38 When Jesus comes, as the True Israel, the historical mission of Israel to function as husband to the nations ceases.

glory to them, so that David's power and glory spread to all his men. Thus, in the second, kingly, hope-oriented phase, the Son is working, while the Spirit is His operative principle. The Son works to bring the Spirit to the brothers.[39]

In the third phase—the prophetic, love-oriented phase—it is the other way around: The Spirit is working, while marriage to the Son is his operative principle. The Spirit works to bring the Son to the bride, and the bride to the Son. The prophets are the Spirit's agents in this. The prophets do not distribute glory, but call us to be faithful to our Husband, to Yahweh, to Jesus.

Thus, in the second phase, the Son gives us glory and hope in the Spirit; in the third phase, the Spirit gives us love for the Son. We move in the second phase by the Spirit's hope, given us by the Son, and in the third phase in the Son's love, given us by the Spirit.

Let us remind ourselves that we are always both brothers and the bride of Christ and that all our lives we live by faith, hope, and love. Yet, these come into focus at particular times, and that is what we are interested in as we consider history, biography, and ritual. The order in Canticles is "my sister, my bride," not the other way around. At the end, the holy city in Revelation 21–22 is bride, not a collection of brothers. Sonship from the Father and brotherhood from the Son are only stages toward marriage to the Son by the Spirit.

How does the Son give us the glory and hope of the Spirit? By going before us. David had glory as Saul's adopted son, as crown prince, but he gave it up and then gained new glory as king. Now he spreads this experience to others, thereby imparting the Spirit to them. Similarly, Jesus had glory as the Son, but gave it up and then became King at God's right hand and now sends the Spirit to us.[40]

---

39   We are all, male or female, brothers of the Older Brother.

40   Compare Moses also: prince of Egypt, exiled for forty years, and then leader of a new nation. Then the Spirit is taken from him and distributed to other (Num. 11:17).

How does the Spirit give us love for the Son? Because the Spirit is sent by the Son originally, He is able to bring to our minds who the Son is, not only as our Older Brother and King, whom we emulate, but also as our Husband, whom we love.

Thus, it is entirely correct to think of the order of priest, king, and prophet as an order of Father, Son, and Spirit. Since, however, we are primarily interested in the course of life from faith to hope to love, we shall focus our attention on the order Father, Spirit, and Son.

As we conclude this essay, let us look back at the our ritual again. In chapter 3 we saw that the movement from bread to cup is a movement from priest to king, with the prophetic outflow implied as an effect of that movement. We have now added a second, slightly more detailed perspective on the ritual. Taking the bread in hand speaks of God's election of us to holiness, making us the children of the Father, making us priests. Breaking the bread speaks of the passage through death, by hope, through which the Spirit moves us. The breaking of the bread releases the wine, and the gift of the wine makes us kings. Third, after we have drunk the wine, which is sharp in the mouth, we find that it is lovingly warm in the stomach. It imparts rest, peace, love, and thereby matures us as kings into prophets. We now have peace in ourselves, which we can carry forth as we depart.

Thus, the ritual duplicates true human life. We mature from priests to kings, and from kings to prophets; from children to adults, and from adults to elders. By giving us His own exemplary life, Jesus makes it possible for us to live true human lives after the pattern of His own.

5.

From Three to Five

In the preceding chapter we were reflecting on the sequence of faith, hope, and love, and how these play out in history, biography, and ritual, as these manifest the inner life of God. We can summarize our findings by saying that as small children we have not learned to love, but we do trust our parents that they will comfort us when we are distressed. This is how we relate to the Father, primarily. As we pass through the troubles of this life we live by hope, and that hope-in-trial is primarily the gift of the Spirit. Finally we come to mature love and marriage, to our Husband, the Son.

The stress must as always be on the word "primarily." When God acts outside of Himself, all of God does all that God does, but also one Person is highlighted in each action. Thus we grow in faith, through hope, to love of the Father and of the Son and of the Holy Spirit. Yet, as I have pointed out, there is a kind of special relationship of the Father to faith, of the Spirit to hope, and of the Son to love.

We have seen that each Person of God gives Himself to the other two and that the Spirit is the Motion of God. It follows, then, that it is by the Spirit that the Father gives Himself to the Son, and vice versa, just as it is by His own property of Motion that the Spirit gives Himself to the other Persons. The Spirit is the means by which this giving takes place. From this fact we can see that the Father sends the Spirit to the Son (gives Himself to the Son by means of the Spirit), and vice versa.

THREE, FIVE, AND SEVEN

Recent theologians, particularly John M. Frame and Vern S. Poythress, have called attention to the fact that theology is enriched by an awareness of multiple perspectives. We can look at a given subject, or at a given historical sequence, from more than one completely valid perspective. For our purposes, we can look at history, ritual, and biography from a Father-perspective, from a Son-perspective, and from a Spirit-perspective. Each is equally valid, and each perspective embraces all the phenomena of history, biography, and ritual.

In what follows, we shall present history, biography, and ritual in three, five, and seven phases. Each perspective covers the whole of history, biography, and ritual, but does so from a particular standpoint. Seeing history, etc., in a *three-phase* way has its root in the Father, focuses on holiness, and climaxes in marriage. Seeing history, etc., in a *five-phase* way has its root in the Son, focuses on righteousness, and places marriage in the center. Seeing history, etc., in a *seven-phase* way has its root in the Spirit, focuses on glorification, and places marriage toward the beginning.

The three perspectives are different, as the three Persons of God are different from each other, but all three perspectives look at the same thing, at the same sequence of history, biography, and ritual. To this let us now turn our attention.

When we think of the three Persons of God and of the movement from faith to hope to love, we are thinking in terms of three. Since the Father is the root of Personhood, identity, or particularity in the Godhead—in a word, holiness (see previous chapter)—this threefold perspective is closely associated with personhood, with the Father. The numerous triadic formulations in the Bible have their root in this triunity of God (i.e., faith, hope, and love; priest, king, and prophet). To follow up on one of my suggestions, this triadic way of looking at history, biography, and ritual is a way of seeing how we develop from holiness through glory, which we must give up, to righteousness; from faith through hope to love; and all of this with an emphasis on holiness, on the personal dimension. In the triadic perspective, holiness *implies* glorification and covenant loyalty (righteousness).

We can make another ritual application of this perspective by noticing that there are basically three kinds of offerings in Leviticus. When we draw near to God as sinner, we first bring the Trespass and Purification (Sin) Offerings. These focus on our faith in God, the God who forgives sins. Next, we bring the Ascension (mistranslated as Burnt) Offering, with its Tribute (mistranslated Cereal or Meal) Offering.[41] The emphasis here is on the chopping up of the animal, the breaking up of the bread, and the pouring out of the wine, so the focus is on hope through tribulation. Third comes the Peace Offering, including the variants of Thank and Vow Offerings, which highlight a meal with God and focus on love. In terms of what we have seen previously, the movement is from Father to Spirit to Son. The movement enables us to follow what is commanded: "Be holy as I am holy."

Christian worship has the same form:

1. *Entrance and confession of sin*. Renewal as persons, forgiven and made holy by the Father.

---

[41] Though the Ascension offering is indeed all burned up, the word in Hebrew (*'olah*) means "go up" or "ascend." We need to link this offering with all the many times when people go up on a mountain to meet God, up into an upper room, or up to a rooftop, or "up on the altar." Similarly, though the Tribute offering in Leviticus 2 consists of grain, the Hebrew word (*minchah*) means "gift or tribute," and "tribute" is the better word to use when presenting a required gift to a king. Moreover, in Numbers the Tribute offering has wine added to it, so "Grain/Meal/Cereal offering" is not a good term to use for this offering. The sequence of the two offerings means that we ascend to God's throne and present our gifts to Him, which He accepts. This fundamental meaning of the offerings is completely obscured by the common mistranslations of the two key terms.

2. *Ascension and the hearing of the Word, both empowered by the Spirit.* The Word chops us up (Heb. 4:12).

3. *Fellowship at the Table, with the Son/Husband.*

We can add that with the coming of the creation, of humanity, we have a fourth "person" in existence, and that this is the root of all the fourfold lists and patterns in the Bible—which brings us to a last part of Christian worship:

4. *Blessing and Sending Forth.*

Turning now to the fivefold structure with which we began this chapter, I suggest that it is primarily associated with the Son, the Word of God, the root of "spatial structure." I associated the Son with righteousness, with covenant loyalty. When the covenant takes the form of a written document, it has five aspects, and the Law of the covenant is at the center.[42] Those five aspects can be summarized in various ways, for instance as:

The King
The King's Gift
The King's Law
The King's Blessing
Inheritance with the King

To be sure, our interest in these essays is in the order or sequence of these five elements, as our interest is in biography, history, and ritual; and after all, the Spirit gives time and motion to the Son, so that the Son's structuring "work" also has the aspect of time and sequence.

This "five" is how the covenant is usually expressed, and we are in covenant particularly with Christ Jesus, the Son. It is He who, as Yahweh, made the covenant with Israel. Thus, the "five" has a particular association with the Son.

---

42 I've discussed this and given all the bibliographical references in *Covenant Sequence in Leviticus and Deuteronomy* (Tyler, TX: Institute for Christian Economics, 1989).

If we add humanity to the fivefold set we began this chapter with (Father-Spirit-Son-Spirit-Father), we see humanity as a sixth element in the whole, providing another perspective on the biblical use of the number six as the number of man.

Christian worship can also be seen as having a five/sixfold structure:

1. The Father, Supreme King, calls us to worship.
2. The Spirit cleanses us and moves us in transition from sin to forgiveness again, into the King's gift of the kingdom.
3. The Word/Son preaches to us the law of the Kingdom.
4. The Spirit gives us new life and blessing in the Supper.
5. The Father commissions us to go forth and take His Son to the world, our inheritance.
6. We go forth into the new week.

Finally, anyone familiar with the book of Revelation knows that the number seven is associated with the sevenfold Spirit of God. The Spirit enters creation along with the act of creation itself and travels with it always. His sevenfold work, a pointedly temporal sequence, begins with the seven days of Genesis 1. Also, it is the Spirit who comes alongside us to provoke us to and guide us in worship, or liturgy. These sevenfold sequences move us from glory to glory, as glory is the peculiar property of the Spirit. Thus, our preliminary investigation of a biblical Liturgical Theology will not be complete until we get to a discussion of worship in seven steps and its theological root.

And, if we add humanity to what we shall see as God's sevenfold work, we come to an eight, and it is on the eighth day that humanity is said, repeatedly in the Bible, to enter into the human week following God's first week (circumcision on the eighth day, etc.).

A discussion of this sevenfold flow and its place in Christian worship will come in a later chapter. For now, let us look at the fivefold pattern as it comes to expression in biography, history, and liturgy.

A Double Sequence

The Spirit moves from the Father to the Son and back again. One manifestation of such a fivefold sequence of human life is this:

1. Childhood faith.
2. Early trials and hope.
3. Marriage and love: a new childhood.
4. Further trials and hope.
5. Final marriage to God and love.

Consider that newlyweds are like children. They have not yet begun to experience trials, at least not usually. Yes, there may be trials from the outside, which may have brought them together in the first place, but not trials inside—at least not many. The trials inside the marriage, which force us to a new kind of hope, come with children. The psychology of married people without children is quite different from the psychology of married people with children. Rearing children is hard work: full of fear, conflict, doubt, and worry. Husband and wife usually experience tension between themselves as they rear their children. This is the new course of trials, which we must bear with hope.

It is not the end, however. The children are eventually grown and gone. In the autumn of our lives, after we are once again only husband and wife for a time, we may experience a mature kind of love and peace—if only our sin did not cripple this experience so often, leaving so many people old and bitter.

Thus, the movement is from initial faith, to tension and trial, to a time of rest, love, and peace when we marry. This is followed by more tension and trial, and a final time of rest, love, and peace before we die. That is, there is a movement from the security of childhood (faith), to the tribulations of adolescence (hope), to the joys of marriage (love);

and then to the tribulations of midlife, often culminating in some kind of midlife crisis, which we must persevere through hope, and then to the autumn of life, when we have learned to love the Father fully, and we prepare to go and be with Him.[43]

Using this model of human life, we can go back to the discussion with which we ended the previous chapter, where we noted a certain ambiguity in the revelation of the Son and the Spirit in the "kingly" and "prophetic" times of life. Expanding the threefold sequence to five enables us to expand our understanding of this:

1. *Childhood.* Time of faith and of interacting with the Father, with adults. Compare the Patriarchal era, when the emphasis is on fathers and sons. This time of faith climaxes with the giving of the Law, where the emphasis is on holiness (liturgically in Leviticus, practically in Deuteronomy).

2. *Adolescence.* Time of transition through hope, by the Spirit, which leads to a time of kingship and marriage. Compare the Mosaic era, from the giving of the law through the book of Judges. This time of hope climaxes with the Psalter, which is all about maintaining hope through the difficulties of life. Notice that at this time the sons of Israel are priests, a priestly nation, and this is pointed in the "sons of Aaron." Thus, we can say that the Son is revealed as Priest and then carried by the Spirit through trials.

3. *Marriage and Calling.* We have arrived at kingship and marriage, when we begin to manifest the qualities of the Son more fully. But rather soon, we find that we are in trials, learning wisdom through trial and error, and our loves are refined through hope by the Spirit again. Compare the Remnant era, when the crisis begins to come upon the Kingdoms of Israel and Judah. The climax is the exile, when the glory must be given up. Notice that at this time the sons of Israel are kings,

---

[43] I trust it is obvious that I am simply using the "normal" human life as my fundamental illustration. Not everyone marries, of course. Not everyone experiences things in exactly the way I'm describing for illustrative purposes. Not everyone lives to be seventy or eighty years old. In all human life, however, these fundamental principles of the Divine life are played out in some fashion.

a kingly nation, and this is pointed in the "sons of David." Thus, we can say that the Son is revealed as King and then carried by the Spirit through trials.

In our last chapter, we associated this period with the king as Older Brother and marriage with the third and last, prophetic phase. Here we are associating this kingly period also with marriage, the third and middle phase of five. When we get to the sevenfold course of life and history, we shall associate marriage with the priestly period, early in our lives. Marriage is associated with our priestly calling at Mount Sinai, when Israel married Yahweh. Marriage is associated with kingship in Psalm 45, as the king marries Israel. Marriage is associated with our marriage to Jesus after He has finished His priestly and kingly sufferings and entered into His full prophetic office at the right hand of God as His chief counselor. We shall explore the dimensions of our marriage to Jesus more fully as we move along in these essays.

4. *Time of Crisis*. It would be nice if the crisis were sudden and quickly finished, but it is actually more of a period in a person's life. Menopause does not happen for women in a day, and neither do the midlife trials a man goes through. Here again, it is the Spirit who is refining us, and we must persevere by hope, especially since love and kingship often seem to have departed from our lives to a great degree. The departure of children from home means husband and wife have to learn about each other again, in a new way, and this is usually stressful. Compare the Restoration era, when the Jews were dispersed among an empire as prophets awaiting their king. The climax of this time is the coming of Jesus, the great Prophet, who brings kingship and marriage in its fullness. Notice that at this time the sons of Israel are prophets, a prophetic nation within the empire, and this is pointed in the phrase "sons of the prophets." Thus, we can say that the Son is revealed as Prophet and then carried through trials by the Spirit.

5. *Eldership*. Ideally, this is the time when love of the Father becomes once more manifest in our lives, in a fullness that can only come as a result of the course of our lives from childhood to eldership.

We have, to some degree, learned to love the Father in the way the Son loves Him. Compare the New Covenant era, when Jesus is leading us, by the Spirit, to pray "Our Father."

So, looking at this fivefold sequence, we can schematize it as follows:

Childhood	faith	before priesthood; holiness as persons
Adolescence	initial hope	priesthood (servants); initial glory
Adulthood	initial love & more hope	kingship; full glory
Crisis	full hope	prophethood; abandoned glory
Eldership	full love	full maturity as images of God; mature righteousness/loyalty

Let us now discuss all this in a bit more detail.

In his essay "Liturgical Thinking,"[44] Eugen Rosenstock-Huessy points out that adolescence is the time when reason develops and argues that we need to move beyond reason to wisdom if we are to mature. Reason is closely associated with hope, for when we experience the trials of adolescence, marriage, and the midlife crisis, we often have to reason with ourselves and argue with ourselves, to persuade ourselves that God is really on our side and has not turned against us. Notice how David reasons with himself about God's faithfulness in the Psalms, which are all about being carried through trials by hope. On how Jesus did this, see Heb. 12:2.

---

44 Originally published in *Orate Fratres* (November 1949 and January 1950); republished in *Rosenstock-Huessy Papers*, vol. 1 (Norwich, VT: Argo Books, 1981) and as Views and Reviews: Open Book Occasional Paper 22 (Niceville, FL: Biblical Horizons).

Now this movement in our lives is a reflection of the movement of the Spirit from the Father to the Son and back again. The Spirit carries the creation (us) from the Parent we trust (the Father), through trials, to the Son, whom we marry. This is the history from Adam to Jesus. Then the Spirit carries us in our marriage to the Son back to the Father. This is the history from Jesus to the end of history, when the Son gives all He has back to the Father.

This world history is set forth in a type in the Bible history. We begin with the creation of Adam as a creature-son of God the Father. We move through a difficult history until we come to Sinai, where we marry Yahweh, the preincarnate Jesus. After this we pass through another difficult history until we come at last to the Father, as He is revealed by the incarnate Jesus Christ, who teaches us to pray "Our Father." Or, to see the type differently, we move from Israel's "creation" at Sinai through trials to Solomon, and then through more trials to Jesus. The first, Sinai-centered type speaks of our marriage to the Son as God, and the second, Solomon-centered type speaks of our marriage to Jesus, the Son of Man.[45]

This fivefold movement is seen in the establishments and renewals of covenants in the Bible. First comes a call from God, an announcement of who God is, whom we are to trust. Then comes an historical narrative, detailing how the Father's Spirit has brought us to the Word through a time of "adolescent" difficulty. Third comes the

---

45 More fully we find a sevenfold movement, which will be discussed in due course: From creation through trial to Sinai, through trial to Solomon, through trial to Jesus. Or, from "creation" at Sinai, through priestly trials to Solomon, through kingly trials to Daniel, through prophetic trials to Jesus. Putting these together we have a sequence of nine, implying ten: 1. creation, 2. patriarchal trials, 3. Sinai marriage, 4. priestly trials, 5. Solomon marriage, 6. kingly trials, 7. Daniel, 8. prophetic trials, 9. Jesus, and then, 10. the world to come. The fivefold movement, Father-Spirit-Son-Spirit-Father is the root of all of this.

Additionally, it can be noted that Solomon and the marriage celebrated in Canticles is itself the climax of a three-phase movement from Saul to David to Solomon. With David, the stress is on his mighty men and on David as Older Brother. With Saul, the stress is on father-son relationships: Saul as adopted son of Samuel; Saul as mistreating his adopted son David.

revelation of the Word, the grant of the Kingdom (marriage), and the rules of our Husband (Jesus). Fourth comes another historical period of historical applications of the rules of the Kingdom in the form of blessings and judgments, which involve more trials that we must move through by hope. Finally comes the sabbath rest, the promise of the future.

We can make a further application of this sequence to biography by building on Dorothy Sayers's essay "The Lost Tools of Learning."[46] She points out that children pass through a phase of delighting in learning facts and rules, to a phase of arguing about everything, to a phase of being interested in artistic expression. In my lecture series "Your Child in God's World," I expand this to include two other phases at the beginning.[47] First, the baby is given lots of love and is held and warmed a lot. This is a time when assurance of acceptance is paramount. Then the child moves into a period of story-hearing, when he is inculturated further into human life by stories. Let me now take this up in more detail.

First in the covenant sequence as delineated above, we have revelation of the King, of the Father: "I am Yahweh, your God." This corresponds to the time of assurance in the baby's life. We should link it with baptism. The baby learns to trust by faith his parents, for he is helpless and needy.

Second comes the King's Gift: "who brought you out of the land of Egypt, out of the house of bondage." This is an historical transition, and it is a story. The story tells of a time of distress and sorrow, which we needed to pass through by hope, the gift of the Spirit.

Third comes the King's Law, which in Exodus 20 is the Ten Words. This corresponds to what Sayers calls the "parrot" stage of childhood development. Small children become very interested in rules and

---

46 This essay has been reprinted dozens of times and can be found online at many places. Sayers first issued it in 1947. Years later it was published in *National Review*, and that is the form in which it is reprinted.

47 These recordings are available from WordMP3 (http://www.wordmp3.com/product-group.aspx?id=131).

become very upset when another child breaks the rules during a game. Children delight in these things, as Psalm 119 delights in the Law, and thus it is a time of love, of "marriage" with the Son, the Word.

Fourth comes what Sayers calls the "pert" stage, around the ages 9 to 14 or so, when the child enjoys arguing and debating. He becomes interested in contrasts. Boys no longer play with girls, and vice versa. We know the rules, but now we become interested in breaking them, as sinners, or at least in coming up with arguments as to why the rules don't apply in this or that situation. Anyone who has ever taught a Junior High School class has seen how formerly tractable children become rebellious and feisty during this period of their lives. Reason starts to develop, Rosenstock-Huessy points out,[48] as we begin to make all kinds of contrasts, primarily boys versus girls. This pre-adolescent and early-adolescent state is a time of trouble, and increasingly we must move through it in hope. It corresponds in the covenant sequence with the announcement of blessings and curses, which are, of course, contrastive.

Finally comes what Sayers calls the "poet" stage, when the child becomes more interested in artistic expression. Rosenstock-Huessy points out that art and wisdom—which are closely linked; think of how artistic are the wisdom books of the Bible, including the Psalms—are needed to overcome the gap between boys and girls.[49] Boys are now very interested in girls, and vice versa, and they become interested in the arts of wooing. This is all preparation for marriage, which is the climax of childhood: "For this cause a man shall leave his mother and his father, and cleave to his wife" (Gen. 2:24). It corresponds to the inheritance phase of the covenant sequence.

We can link this childhood development with the first phase of history, the Old Creation phase of childhood, as follows:

1. God's loving claim is seen in His covering the sin of Adam and Eve and in His spanking the human race at the Flood.

---

48   Rosenstock-Huessy, "Liturgical Theology."

49   Ibid.

2. The great story is that of the patriarchs and the exodus from Egypt.

3. The marriage to the Law comes at Mount Sinai, and the period thereafter, which is concerned with obedience.

4. An interest in what the Law means in its more subtle ways comes with the Kingdom and the production of wisdom literature; and the blessings and curses are highlighted in the work of the prophets who write and preach during the Remnant era, during the latter part of the Kingdom era.

5. Preparation for marriage is highlighted in the Restoration, as the prophets now focus on the glories of the greater Kingdom to come, and this climaxes in the work of Jesus, the last and greatest Prophet. Then comes the marriage, as we are drawn, Eve-like, from the side of the Last Adam as blood and water.

World history provides a larger manifestation of the whole sequence, as does the entirety of human life:

1. Initial faith in our parents, which carries through the "parrot" stage of childhood, from Adam through Moses. Here we are receiving things from parents and authorities whom we trust.

2. The doubts and difficulties of pre-adolescence and adolescence are our first "story." In world history, this moves from Moses to Jesus, the whole time of the Law.

3. Our marriage to Jesus, the incarnate Logos or Law, brings us to the middle of life and to our earthly marriage. Note that in marriage we take vows to be covenantally faithful.

4. From marriage to old age is another time of difficulty, including the "midlife crises." Here we must act more as kings and make hard decisions, experiencing blessings and curses and learning from them. Wisdom succeeds Law in world history, and this, more than sheer obedience, is the concern of the Epistles.

5. Before Jesus returns, of course, there will be a time when righteousness covers the earth as the waters cover the seas. This is the time of old age, of eldership. Following this is the eternal rest.

I trust that enough has been said to indicate the reality of this fivefold sequence in human life and in history. We have laid out several sequences, and could lay out others, but in every case we see that we are moving from childhood to some kind of priestly adolescence, to some kind of kingly marriage/calling period, to some kind of prophetic trial, to a final peace and rest. Whether we locate the central marriage/calling period at Sinai (when we are made priests and married to Yahweh), or with Solomon (when we are made kings and married to the King), or with Jesus (when we are made prophets and married to the incarnate Son), the movement is the same.

Returning, then, to the Lord's Supper, we can see that this ritual encapsulates this movement and teaches us something about its meaning.

1. Jesus takes bread. Here is childhood.

2. Jesus breaks it and we eat it. Here is the trauma of adolescence, our priestly trials, which are sustained by the body of Christ.

3. Jesus takes the cup. This is our entrance into adulthood, kingship, marriage, calling.

4. Jesus says that the wine is poured out for us. Drinking wine is our kingly privilege, but such shed blood speaks of our giving up our kingly glory and moving through the difficulties of our later lives as we are fitted to become prophets. What the king drinks from his cup is the wine provided him by the prophet, and drinking it begins to make him into a prophet also.

5. Drinking the wine also provides peace and rest in our bodies, and this speaks of the final rest.

6.

THE RITUAL OFFERINGS

We have seen that in the life of God the Spirit moves from the Father to the Son, and back again, forming a sequence of five steps. We can see this duplicated in the ritual of the offerings. We shall use Leviticus 1, which provides the ritual for the Ascension Offering, as our model, since this offering, being discussed first, provides a large model or paradigm for all the others.[50]

Three persons are involved in the ritual: the worshiper, called "son of Israel"; the priest, called "son of Aaron"; and the animal, called "son of the herd" (Lev. 1:5, in Hebrew). These three "sons" are one, in that all speak of the work of Jesus, the son of God, in three aspects or dimensions. The Father is represented by the enthroned Yahweh,

---

50 Some readers may wish to skip, or only skim, this chapter. It is integral to my thesis that the rituals God has given are connected to the course of human life and history, but it may be a bit too technical for some readers.

before whose face the ritual is performed, and the Spirit is represented by the fire sent by the enthroned Yahweh to the altar. Yet, the three sons also replicate the Trinity as follows: The worshiper is like the Father, in that he brings his animal-son for sacrifice. The animal, of course, is like the Son, in that he is sacrificed. The priests are like the Spirit, in that they display the blood, build up the fire, and mingle the husband and wife pieces together in the fire (more on the marital aspects below).

Another aspect of the ritual that we must bear in mind is this: While the enthroned Yahweh represents, in one way, the Father, He is in fact the pre-incarnate Son. It is the Son, bearing the regal property of the Father, who sends the Spirit-fire to the altar. The Tabernacle has been built, and the Son has come to His throne as King of Israel. Then the (pentecostal) fire is sent down and the worship commences in the Tabernacle area. In terms of the historical events, the Son has been sacrificed in the original Passover, in Egypt. Then the Tabernacle is built as His throne-house, and He moves into it. This corresponds to the crucifixion and ascension of Jesus. Then the ritual offerings commence.

What this means is that these offerings are all memorials of the original Passover. This is clear from the fact that the altar is considered to be positioned at the "doorway" of the Tabernacle, and the blood of the offerings is daubed, dashed, or sprinkled upon it, just as the blood of the original Passover was put on the doorway of the Hebrew dwellings in Egypt. All the various sacrifices look back to Passover and provide detailed explications of the original, simple Passover ritual. They also memorialize Passover, by doing Passover again before God, thereby reminding Him of the original, once-and-for-all Passover event. While only the Tribute Offering is specifically called a memorial, since it itself looks back to the preceding bloody offering that it follows, in a larger way all the offerings are memorials of the original Passover.[51]

---

[51] Recall that in Luke 22, Jesus does the Passover with lamb and cup, and then institutes the Lord's Supper as a memorial, not of the original Passover event, but of the greater Passover that He is about to accomplish.

The Ritual Offerings

The reason this is important is that it tells us that the early church was absolutely correct to consider the Lord's Supper as a memorial sacrifice or offering. The blood of bulls and goats could never take away sin, and such offerings were always only symbolic memorials of Passover and symbolic pointers to the future cross. In the same way, the Lord's Supper is a memorial sacrifice not because it takes away sin, or because it crucifies Jesus again, but in that it is a symbolic memorial of His finished work. The ritual of the Lord's Supper is a New Covenant form of the rituals of the Levitical offerings. Both were memorials. Both cover the same ground. Both ultimately mean the same thing. But the Old Creation memorials were usually bloody, while the New Creation memorial is unbloody.

With this in mind, we can see that it is entirely proper and important to draw parallels between the memorial offerings of the Law and the memorial offering of the Gospel.

Now, what do these two memorials signify? The answer is: many things. But one thing they both signify is the entire course of human history, and another thing they both signify is the entire course of human biography. This is why they are rituals, temporal sequences that are microchronic replicas of larger (macrochronic) temporal sequences. The rituals of the Law duplicate, microchronically, the sequence of events by which Yahweh came to be married to Israel as her King and impart the meaning of that kingship afresh to the worshiper. The Lord's Supper duplicates, microchronically, the sequence of events by which the incarnate Yahweh came to be married to the new humanity as her King and imparts the meaning of His life to us. The two events are parallel, as are the rituals that duplicate them. And, since Jesus' life is the key to human biography and history, the ritual of the Lord's Supper also duplicates human biography and history.

With this in mind, then, let us turn to the ritual of the Ascension Offering. The actual rite, taking every event into consideration, can be seen as having the following steps:

1. Yahweh enthroned in the Tabernacle (Exod. 40; 2 Chron. 5)
2. Spirit-fire sent into the Altar (Lev. 9:24; 2 Chron. 7:1)

3. Son-of-the-herd (Lev. 1:5) brought near (Gen. 22: animal as Isaac), by worshiper
4. Hand laid on animal-son, by worshiper
5. Animal-son slain, by worshiper
6. Blood displayed, by priest
7. Animal-son skinned, by worshiper
8. Animal-son cut up, by worshiper
9. Fire stoked up, by priest
10. Clean pieces put into fire, by priest
11. Unclean pieces washed, by worshiper
12. Cleansed pieces put into fire, by priest
13. Ascension in smoke
14. Sweet savor to God
15. Worshiper departs

We shall condense this rite into five stages eventually, but to begin with we need to consider it in two aspects, past and present.

First of all, the ritual looks back into the past to the once-for-all Passover event in Egypt. In the original Passover, the worshiper and the priest were one and the same person, while the lamb or kid represented someone apart from him who was being offered for him. That is, the animal was someone else, not a symbol of the worshiper himself. The ritual duplicates and memorializes this event. But it does something else also. It points to the present state of the worshiper, for in the memorial the animal is both the substitute and the worshiper. Considered this way, the worshiper is identified with the animal, and what happens to the animal is happening to him. In the same way, the Lord's Supper looks back to the life and death of Jesus apart from us and also looks to our present life and death in union with Him.

Let us consider both aspects of the ritual in Leviticus 1. The ritual only looks partly back to Passover; some aspects of the ritual are not found in Passover. The ritual in its fullness is a present event, which memorializes the past event and also applies it in the present to the worshiper. The ritual also points prophetically to the future work of

Jesus Christ apart from us, as the supreme Passover. Thus, to begin with we shall consider the ritual as showing the work of the substitute apart from the worshiper:

1. *Yahweh enthroned in the Tabernacle* (Exod. 40; 2 Chron. 5)
2. *Spirit-fire sent into the Altar* (Lev. 9:24; 2 Chron. 7:1)

God, enthroned in heaven, gives the commands for the original Passover. Prophetically, the Father sends the Spirit to baptize Jesus for His work.

3. *Son-of-the-herd* (Lev. 1:5) brought near, by worshiper

The animal is set apart for four days (Exod. 12:3-6). The worshiper here is acting for the Father, for God. Prophetically, these four days represent the three and one half years of Jesus' ministry.

4. *Hand laid on animal-son, by worshiper*
5. *Animal-son slain, by worshiper*

In the Passover ritual, hands are not laid on the offering. The worshiper does not "mingle" with the animal, which is offered apart from him. But, acting again for God, the worshiper does slay the animal. Prophetically, the Father slays Jesus on the cross, but the Father does not lay His hand on Jesus so as to participate with Him. Jesus dies alone, separated from Father and Spirit for three hours. Acting as the Father's agent, human hands were involved in what was done to Jesus.

6. *Blood displayed, by priest*

The Passover blood is displayed on the doorposts of the house, and God is satisfied. Prophetically, this is the blood of Jesus displayed on the cross. Notice that while human hands displayed the blood of the Passover, no human hands were involved in the display of Jesus' blood on the cross. In this we can see part of the difference between what is done by the worshiper and what is done by the priest in the ritual.

7. *Animal-son skinned, by worshiper*

Exodus 12 does not say that the Passover was skinned, but 2 Chronicles 35:11 shows that it was. The verb for "skin" is also used to strip a person of his garments. Prophetically, this happened to Jesus at His crucifixion, and especially in that He left His old garments behind at His resurrection, in preparation for receiving new garments of glory. In both cases, this removal of skin/clothing was done by human hands, human agents of the Father.

8. *Animal-son cut up, by worshiper*

In the case of Passover, and in Jesus' death, the offering was not cut up into pieces; there is no unclean part of the Passover, of Jesus. This aspect of the rite applies only to its present meaning, where the animal represents also the worshiper.

9. *Fire stoked up, by priest*

The fire used to cook the Passover was made by human hands originally, while in the prophetic dimension this event corresponds to Pentecost, where the fire fell without human hands. Now, since the fire is inside the altar, which represents the human person (since blood is put upon it), this speaks of the coming of the Spirit into the believer, so that he can receive the offering into himself.

10. *Clean pieces put into fire, by priest*

The entire Passover is considered clean, even the entrails (Ex. 12:9). No distinction is made. Similarly, Jesus was wholly clean. Again, while in the first Passover human hands cooked the meat, in the prophetic dimension Jesus' entrance into the glory of the Spirit was apart from human action. Putting the animal into the fire inside the altar means that the worshiper now eats into himself, by the power of the Spirit, the substitutionary work of the Passover animal, of Jesus Christ.

11. *Unclean pieces washed, by worshiper*

We have to move beyond Passover itself to see what this part of the rite looks back to. Passover, the offering of a substitute apart from us, is finished. The baptism of the unclean aspects of the animal corresponds to the baptism of Israel in the Red Sea. The people themselves moved through the Red Sea; thus, this was human action.

12. *Cleansed pieces put into fire, by priest*

I suggest that the appearance of the Pillar of Cloudy Fire, hovering over Israel and encasing them, signifies their entrance into the communion of the Spirit. The appearance of the Cloud was apart from human action.

13. *Ascension in smoke*

Here we arrive at Mount Sinai.

14. *Sweet savor to God*

God makes covenant with us at Sinai.

15. *Worshiper departs*

Here is the departure from Sinai, the movement back into the world.

Now let us consider the present meaning of the ritual.

1. *Yahweh enthroned in the Tabernacle* (Exod. 40; 2 Chron. 5)

The once-for-all Passover event is over, and Yahweh is enthroned on high. Similarly, Jesus has ascended to His throne and now institutes His memorial-worship on the earth.

2. *Spirit-fire sent into the Altar* (Lev. 9:24; 2 Chron. 7:1)

This corresponds to Pentecost, or to a specific application of Pentecost in that it is the presence of the Spirit that makes the worship possible.

3. *Son-of-the-herd* (Lev. 1:5) brought near, by worshiper

The believer brings the animal as a memorial of the once-for-all Passover event. He is acting as a "son of Israel," which means as a son of God and also as part of the daughter of God, destined to be a brother of Christ and His bride.[52] The worshiper brings forward a symbol of Passover, of Jesus, and by his actions will show that he accepts what God has done for him.

4. *Hand laid on animal-son, by worshiper*

The leaning of the hand signifies identification. The worshiper pours himself into the animal, inserting himself into it. Now what happens to the animal is also going to happen to him. The animal will carry him along with itself in the ritual. Similarly, now that Jesus has died apart from us and for us, He now carries us with Him, and His death and new life become ours. We cannot ascend to the throne

---

52 Sonship imagery in the Bible is individualistic. Whether male or female, we are each sons of God. Daughter/bride imagery is corporate. Together we are all the daughter and bride, but individually we are not considered such.

by our own power; we must be carried. Similarly, we cannot grow to maturity on our own power; we must live our lives by faith, hope, and love in the one who carries us.

5. *Animal-son slain, by worshiper*

The worshiper kills himself. He puts to death his own "old man." He does this by identifying with the perfect sacrifice, the unblemished animal, the Son of God slain for humanity. By killing the spotless animal, the worshiper confesses that his own death is not adequate and cannot please God or have the effect of bringing about a resurrection. It is only in union with the perfect offering that his own death can have that result.

6. *Blood displayed, by priest*

The priest represents the Spirit in this aspect of the ritual. The Spirit shows our actions to the Father. The Spirit displays to the Father that we have accepted Jesus' blood on our behalf and that, in union with Him, we have killed ourselves.

7. *Animal-son skinned, by worshiper*

The worshiper takes off his own old garment, so that he can receive new garments as God's son, as Christ's bride.

8. *Animal-son cut up, by worshiper*

The animal is cut up into parts, some of which are clean and some of which are unclean. It is at this point that it becomes apparent that the animal represents both the savior and the saved, both the sinless substitute and the sinful worshiper. While these have been united in the rite up until this point, they must be briefly separated before they can be reunited in the transfiguring fire. The fact that the worshiper does the cutting indicates, I believe, that the worshiper must distinguish between his unclean self and his perfect savior. (There are other dimensions of the cutting up of the animal that we shall examine in due course.)

9. *Fire stoked up, by priest*

The fire of the Spirit, of God's presence, which has been present all along, is now made more manifest. The Spirit comes, so to speak, to do His work.

10. *Clean pieces put into fire, by priest*

The priest and fire, the Spirit's agents, accept the sinless aspect of the offering first.

11. *Unclean pieces washed, by worshiper*

The water used to wash the pieces comes from the Laver of Cleansing, which is a shell of water held off the ground on a pedestal that is not connected to it. The Laver represents the firmament, and the water represents the heavenly water. Thus, the water comes down from the clean parts of the animal that have already ascended. In this way, the unclean parts are cleansed by the work of the clean parts and are reunited to them judicially by baptismal water. The worshiper does the washing, showing that he accepts the finished work of the clean part of the animal on his behalf.

Heavenly water is water permeated by the heavenly rainbow, sign of the covenant. The glistening water on the animal, and on us at our baptisms, is the first form of our new garments of glory. The fire will be the second form thereof.

12. *Cleansed pieces put into fire, by priest*

Now the cleansed pieces are joined to the clean pieces in the fire, where they mingle in transfigured fellowship. It is the priest, the Spirit's agent, who does this. The animal, judicially reunited in baptism, is now really reunited in the fire. The fire completes the reclothing process. The worshiper is glorified together with Christ.

13. *Ascension in smoke*

Now reunited, the cleansed and clean pieces together ascend to the throne of God in heaven.

14. *Sweet savor to God*

God is pleased to accept the worshiper.

15. *Worshiper departs*

The worshiper goes forth transformed into a new man, to take dominion over all the earth.

This large rite passes through our five stages, but to understand this we shall have to group various specific events, as follows:

A. (1. above) God is enthroned in the Tabernacle as Yahweh, who is the Son of course, but in this kingly position He reflects the Father's attributes.

B. (2.) The Father sends the Spirit, the fire, to the earth, the altar.

C. (3–12.) The Spirit's presence calls forth the Son, and then comes the marriage (see below).

D. (13.) The Spirit's fire carries the Son and Bride to the Father.

E. (14–15.) The Father accepts both and sends the worshiper out renewed and restored.

If we look at the rite from the perspective of the worshiper, we can also find a sequence of five zones:

A' (3–4.) The animal-son is brought near and the worshiper leans on it with his hand, identifying with it. In a sense, the animal-son is Groom, and the worshiper is Bride, as we shall see.

B' (5–6.) The animal-son is slain and the proof of its transition through death is displayed on the altar, which also symbolizes the worshiper and signifies that the blood is applied to him and that he accepts it. In union with the animal-son, the worshiper has also died and gone through death.

C' (7–12.) The animal, having gone through this passage, is now united, Groom and Bride.

D' (13.) There is another passage through another kind of death, this time in the fire and the ascension through smoke.

E' (14.) The animal enters God's presence.

The marriage stage, which is the C section of both sequences, calls for a bit more comment. The animal is divided into its clean parts (the Husband) and its unclean parts (us), which are washed. All are united in the fire on the altar. This is marriage, and a pointed revelation of the Son as Husband. The cutting up is by the Word, the Law (Heb. 4:12). The washing is also a washing by the Word, and we have associated marriage with the giving of the Law in our preceding chapter (John 15:3, and especially Eph. 5:26; cf. Ezek. 16:4–13).

The animal-son must be male. The rite might have included a male and a female animal, both slain and then mixed in the fire. To understand the fact that part of this male animal represents the Bride, recall that Eve was taken out of Adam. Adam contained Eve to begin with. The animal is essentially a son, not a daughter, pointing back to Isaac and forward to Jesus; but the animal contains the Bride in essence, and thus when it is cut up, it is divided into male and female parts, clean and unclean, Jesus and sinners, Husband and Bride.[53]

The three fundamental sacrifices, as discussed previously, are set out as five in Leviticus. The order, when all are offered, is this:[54]

1. *Trespass Offering.* This is to satisfy God and thus to enable us to draw near to Him.

2. *Purification Offering.* This is a form of cleansing, associated with the Spirit for that reason, and the disposition of the blood is highlighted in the rite. Blood is associated with life (Lev. 17) and in all the rituals it flows downward, either splashed against the side of the altar and dribbling down, or placed on the horns at its top and then poured out at its base. This downward movement speaks of the descent of the Spirit. Blood, like water, is a purifying agent in the Law. (The outer shell of the altar corresponds to the skin of the worshiper; thus, the blood is put upon him.)

3. *Ascension Offering.* Here the flesh is highlighted, and putting the clean and the cleansed flesh together into the altar relates to marriage; thus the Son is highlighted. (The inside of the hollow altar is the inside of the worshiper; thus, he eats the offering.)

---

[53] The fact that the woman is initially "contained" in the man helps explain why the circumcision of men under the Law carried their women with it into God's priestly nation.

[54] The order can be seen clearly in Leviticus 9, save for the Trespass Offering. A man who must bring a Trespass Offering for some serious sin must do so before he can bring a cleansing Purification Offering, so that the Trespass Offering comes first.

4. *Tribute Offering.* Tribute is what we bring to God, so that we are returning upward to Him, a point specifically made by the burning of incense on top of it. This offering is also called "memorial," which means it points back to the Ascension. The memorial is what sustains us as we move into life after our marriage to the Son.

5. *Peace Offering.* The meal is what is highlighted here. We have fully entered God's palace and now sit down with Him.

Before moving further, let me point out that our Christian worship is a sacrifice of praise and that the order of the sacrifices has long been understood as providing insight into the order of Christian worship. Briefly:

1. *Trespass*: Crossing the threshold into God's presence by means of His forgiving us of original sin. Thus, the call to worship.

2. *Purification*: Cleansing from sin; the confession of sins and absolution.

3. *Ascension*: Being cut up by the Word; the Word and sermon.

4. *Tribute*: Consisting of bread and wine, this can be linked to the first part of the communion, which is the offertory, when the bread and wine (and tithes) are brought forward.

5. *Peace*: The meal: communion.

6. *The worshiper departs*: commissioning and benediction.[55]

---

55 For further comment on the order of offerings and the sequence of Christian worship, see Gordon Wenham, *The Book of Leviticus*, NICOT (Grand Rapids: Eerdmans, 1979), 66; R. K. Harrison, *Leviticus*, Tyndale OT Commentaries (Downers Grove: InterVarsity Press, 1981), 106–107; James Gracey Murphy, *A Critical and Exegetical Commentary on the Book of Leviticus*, International Critical Commentary (Andover: Draper, 1872), 20–21; C. F. Keil, *Leviticus*, trans. James Martin (Grand Rapids: Eerdmans, 1973), 345–346, on Leviticus 9:8–21; Samuel H. Kellogg, *The Book of Leviticus* (London: Armstrong, 1899), 222, 228; John Peter Lange, *Leviticus*, trans. Philip Schaff (Grand Rapids: Eerdmans, n.d. [reprint, 1876]), 80. See also Jeffrey J. Meyers's *The Lord's Service: The Grace of Covenant Renewal Worship* (Moscow: Canon Press, 2003), especially pp. 20ff., where Meyers provides full bibliographical information and extensive quotations from the commentaries listed above, and others as well.

THE LORD'S SUPPER

Before attempting to make any applications of this model to our ritual, some general remarks are in order. The flow of events, the sequence in time, can be seen as moving through three, five, or seven general zones. I trust that I have made the first two of these perspectives clear enough by this point. Yet the fact that the same sequences of biography, history, and ritual can be "seen" in three, five, seven, or even ten phases indicates that we do not have "hard and fast boundaries" between the stages within history, biography, and ritual. Rather, we have a general flow that can be, and should be, considered in each of these ways, because the Bible teaches us to consider them in such ways. But this also means that there may be, and in fact is, more than one way to look at life, history, and ritual in each of these ways.

For instance, when we considered human life in five phases, we considered the following general sequence:

1. Conception/birth
2. Adolescence
3. Marriage
4. Adult life and crises
5. Death

But we could also do it this way:

1. Conception
2. Initial days after birth, transition to:
3. Baptism
4. Post-baptismal life, transition to:
5. Death

. . . since our baptism is our washing and marriage to Jesus and a definite transition in our lives. Our life before baptism is, so to speak, a time of suffering under Adam's judgment. Our life after baptism is a time of suffering in union with the sufferings of Jesus. Thus, these are two "hope" periods.

In my essays called "Crisis Time: Patriarchal Prologue,"[56] I look at the midlife crises of Abraham, Jacob, Joseph, and Moses. We can lay out their lives easily in these five stages, as follows:

1. *Initial promises:*
    Call of Abram
    Promise to Rebekah that Jacob is to inherit
    Visions of Joseph as a youth
    Moses' rescue by the daughter of Pharaoh

2. *Early life and struggles*:
    Abram: Genesis 12–14
    Jacob and Esau
    Joseph sold into Egypt
    Moses in Pharaoh's court, eventually being driven out

3. *Meeting with God and receiving something from Him*:
    Abram/Abraham: Genesis 15 & 17
    Jacob at Bethel and getting his wives and sons
    Joseph elevated by Potiphar
    Moses' marriage and happy life in the wilderness

4. *Dying to that gift*:
    Giving up Ishmael and then offering Isaac
    Jacob at Peniel, then losing Joseph, and then his sons massacring the men of Salem/Shechem[57]
    Joseph in prison
    Moses sent back to Egypt and forced to lead wicked people for forty years

5. *Receiving back something better in the later part of life*:

---

56 In *Biblical Horizons* 109–113 (September 1998–January 1999).

57 A study of the chronology of Genesis shows that this event happened after Joseph was sold into slavery. When Joseph was sold, at the age of 17, Dinah was at the most about 10 years old (Gen. 30:21, 25; Joseph's birth is out of chronological order, because of the theology of the passage: He is the miracle son. Leah could not have had seven children, and also a period of barrenness, in only seven years.)

> Abraham receiving Isaac back, and then six more sons
> Jacob receiving Joseph back and moving to happy Goshen
> Joseph elevated to Pharaoh's right hand
> Moses' death and entrance into God's presence

All the same, one might lay out these lives in other ways, which would display the same fivefold sequence. One might, for instance, see the center of Moses' life as the wonderful giving of the Law at Mount Sinai. As we shall eventually see, a fuller display of these lives involves a sevenfold sequence.

We saw that there are at least two ways of looking at the individual sacrifices, one beginning with God's enthronement in the Tabernacle, and the other beginning with bringing the animal and laying hands on it. These cover mostly the same ground, but with different emphases.

With these general observations in mind, we can now turn to the Lord's Supper and consider it, in more than one way, as a move through five zones of ritual sequence.

We have seen that the movement from bread to breaking to wine can be seen as a display of human history from the Old Creation through the crucifixion to the New Creation, and as a display of human biography from early priestly life through midlife crisis to eldership. Let us now expand the three to five.

History as a whole can be considered this way:

1. God takes hold of the loaf. This is the impregnation of Adam's dust with the Spirit.

2. The Spirit matures the loaf to the mid-point of history.

3. The loaf is broken at the cross, and wine (blood) is given. Here is the marriage: The water from Jesus' side speaks of cleansing by the Word, and the blood speaks of marriage.

4. The Spirit matures the wine to the end of history.

5. The wine is finally poured out in the final tribulation, and we come to the final resurrection.

Similarly as regards biography:

1. God gives life to the united ovum and sperm, laying hold of it.

2. The Spirit matures the loaf from fetus through adolescence.

3. The loaf is broken in marriage. Recall that Eve was taken from Adam's side, from the broken loaf/body of Adam. Compare this to the blood and water that flowed from Jesus' side, forming the new Church. The "wine of joy" comes with marriage; but

4. The wine must be matured through the rest of life, through new trials and difficulties.

5. Finally the wine is poured out, as we share our wisdom with others in the twilight of our lives, and finally as we die gloriously in union with Jesus.

When we look at our ritual, it is difficult to find five zones of general meaning that correspond nicely with what we have discussed thus far; although, as mentioned, the flow covers the same ground.

1. *Jesus takes bread.* This links with the enthronement of God in the Tabernacle, step 1 of the Ascension Offering in our first consideration discussed above. This is the rite considered from God's side, in terms of His actions upon us. It's the beginning of human life and of human history. In Leviticus, the worshiper leans his hand on the animal-son, identifying with it. In the same way, Jesus' taking bread identifies Him with it, and since the bread also represents the Church as His body, it signifies His identification with us.

From the standpoint of the worshiper, it is the minister or his appointed agent who takes hold of the bread. This links with steps 3 and 4 of the rite, in our second consideration above, from the standpoint of the worshiper. Just as Jesus takes hold of the bread, taking hold of us and identifying with us, so we take hold of the bread, taking hold of Jesus and identifying with Him.

2. *Jesus gives thanks and breaks the bread.* Remembering to give thanks is how we persevere through trials. We must remember what God has done for us and reason that He has not abandoned us. This is the transition between our beginnings and our marriage. Compare step 2 above: The purging fire comes down on us, for we are the altars (compare the day of Pentecost).

From our standpoint, that of the worshiper, the minister or his agent breaks the bread, showing that the congregation is broken in union with the brokenness of Christ. Compare steps 5–6 above: The purging blood flows down the sides of us as altars, after the animal-son has been slain. In the bloody offerings, the display of the blood shows that we accept the death of the animal on our behalf. Breaking the bread shows that we accept Jesus' death on our behalf and that we are ready to die in union with Him.

The breaking of the bread also links with steps 7 & 8, the skinning and cutting up of the animal-son. Jesus is the Loaf of humanity, and His being ripped in half also means that humanity is ripped in half. The two halves, in the animal sacrifice, represent the whole of humanity divided into Groom and Bride, as we have seen. Consider again that it is in pre-adolescence and adolescence that boys and girls separate from each other. The breaking of the bread not only signifies the death of Jesus, but also His separating from us so that He can save us and then return to us and marry us.

It is no accident that this parallel exists: Boys separate from girls and then seek them out, and Jesus separates from His Bride on the cross and then seeks her out. The order of redemption follows the order of creation.

What is added in the order of redemption is that the Groom is clean, while the Bride must be cleansed. Notice in the Ascension Offering that first the clean pieces are put into the fire, separate from the unclean ones. This is part of the time of separation, when Jesus ascends to the Father first. Then, on the basis of that sacrifice so to speak, the unclean pieces can be washed. Then the clean pieces join their Husband in the Spirit's fire, to ascend with Him.

This part of the Supper also links with step 9, the stoking up of the Spirit's fire within the altar. As we join in prayer and thanksgiving with Jesus, the Spirit prepares us to eat the food given us. The fire "desires" the reunification of all the parts of the animal, just as the Spirit brings boys and girls together as the Divine Matchmaker.

3. *Jesus gives it to us with a command to eat it.* We eat it and finish out the supper with Jesus, after which He takes the cup and gives it to us. Thus, there is a "honeymoon" after we eat/marry Jesus. (This short period of time tends to evaporate into virtual nothingness in the way the Supper is usually done in worship, but suppose we sang a few hymns between the bread and the wine?) Law is also present here, for Jesus gives a command, without any explanation.

In the older rite, the altar eats the sacrifice as the animal parts are put inside of it (steps 10–12). The animal rite separates the two parts of the animal-son, clean first and then unclean. In our ritual, these two actions are put together. The bread we eat is both Jesus and His Church (1 Cor. 10:16–18). We don't individually eat from both sides of the broken loaf, but the congregation as a whole does so. The congregation as a whole eats the marriage into itself.

I suggest that Jesus' taking the cup of wine fits here also. Being given wine is the sign of being a king, and wine is associated with marriage (John 2). This is the beginning of our marital kingship.

4 *Jesus gives thanks for the wine.* Here is our married life with Jesus, and the giving of thanks points again to the trials and difficulties we experience in our marriage to Him, as He perfects us. It corresponds to the ascension of the reunited animal-son in smoke as it journeys back up to God (step 13). Once again, the fire of the Spirit is both our trials and the hope He gives us as we pass through them, as we move through the rest of our life on our way to heaven.

Next Jesus gives the cup. We have become bread, and now Jesus intends to add wine to our lives.

Jesus not only commands us to drink it, but also explains that it is shed. We notice that this time we get both Law and Wisdom, explanation. Jesus tells us that the blood is the (New) Covenant and that "as often as you do it," we are to do it as His memorial. Thus, we are given some more liberty and discretion about when to do the second half of the ritual. For instance, the wine might be omitted sometimes by a poor congregation that is able to bring bread every week but to purchase wine only occasionally.

When we drink the wine, we are accepting the suffering that is our privilege as people united to a suffering Savior. While I cannot recall any Bible passage that specifically links wine with fire, the fact is that the alcohol in wine provides a slightly burning sensation. Thus, we drink the fire into ourselves.

5. *Peace with God*. Though it is not pointed specifically in the rite, the fact is that wine gives us rest and pleasure in our stomach, though it may be somewhat sharp in our mouths. It is a "sweet savor" to us, just as the older sacrifices were a sweet savor to God (step 14). Here is the autumn of our lives, corresponding to our peace with God. Notice that after the wine, the disciples sang a psalm with Jesus before departing.

As we approach death, and at our death, we are poured out as a drink offering. Consider that the wine that has been poured into us over the years—replacing our old blood with new, so to speak—is now poured out for others.

Once again, the entire rite of the Supper is more detailed than this survey, but the details flow through this fivefold sequence. We can do more with the details if we look more closely at the two halves, and in doing so we shall make further applications of the fivefold sequence to life and history. We shall apply the bread rite to our lives up to marriage and the wine rite to our lives after marriage, and to history up to the cross and to history after the cross.

1. *Jesus took bread.* As always, this is the beginning.

2. *Jesus gave thanks.* Biographically, this is the time of learning stories and of being spanked as small children. Historically, this is the period before Sinai.

3. *Jesus broke it and gave commands.* We'll link this historically with Sinai and biographically with the "parrot" stage, the time of law.

4. *We eat it.* We can link this historically with the Kingdom era, when men like David and Solomon, having eaten the Law and meditated on it, give forth wisdom. Biographically we'll link this with the "pert" stage, the time of arguing about the meaning of the rules. Since what we eat is broken bread, we are eating tribulation and thus must move through this time by hope.

5. *We relax and enjoy it*. Notice that Jesus took the cup "after supper," so that there was originally a time of peace before the second half of the rite began. Biographically, this is the time of joy when we marry. Historically, I suggest we link it with the Restoration from exile, when the Jews initially enjoyed a time of peace with God.

1a. *Jesus took the cup*. Here Jesus can be seen as laying hold on the Church at Pentecost, taking hold of us as newlyweds, in order to move both history and life to their appointed ends.

2a. *Jesus gave thanks*. Here is another time of trial, by implication. Consider it biographically as the time of child-rearing and historically as the whole period from the death of Stephen until the latter-day glory, when the kingdom of God covers the earth.

3b. *Jesus gave the wine, explaining that it was His shed blood, and gave command to drink it*. Historically I think this is reflected in what the book of Revelation teaches us, that it is through the blood of the martyrs that the kingdom comes fully into history. When the Church has learned to drink Jesus' suffering and death into herself, the latter-day glory will come afterwards. Similarly, I suggest that biographically this is the beginning of what I have called the midlife crisis. As these times of trial come on us, Jesus tells us to go ahead and drink them and not to reject them, just as He did not reject the Father's cup in Gethsemane.

4b. *We drink it*. Only in this way will we acquire the "prophetic" wine of kingly wisdom, so that we have something wonderful to impart to others in the twilight of our lives, when we are elders. Historically, as I said above, the Church must drink the suffering Jesus sends her.

5b. *We relax and enjoy it*. Wine may burn in the mouth (the moment of suffering), but it warms and relaxes us inside. This is the twilight of life, and the latter-day glory.

All of this may seem "allegorical," and in a sense it is, but in a biblical sense. I shall take up the question of allegory later on, when we get to the sevenfold sequence. For now my point is that the rite of the Lord's Supper is designed, from one perspective, to put us back into a true and right way of living our whole lives and to a right way of understanding history. The rite covers not just the whole of Jesus' own life, but of all humanity's life as well, since we are all living "in Him."

7.

Death and New Life

At this point it will be helpful to think a bit more about the Spirit's work in the liturgy. We have seen that the "tribulation" phases of the ritual are particularly associated with hope, reasoning with ourselves so that we give thanks, and with the Spirit. I have made the point that it is the Spirit's motion that is given to the Father, so that the Father gives Himself to the Son, and vice versa. And we have seen that this self-giving on the part of each Person involves a kind of death to His own things, a giving up, a self-denial, whereby each Person lives by hope in the other Two that what He gives up, He will receive back abundantly from Them.

With this in mind, we might well say that "death" is the gift of the Spirit. The Spirit enables humility and self-giving, dying to our own things for the sake of others.

Yet, the Spirit is associated with life in the Bible, as expressed in the Nicene Creed, where He is the "Lord and Giver of life." We think of life and death as opposites, and in the sense of the curse for sin, death is indeed the opposite of life. But there is something more involved, for the imagery associated with the Spirit, such as blood, water, and fire, speak of both life and death. What this means is that it is by means of a passage through death that we come to experience greater life.

It is important that we come to understand this, because without understanding it we shall not understand the full meaning of the death of the animals in the Old Creation rituals, the death of Jesus, and the application of His death to us in the Supper.

The premier example of this "good death" in the Bible is perhaps in Genesis 2. What we are about to look at happened *before* the rebellion of Adam and shows us the aspect of "death" that is a positive blessing, not negative and qualified by the curse.[58]

"And Yahweh God caused to fall a deep-sleep (tardema) upon the man, and he slept (yashan)" (Gen. 2:21a). As you can see, the Hebrew verb and noun for deep-sleep (radam and tardema) are not related at all to the ordinary verb for sleep (yashan). We might render deep-sleep as unconsciousness, but as we shall see, such a translation will not work. We ask the question, then, why does the Hebrew use a completely different word? Why not just say "deep sleep," using the adjective "deep" to modify the ordinary noun for sleep?

An investigation of the usage of the peculiar verb translated "deep-sleep" will reveal that it has a special meaning associated with de-creation or death, especially in covenant-making acts of God. The first instance of it is here, where we see God separate the woman from the man and then join them in covenant.

Deep-sleep is close to death and is the place where covenants are made; it is de-creation preceding either total death or resurrection. The term occurs in Judges 4:21, where Sisera falls into deep-sleep just before his head is crushed. Building upon this incident is 1 Sam. 26:12,

---

58 The following is taken, with modifications, from my *Trees and Thorns: Studies in Genesis 2–4* (Niceville, FL: Biblical Horizons, 2005).

when David finds Saul in deep-sleep and is given opportunity to crush his head, but merely removes items from around his head instead. Coming back to life from deep-sleep, Saul renews covenant with David (1 Sam. 26:13–25).

Jonah, fleeing from God, is found in deep-sleep in Jonah 1:5–6 (the word is found in both verses). Soon he will be cast overboard and experience death and resurrection in the belly of the great fish, renewing his covenant with God therein.

Some, like Sisera, move from deep-sleep to the total sleep of death. The Egyptian army was in deep-sleep in the Red Sea, but unlike Jonah in the sea, they were not raised to life again (Ps. 76:5–6). Such is the case also in Isaiah 29:10: "For Yahweh has poured over you a spirit of deep-sleep." Similarly, the sluggard in his laziness is moving into a deep-sleep condition near death and may starve to death (Prov. 19:15). The same fate awaits him who deep-sleeps during harvest (Prov. 10:5).

The man who is in deep-sleep and is headed for full-death is not conscious, but the man who is in deep-sleep and is headed for resurrection may be in a vision. Eliphaz claims to have had a vision while in deep-sleep (Job 4:13), and Elihu states that God visits men with visions while they are in deep-sleep (Job 33:15). As we shall see, Abraham's experience lies behind these two men's observations.

The association of deep-sleep with death and resurrection is clearly seen in Daniel. In Daniel 8:18, Daniel is told that he is going to be shown the end. Immediately he falls into deep-sleep, but then is raised to stand on his feet to be shown the vision. Similarly, as soon as Daniel hears the Angel of Yahweh speaking to him in Daniel 10:9, he falls into deep-sleep, from which he is raised to hear the message. This event is a type of the death and resurrection of Israel that is prophesied in the message. An identical death-resurrection sequence is found in Revelation 1:17, where John fell at Jesus' feet "like a dead man" and then was raised again. John's death and resurrection is a type of the death and resurrection of the Church described in Revelation.

In our survey we skipped Genesis 15, because it perhaps gives the fullest picture of this kind of event. At the beginning of this chapter, Abram has become aware that though God has promised him the land, he does not possess it. The land has refused to yield anything to him, forcing him by famine into Egypt. Then, when he finally returned to the land, a civil war raged over it, during which is became clear to him that he was not in charge of the land at all. Yet, Abram had defeated Chedorlaomer and had delivered Lot.

Now Abram is afraid Chedorlaomer will return, and God appears to comfort him. During the night God tells him that his seed will be like the stars and that he will possess the land. Abram asks for assurance, and God tells him to cut three animals in half and to kill two birds. During the next day, Abram does this. The birds seek to devour the carcasses, but Abram drives them away. Notice that the animals are dead but are not devoured. They are in deep-sleep, but not yet dead, symbolically speaking. They are dead, but not under the curse-judgment of the covenant. Then Abram himself falls into deep-sleep (Gen. 15:12). While in this condition, Abram sees God pass between the parts of the animals.

This event is often misunderstood today. God is not saying, "May I be ripped in half and devoured by the birds if I don't keep this covenant." Rather, God is making a covenant between the two parts of the animals, which signify Abram on the one hand and the land on the other. This symbolism is possible because both man and the animals are made of soil, so animals can represent both soil and man. God's fiery Spirit will reunite the two halves of the broken covenant. Adam was cursed from the soil, and up to now Abram has experienced that curse. Now, however, God will resurrect that relationship by His Spirit, and on the basis of the death-sacrifice of a representative.

Thus, the covenant is made through death and resurrection. When we apply this sequence to Jesus, we can see immediately what it means. Jesus is the animal torn in half (not literally, but as signified by the tearing of the Temple veil), but not cursed in His death. He died, but did not undergo corruption. The birds did not devour Him, though he was hanged up and made available to them by His crucifixion (compare 2 Sam. 21:9–10). Then, God's Spirit raised Jesus from the dead, passing between the parts and granting covenant renewal. Jesus' spirit was reunited with His flesh.

Death and New Life

For Abram to appreciate this, Abram too must die. He must enter deep-sleep and then awaken. So must we. We must die to the old broken, cursed, shattered covenant in Adam and be raised into the new covenant in Christ. Then we are restored to God, to one another, and to the world. Then the soil no longer curses us. God Himself is the bond of the new covenant.

The instances we have looked at all happened after the fall of man, and thus deep-sleep carries with it the possibility of final death or of resurrection to the new creation. Before the fall, however, it did not carry this precise meaning. Adam goes into deep-sleep and "dies" to his state of being alone. Then, from his side, God makes a partner for him. When Adam awakes, he is in covenant union with his wife. This covenant is made through blood, for it is not just a rib but a whole flesh-and-bone (and blood) piece of Adam that is made into Eve; as Adam says, "This is flesh of my flesh, bone of my bone." And Adam also says that man must "die" to his old family to make a new one: "For this cause a man shall leave his father and mother and cleave to his wife."

Thus, dying to the old and moving by resurrection into the new is not just something that comes into being because of the fall of man. Human life has involved such passages even apart from sin. After the fall, of course, such transitions become much more traumatic, and in the greatest such passage what must be left behind is an old world of sin, while what we are raised to is a new world in God's kingdom.

The formation of Eve from Adam's side is fulfilled when the soldier pierces Jesus' side and blood and water come out of it. Jesus has died, but is not to be cursed. In that place of deep-sleep, His bride is formed. The Church is created on the basis of the blood of Christ, and by the water of baptism that comes from His side. It is the Spirit, the paraclete, the "side-comer," who comes from Jesus' side in baptismal water, and it is the Spirit who forms the bride.[59]

---

[59] This concludes the material from *Trees and Thorns*.

I have included this discussion to establish more fully that there is a kind of "death" that does not reflect God's curse but is entirely a positive and glory-producing event. Its root is in God, as I have argued, as each Person "dies" to His own properties for the sake of the other two. And I have argued that what each Person receives back, since it comes from the two, is therefore double. What needs to be added is that this "death" experience leads to a birth and to a marriage, as Eve was born from Adam's side to be his bride.

We have to bear in mind always that in God these things are eternal, atemporal, or, better, that God possesses the fullness of uncreated time and of uncreated life. These transitions are "conditions" in eternity, while they are manifested in time as events. (The root of time is in God, in the Spirit's Motion, but what we experience as the flow of time is not what God experiences.)

Yet with this in mind, and since we cannot think in any way other than temporally, we can say that each Person gives a "new birth" to the other two when He "dies" and passes on His property to Them. The other two already exist, so that the bare existence of the Persons does not depend upon receiving anything from the others. It is a "new birth" that they receive, and the new birth is an enhancement of their "previous" existence. Similarly, while the Three "already" exist in a relationship with each other, there is a fuller "marital" relationship that comes as a result of the "death" of each for the others.

I suggest that the "new birth" that each Person gives the others possibly resolves the problem of the "generation of the Son from the Father," especially since the "birth" of the Son is actually usually associated with His new birth, or resurrection, in the Bible. "You are My Son; this day have I begotten You" (Ps. 2) does not refer to the birth of David, nor by implication to the birth of Jesus, but to their enthronements after a time of trial. This is quite along the lines that we are considering, that in the Godhead the "death" of each person results ultimately in His own receiving more, and that our various "deaths" make us into priests and kings and prophets. The Son does not receive bare existence, as God, from God the Father; but He receives a "new birth" into a greater fullness of God-hood.

Since the Spirit has the property of Motion and Life (and therefore also of "death") in God, it is the Spirit's eternal work to provide these new births and these marriage linkages.

These phenomena in God are played out in His images, humanity, in biography and history. Adam was in an important way alone before Eve was born from his side. He was not fully alone, but there was more fellowship in store for him. Passing through "death," Adam gave birth to Eve and found her a closer partner than any creature he had previously encountered. Here we have the first part of the fivefold structure of biography, history, and ritual. Adam was (1) alone, and God laid hold on him. Adam (2) passed through the Spirit's gift of death and life. Adam (3) gave birth and found a wife, a double, from his side.

There is a second phase, however, that is equally important for us to understand. God told Adam to refrain temporarily from the Tree of Knowledge of Good and Evil, which was associated with death. The prohibition was temporary, as we see from Genesis 1:29 ("I have given you ... every tree whose fruit yields seed; to you it will be for food"), so that eventually Adam would indeed eat of this tree and "die." This would be a second passage through some kind of "deep sleep," and this would result in greater glory than before. Since "good and evil" are associated with full maturity and kingship (Heb. 5:14), this passage through "death" must be linked with the crisis that comes upon us after we have been married for a while and that fits us for kingship.

We shall not rehash all the various fivefold sequences we have already examined, to make the point again that a kind of death, a passage through hope-filled trials, is found in the second and fourth zones of the sequence. At this point, I simply want to reinforce how such passages result in new births and marriages. A few illustrations will have to suffice.

Jesus said that the essential sign of His work would be the "sign of Jonah." Notice that after his passage through deep-sleep (good death), Jonah was born again by being cast upon the land, and then a great multitude of Gentiles were converted. Since conversion is marriage to God, we can see that a marriage resulted. This is also a doubling, with Assyria now a second nation belonging to Yahweh. Jonah was the surrogate husband in this marriage, and in Jonah 4 he initially rejected that glorious task until God persuaded him to accept it.[60]

Similarly, after the trauma of his time in prison, not only did Joseph ascend over Egypt, but also, as the same passage (Gen. 41) is careful to tell us, he married an Egyptian convert. The converted Egypt is a doubling of God's people.

Abram's experience in Genesis 15 was designed to marry him to the land, from which he had previously been estranged. It is interesting to note that the birth of Ishmael follows after this event; and after the trauma of circumcision (another death experience) in Genesis 17, we come shortly to the birth of Isaac. These sons are each a doubling of Abram.

After his trauma in the wilderness apart from Saul, David was married to Israel as her king.

We could easily go through the entire Bible and show that after a passage through death, God's people not only receive back double, but also experience some kind of new birth and enter into some kind of new and fuller covenant "marriage." The exceptions, like Jeremiah, only serve to highlight the principle by way of contrast—though if we consider Daniel and Ezekiel as Jeremiah's disciples, as we must, then we can see in them a doubling of his life after his unhappy and semi-vicarious death experiences.

With all this in mind we can see that the passage through death that the animal experiences in the sacrificial offerings is not only a sign of judgment on humanity for our sins. It is deeper than that and points to the fact that only by going through some kind of deathlike experience do we come to greater glory, new birth, and marriage, one

---

[60] Notice that Jonah passes through a second and arguably a third death experience in Jonah 4: "Death is better to me than life" (vv. 3, 8). Jonah's first death experience fitted him to be a priest, to take God's word to Nineveh. His anger and second death experience should have made him an advisor to the king of Nineveh, but he left the city and rejected that kingly calling (vv. 1–5). His third death experience might have fitted him to be a prophet, to be an elder, but we don't know that it did (vv. 6–11).

way or another. The Ascension Offering is not cut in half (halved) and devoured by the birds, but is cut in half (doubled) and then put into God's fire, made whole again in a more glorious way by the Spirit.

Moreover, as we have seen, the two basic parts of the animal, rejoined, signify marriage. The animal-son starts out as Adam, alone. Passing through death and into resurrection, the animal-son not only comes back to life in a new and transfigured way (in the fire), but also is divided and finds a wife, a partner, a new relationship.

This is why the death of Jesus not only pays for our sins, but also gives us new birth (united to His new birth, His resurrection) and brings Him into marriage with us. It also means that the Kingdom now goes not only to Israel but to the nations: the doubling. If all Jesus did was pay for our sins, we would go back to being like Adam in the garden; but Jesus' death is, more profoundly, this movement through trauma to glory.

With this in mind, we can see that our ritual is not only a display of Jesus' death for our sins, which we memorialize in the Supper, but is also a display of our new birth in Him and of our marriage to Him, as well as a sign of the growth (continual doubling) of the Kingdom. By the Supper, we are given the death-life of the Spirit, enabling us, in Him, to move through distress to greater glory, so that our lives also issue in new births for others, various kinds of "marital" covenant relationships with others in the Church, and various expansions (doublings) of our lives. The Supper shows us the pattern of true human life, and the Spirit inserts us into that pattern, convicting and conforming us to it. Similarly, it shows us the true pattern of history, for as the Church dies from time to time, going through various tribulations, she is born again more glorious and more people are added in to the Great Marriage.

In conclusion, we cannot know fully what our lives would have been like if Adam had not sinned, but we can know that God-like passages through "death" would have been part of them. God Himself "dies" for others, and before he sinned, Adam "died" that Eve might be born. And he would eventually have "died" again to become a king, through the death-dealing Tree of Knowledge. Thus, the traumas that we go through in life and history, as displayed by the many rituals in the Bible, are not only chastisements for our sins (though since we are sinners, they are partly that), but are also ways in which God perfects us for greater privilege and glory.

It is for this reason that the tribulation-phases of the rite are associated with thanksgiving. Jesus gives thanks after taking the bread and after taking the cup, as we have set it out. We have said that reasoning about God's good purposes, and giving thanks despite how we feel, is how we manifest hope in the midst of these times of trial. We now know more about what that hope is: It is the full confidence that after the trial comes not only some kind of doubling of our lives, but also a new birth and a new, fuller "marriage" relationship with God and with the Church.

A final thought. As the Spirit is the Divine Matchmaker, I suggest that the marriage aspect of resurrection is most closely to be associated with the Spirit. As the Father is the Divine archetype of personhood, I suggest that the new birth is most closely to be associated with the Father. And as the Son is the Divine archetype of structure and relationship and is Himself a "double" of the Father, I suggest that the doubling of our lives is most closely to be associated with the Son. Thus, these three interpenetrating manifestations of new and glorified life stem from the three Persons of God, as His gifts to His images.

8.

REPEATING THE RITUAL

We have been considering human life, ritual, and history in five stages. There is a peaceful time of beginnings, followed by a time of trial that issues in a new birth, in a marriage. There follow more trials and final peace with God.

What I am trying to do in this series of essays is to work us gradually into a better way of thinking about our lives, as we image the life of God. What we need to do now is consider the fact that we do not do the Lord's Supper only once, but week after week. Similarly, in our lives there is not just one huge transition from bread to wine, but many such transitions that change us progressively "from glory to glory." We are not just born again once, but as children of God we encounter the Father again and again and receive new births along the way. Similarly, we must renew our marriage to Jesus (and to our earthly spouses) from time to time, and each time the marriage comes afresh and as something new. We pass from faith through hope to love many times in our lives.

We usually link the new birth and our marriage to Jesus with baptism, and rightly so, but when we see the body of Adam broken so that Eve may come from his side and reflect on the breaking of bread in our ritual, we can see that the covenant re*new*al provides us successive new births and new entrances into fuller marriage with Jesus. What starts with baptism is renewed and made new again in the Supper.

There is, in fact, a kind of sevenfold sequence to human life, and it flows from the sevenfold work of the Spirit. Before we turn to Genesis 1, however, it will be useful to consider some exemplary lives in the Bible, and our own lives, along these lines. The reason for this is that making an application of Genesis 1 to human life involves taking its features in a symbolic way (for instance, sun and moon as man and wife), and we will be much better able to suggest such symbolic applications if we first have in mind the sevenfold structure of human life as the Bible sets it forth.

Using the symbolism of the Supper, we move from bread to wine three special times in our lives. Three significant times we are broken so that the wine of wisdom can become more manifest in us.

DAVID, ADAM, AND JACOB

Consider David first of all. We first meet David as a lad in his father's house. As a young child, David enjoyed peace and security. Then, however, he was made a shepherd, and he experienced a time of trial fighting a bear and a lion. As a climax of this time of trial, he defeated Goliath. At this point he left home, which we must see as a breaking of the bread of his previous life and context. He was adopted by King Saul and married Saul's daughter; Saul's son Jonathan gave him his own armor and by so doing gave to David his own position as crown prince and heir. David has begun in Jesse's house, passed through a period of breaking away, and has now become the prince of Israel in Saul's house.

This corresponds to the first three steps of the fivefold sequence we have been considering, as it climaxes with a new birth (adoption) and marriage.

Now, compare this with Adam. Adam went through deep-sleep and then was born again, returned to life, and found a wife. In both these cases, the passage through "death" was not really traumatic at all. Adam was asleep. David evidently experienced no great fear or trauma as he faced bear, lion, and Goliath. When a young man leaves home to get married and to seek his fortune, he does not feel any great trauma. Rather, he is full of expectations. Yet there is a death to the old and a new life in the new.

Now, however, Adam is tested with regard to the Tree of the Knowledge of Good and Evil, which we have seen is associated with wisdom, rule, and authority: with kingship.[61] This is a more traumatic time, since Adam is awake and must force himself to submit to God's command not to eat of the Tree before God is ready to give it to him.

Similarly, David now enters into a much greater time of trial. He has been anointed as future king, but Saul is still on the throne. Saul is wicked and persecutes David, but David must not put forth his hand and seize the throne from Saul. Even after Saul is dead, David must not try to seize the northern tribes from Saul's son Ishbosheth. He is repeatedly tempted to do these things, but he refuses. As a result, he eventually does become king over all of Israel, and this is his marriage to the nation. As we saw last time, Psalm 2 speaks of the enthronement of the king as the begetting of a son by God, the true High King.

As a prince, David is under authority. He is a priest, which means "palace servant," of Saul. The trauma that he undergoes is what gives him the wine of wisdom and fits him to be a king. The first bread-breaking, when David leaves home and marries, makes him a new son, son of Saul. This makes him a priest, a king-to-be. The second bread-breaking, when David ascends to the throne and marries Israel, makes him a new son, the son of God. This makes him a king.

---

61   See Deuteronomy 1:39; 2 Samuel 14:17; 19:27; 1 Kings 3:9; Hebrews 5:14. For a full discussion of this, see my *Trees and Thorns*.

Now, however, David is tested as king, and this time he fails dramatically. He passed the test Adam failed, but now he fails after having been given what Adam did not receive: kingship under God. What David fails to do is to hold the kingdom that he has been given. At the time the kings go forth to war (2 Sam. 11:1), David remains behind in the palace, gets involved with Bathsheba, and murders one of his close companions. He perverts his kingly sonship and his marriage to Israel. Though he repents, trouble never leaves his house, and the trouble comes from his sons. They imitate their father, raping a sister and murdering a brother, and finally rebelling against David. Only after this long time of trial does David finally come to a measure of peace and wisdom in his old age.

The trauma that David undergoes as king fits him for the last stage of life, that of eldership or of aged prophet. It is as an old man that David prophesies. The aged prophet is no longer a man of action, but a man of words, for his body is failing. I am speaking here, of course, not of the bare function or "office" of prophet, which even a young man like Joseph might exercise, but of the aged prophet. The young prophet prophesies what God directly tells him, while the aged prophet prophesies out of his accumulated wisdom and insight.[62]

Thus we have seven steps in the life of David:

1. Childhood.
2. Early trials.
3. New birth as prince, and marriage. (*priest*)
4. More trials as prince, as priest, as servant.
5. New birth as king, and marriage to the nation. (*king*)
6. More trials as king.
7. Final wisdom as elder. (*prophet*)

---

62 Compare Daniel 2, where Daniel receives information from God in order to prophesy, with Daniel 5, where Daniel at about the age of 90 is able to prophesy out of his own accumulated God-given wisdom.

David's life shows us the sequence of the "normal" human life. The David narrative in the Bible carries him from childhood all the way through to death. Let us now look at another full biography recounted in the Bible, where we shall see again the same sequence.

Compare David's life with that of Jacob: Jacob may have had something of a happy childhood, but he experienced youthful trauma as Esau fought him and as Isaac favored Esau. This is a much greater "adolescent" difficulty than David experienced, and it lasts until Jacob is 77 years old. After this, he leaves his father and goes to live as a servant of Laban and marries Laban's daughters. Then come more trials as Laban repeatedly cheats him, climaxing with God's wrestling with him at Peniel. God says that Jacob has prevailed with men and with God, that Jacob has passed the tests God has put before him (contrary to the many expositors who have little good to say about Jacob). Jacob is now able to enter the land as a kind of proto-king, and God gives him peace with Esau. A time of peace follows, but a few years later his sons are committing horrible sins: "killing" Joseph and murdering the men of Shechem, their brothers by circumcision. It is only after several years in this third phase of suffering that Jacob moves to Goshen and experiences peace for the remainder of his life, prophesying at the end.

Now, what these lives show us is the bread of a man's life being broken three times, with more wine resulting each time. David's early trials gave him enough wisdom to serve wicked Saul as a priest. David's trials under Saul gave him enough wisdom to rule Israel. David's later trials as king gave him enough wisdom to become a prophet.

The same pattern is seen in the life of Jacob. Jacob's early trials under Isaac and Esau gave him the wisdom to put up with wicked Laban. His trials under Laban gave him the wisdom to rule his sons well, though they would not listen to him, and he himself failed to make them get rid of their false gods for many years (Gen. 34–35). His trials with his sons gave him the wisdom to prophesy in his old age.

Notice that the first "death" leads to marriage. The second "death" leads to a new birth, as David becomes "son of God" and Jacob is given a new name at Peniel. The third "death" leads to a doubling, as Jacob becomes spiritual leader of Egypt as well as of Israel, and as David's son

Solomon becomes king of a much larger empire. Marriage, new birth, and doubling are not absent from any of these "deaths," but they are highlighted in this sequence.

This leads us to consider yet another order of the Trinity, this time within the sevenfold sequence provided by the Spirit. In this case, the order is Spirit, Son, Father. First, the Spirit as Divine Matchmaker moves us from childhood through "death" to marriage. Then we move through "death" to a new birth as sons, as kings. Finally, we move through "death" to a doubling as elders, as fathers—and consider that the Father is "over" both the Son and the Spirit, who double Him.

Jesus

We can apply this pattern significantly to the life of Jesus. Jesus' first course of trials comes after His baptism and are directly related to it. God proclaims Jesus His Son at Jesus' baptism, right after He leaves home. John shows this as Jesus "rebukes" His mother at Cana in John 2. Then follows marriage, as Jesus meets the Samaritan woman and presents Himself as the right Husband for her and for all humanity (John 4). Jesus calls His disciples and teaches and wrestles with them as a priest, "marrying" them so to speak—marrying this new Israel.

Jesus has been declared Crown Prince, Son of God, but like David, He will not exercise His kingship as long as Saul is alive. Saul is Herod, who is called a king in Mark (though he actually never had the title), but Saul is also the Sanhedrin and the Romans. Jesus acts as a priest, as a servant, paying His taxes to the authorities. At the Mount of Transfiguration, God reiterates to Peter, James, and John that Jesus is the Priest to whom they are to listen (Mal. 2:6, the priest as teacher of God's Word). Jesus begins to act more as a future king at this point and immediately begins a journey to Jerusalem, where He arrives as Prince. But Jesus is rejected by the three Sauls and He refuses to seize the kingdom from them. We are moving toward the second great trauma of His life, when He is tempted not to go to the cross, and then goes through it. (In a larger way, the entire three and one half years of

Jesus' ministry is this second period of trauma, beginning with Satan's temptations.) On the cross He is elevated as King, and afterwards God pronounces Him to be His Son again.

Now, Jesus will experience a third set of "trials" as He wrestles to keep His sons (the Church) in line. Unlike David, whose own sins made dealing with his sons very hard, Jesus is fully able to deal with us. This is the time when Jesus is "doubled" in that His kingdom extends not only to Israel but also to the whole world. At the end, of course, Jesus will enter into the complete fullness of sabbath rest with His Bride and with His Father.

Now to understand Jesus' life fully, we must understand that He died at the age of about 33, but that He lives in the Church, in union with her. Thus, the third set of trials that Jesus undergoes are the trials of the Church. Recall that the bread of a man's life is broken three times, so that more wine can come forth for the next phase of his life. The bread of Jesus' life was broken first when He left home and entered His calling at His baptism. The bread of His life was broken a second time as His disciples began to forsake Him and climaxed in the cross. The bread of Jesus' life is broken for the "third" time every time the Church does the Lord's Supper during this age of trial before the final sabbath. This does not mean that Jesus suffers for us again at the time when the Church does the Supper, but that the fruits of His earlier two finished struggles are applied to those in union with Him. It is we who, as the continuation of Christ, suffer (though since He loves us, He also suffers, as we shall see).

Jacob's two times of trial as child and "priest" gave him the wisdom to rule as king, if only his sons had listened to him. David's two times of trial as child and "priest" gave him the wisdom to rule as king, but he ruled badly when it came to his own sons, and they did not benefit from it. Jesus' own personal two times of trial, as child-Son of God and as prince-Son of God, gave Him the wisdom to rule us as king/prophet-Son of God—and since He sets no bad examples, He will not (like David) lead us astray; and also, since we now have the Spirit within us in full measure, the Church will not be like Jacob's sons, but will listen to her husband and father.

Let us go back and consider Adam's life before we move forward to further contemplations of Jesus'. Adam begins in fellowship with God. Then he goes through the first trauma, the first separation, and receives a wife. This makes him priest of the Garden, and crown prince. Adam leaves his father and cleaves to his wife, which in this context means he separates to a degree from God as his father. This is why God departs and does not return until after Adam has eaten the forbidden fruit. Compare this with Jacob's, David's, and Jesus' departures from home, adoption into a new home, and getting a wife.

Now Adam is tested under Saul, Satan, and he must not seize the temporarily forbidden fruit. Like the priests of Leviticus, Adam must instruct his wife, supervise the food of the sanctuary, and declare the unclean person (Satan) "cut off" from the sanctuary. Assuming he is faithful as priest and crown prince, Adam is "born again" and elevated to new sonship as king, and given the fruit of the tree of authoritative rule.[63]

Now these benefits must be passed on to his future sons, who will double or multiply him into the future. He must rule them as king, moving toward prophetic eldership. They will go through difficulties (not as sinners but as maturing humans), and Adam will be with them as they do, but they will also be faithful and successful. Eventually, all will come to the fullness of joy.

The three extended periods of trauma, with climactic crises, build our lives successively through transformations. The first crisis fits us to be priests, to serve well under the law as obedient crown princes. The second crisis fits us to be kings, to rule well with wisdom. The third crisis fits us to be prophets, to teach others law and wisdom.

---

63 In terms of our discussion in chapter 3 above, notice that Adam's first death consisted of being divided. This is bread-breaking at its essence. It made him a priest. His second death would have involved being given to eat of fruit, which is the source of juice, relating to the liquid in the king's cup. Being given the "cup" of this fruit would have made him a king. Notice also that the fruit of this tree is associated with death, which associates death more closely with kingship than with priesthood.

9.

THE PLACES OF TRIAL AND SUFFERING

We have been considering a sevenfold sequence of human life, and we have seen that there are three times of trial that mature us to new phases of life, to being priests, kings, and then prophets. We continue with that consideration in this chapter.

THE PATRIARCHS

Before moving farther, it will be helpful to consider this pattern as it plays out in the sequence of the patriarchs. Abraham is associated with priesthood, as we see him repeatedly building altars and offering sacrifices. The trials in his life mature him in his priesthood to the point where he is able and willing to sacrifice his only son, Isaac.

Isaac takes up at this point. He inherits priesthood from Abraham and must move toward true kingship. Isaac, however, repeats the sin of Adam and fails in this calling. He prefers the food associated with wicked Esau and rejects the food associated with the "perfect" son, Jacob (Gen. 25:27; the word often translated "peaceful" is actually "perfect"). The name Jacob means "replacement," and Jacob is not the replacement for Esau but for Isaac.

Jacob, as we have seen, moves from priest to king, passing the test that Adam and Isaac failed. His trials under Laban are king-making trials. He is not, however, successful in dealing with his sons. Only after much trauma does he become a prophet.

Being a prophet falls to Joseph, who inherits the priesthood of Abraham and the kingship of Jacob. As a very young man Joseph is able to rule his father's household, and then Potiphar's as well. Joseph's wisdom as king, even as a youth, enables him to become a prophet. And as a prophet, he is able to rule his sons well, which in this case means he rules and redeems his wayward brothers, the sons of Jacob, doing what Jacob had failed to do.

Jesus' Three Testings and the Lord's Supper

The three tests that the devil brings to Jesus at the beginning of His life as anointed (baptized) Messiah follow a particular order, as Matthew sets them out. Mark does not go into the specific temptations, and Luke reverses the second and third. Matthew, being the first Gospel, is providing the "definitive sequence," which the later writers then vary for their own purposes.

The first test involves bread, and thus has a priestly focus. Satan tempts Jesus to make bread and Jesus refuses. Then Jesus begins to call disciples and forms a loaf of bread, a community, out of them: the beginning of the loaf of the Church (compare Matt. 3:9 and 4:3). Jesus now, as priest and crown prince, makes bread: He restores people to life (bread) in many ways, making the people priests with Him, for all the healing miracles have to do with restoring the people as priests, according to the rules of the Levitical law. Having restored Israel as a loaf, with Himself as the priest of that loaf, Jesus allows the loaf to be broken and is isolated from the people at Gethsemane.

The second test involves doing something miraculous, so that people will respect Jesus. It has a kingly focus. Recall that Herod wanted Jesus to do a miracle. Satan says that if Jesus does spectacular miracles, putting His own life at risk, people will follow Him. Jesus rejects Satan's test, but then proceeds to do many miracles, culminating in the most spectacular: the raising of Lazarus. The crowds do acclaim Him, as Satan said they would, but not for long: The crowds refuse to understand that the king must give up his glory, and that "miracle" is the opposite of the glory-abandoning humility to which the king is ultimately called. The paradox of humble glory is seen as the soldiers crown Jesus with thorns and mock His kingship, and also as Jesus reigns from the tree of the cross. Continuing to reject Satan, Jesus refuses to come down from the cross (to cast Himself down from the pinnacle of the Temple into the arms of the angels), and dies that He might become True King, the king who is not for himself only but also for others. Jesus now, as king, makes wine: He gives His "prophetic" wine-blood to make us wine, to make us kings with Him.[64]

The third test involves worshiping Satan in order to gain the whole world. It has a prophetic focus, for it is only when we get to the prophetic literature that we get messages to the nations. It is hard to understand how the incarnate Son of God might face this as a real temptation (though in some sense, He did), but it is clear that it is the temptation that faces the Church as she now passes through this third phase of trial and crisis. She is called to world dominion and is continually tempted to compromise with the devil, to worship and serve him, in order to gain it. Only as she suffers and sheds her own blood, pouring out the wine given her by Jesus, does she become truly prophetic and gain real world influence. Jesus did not go to the world; He sends us to do that and fits us for it by giving us His life and death, His bread and wine.

---

64   Remember that prophets advise kings.

We can now make a powerful application of all this to the Lord's Supper. The Supper gives us what Jesus accomplished in Himself, giving us bread and wine. Then we are sent out to shed that wine, our blood, to bring the Kingdom to the world. The wine, as blood, is both joyful witness and also suffering. (The life and work of Paul is the great example here.) As sons, we apply what our father, Jesus, has gained for us. The bread (priestly) and cup (kingly) traumas of Jesus are given to us, and we now pass through the third phase of trauma on our way to becoming full prophets. Jesus died at 33, while we carry His life forward to old age, in union with Him.

The broken bread and the shed wine form our witness. We are prophets, but only because in union with Jesus we are priests and kings first. The Supper weekly restores us as priests and kings, so that we can go forth as prophets, led by the Spirit of Prophecy. To put it another way, in the Supper we are given the Old Creation, the time of the Law, as found in the Old Testament and Gospels, broken as bread for us. And we are given the New Creation, the time of wisdom, as found in the New Testament epistles and Acts, which begin the outpouring of wisdom-wine to us. Now we move forward with these two gifts and write the third book of history, the history of the Church.

Bible History

The history in the Bible displays this same sevenfold pattern, with its three great crises or traumas. Notice that as we begin with the book of Genesis, there is a continual emphasis on fathers and sons. This is the childhood leading to the first great trauma, which comes in Egypt. This is when we leave home, leave the promised land of Canaan. The Egyptian crisis forms us as a loaf, as a nation, and as a nation of priests. At Sinai we are married to Yahweh. We are tempted with disobedience for forty years in the wilderness, which is where Satan tempts Jesus later on, but eventually we pass the test and enter the promised land.

We are also crown princes, as we are told in Deuteronomy 17 that eventually we shall have a king and be a nation of kings—but not until God is ready. The book of Judges and the calling of Saul as king show that we are not willing to wait, but seize the fruit of the Tree of Knowledge repeatedly, frustrated that there is as yet "no king in Israel" (ignoring the fact that Yahweh is our king). Eventually the loaf of the kingdom is ripped in half, signified by the rending of the Tabernacle into two separate tents between the death of Eli and the temple of Solomon. This second great crisis, this death of Israel as crown prince, leads to the establishment of the kingdom, a new birth for the nation.

But there is a third set of traumas and crises, as we prove unfaithful to that kingdom. The kings, the fathers, are unfaithful and rule their sons, the kingdom, badly. Eventually the temple is destroyed, the city burned, and we are exiled. This third death of Israel, however, leads to the latter-days, in which we as prophets are sent out all over the known world, even before the coming of Jesus. In this third phase, we apply as prophets what we have learned from our priestly and kingly history to our sons, which are now the other nations. Those of us who willingly eat the bread of the law and drink the wine of wisdom, accepting Israel's history and God's judgments, can now impart this to others.

Our Lives

Our own biographies have the same shape, the same sequence. From the ease of childhood we pass through the traumas of adolescence to marriage. That's the first breaking of bread, the essential bread-breaking. After this (normally, of course), we enter into a new life as employees, as servants of some other king or master. We are priests, and crown princes in terms of what we might become later on, and during this time our children are born and grow up. We learn wisdom, but must not seize authority.

This is often difficult and moves forward to some kind of midlife crisis, when our priestly work seems to be broken. The woman goes through menopause. The man finds he cannot bear continuing in his situation any longer. This second time of trauma often sees a man moving to another place or position, forsaking his earlier hopes and dreams, so that he can exercise authority out of the wisdom he has learned. By this time our children are grown, and we may not direct their lives very much, but we may have employees of our own. They go through their struggles, but we can guide them, and we will experience some of their pain because we love them. We function as kings so that they can carry forth our teachings and wisdom into their various tasks.

We move through this last time of suffering (in union with our subordinates) to become elders, aged prophets. Only by moving through this time do we acquire the ability to teach well, to take what we have learned outward "to the nations."

Of course we find exceptions to the pattern, but the pattern is still there as the "normal" pattern. It is the pattern we have seen in Jacob, David, and Jesus. We can cover the same sequence with different words, in summary fashion:

1. Childhood.
2. Bread-breaking: adolescence, leaving home, marriage.
3. Wine-drinking: Time of priestly obedience and gaining wisdom.
4. Bread-breaking and wine-outpouring: midlife trauma, occupational difficulties.
5. Bread and wine sharing: Time of kingly rule by the wisdom we have gained and keep gaining.
6. Participation with the traumas of others, which gives us more wisdom, this time the wisdom how to teach and share better.
7. Eldership, when we now have much to share and the ability to share it well.

Suffering With Those We Love

At this point, we must think a bit more about this third period of suffering. The first two times of suffering or trauma or "death" are things we ourselves experience directly: adolescence and the midlife crisis. The last is a time of suffering or trauma that we experience because we love others, our "children," who are going through their own traumas. The "deaths" that lead to marriage and new birth are individual, but the "death" that leads to doubling/multiplying is something we go through with those others that constitute our doubling. In this sense—and it is important for us to understand this—Jesus continues to suffer. He suffered *for* us on the cross, once and for all, and that breaking experience is finished. But He suffers *with* us during the present age until the end. Thus, when Saul (Paul) attacked the Church, Jesus appeared to him and said, "Saul, Saul, why do you persecute Me?" Thus, we can grieve or wound the Spirit, and the Spirit is the Spirit of Christ.

It is not true to say that Jesus in heaven is experiencing nothing but enthroned bliss. When someone we love suffers, we suffer. When our children hurt, we hurt. When our wife suffers, we suffer also. And in this sense, Jesus suffers with us because He loves us. We are His wife and His children. Also, we are His body, and when the finger is in pain, the whole person suffers.

Traditional Roman Catholicism tends to confuse these two kinds of sufferings, so that Jesus is still somehow on the cross suffering *for* us until the end of time. That is not correct. His suffering apart from us, and for us, ended at His death. But traditional Protestantism has tended to deny that Jesus still suffers alongside of us, *with* us, as we suffer. That is also an error.

Jesus wept over Jerusalem, and He still weeps today over the Church, as He intercedes for Her. If we are to weep with those who weep, surely Jesus does also. But He will not weep forever. When His Bride is perfected and the end comes, both He and His Wife will enter perfect bliss and joy forevermore, and there will be no more weeping, ever.

Two other points on this. First, often all we can do for our grown children is pray for them, because they won't listen to us. That's what Jesus is doing in heaven: interceding for us.

Second, the Bible shows us that there is joy in the midst of suffering, because we know the outcome is glorious. Thus, Jesus in heaven does suffer with us, but it is a fully joyous suffering.

Conclusion

Since the Supper is done not once but repeatedly, it speaks of the progression of crises in our lives and in history. In an important and significant way, there are three such crises. The first breaks bread that wine may come. In the second, bread is again broken, but wine is also poured out. In the third, we share in the brokenness and the outpouring of those we love.

The first of these crises is not hideously traumatic. Children around the age of 20 are quite ready to make the break and leave home, to enter into a new life. They don't suffer when they do so, ordinarily. It is like Adam's pleasant deep-sleep. This first crisis is accompanied by *faith*, faith that a good future awaits us. It is normally accompanied by marriage.

The second crisis is personally traumatic for us. Menopause is traumatic, and it is traumatic for a man to forsake his job and all that he had hoped to accomplish. We suffer here, as Jesus did on the cross. We feel isolated and alone, and often lose our sense of the nearness of God, passing through what older writers called a "desolation" or a "dark night of the soul" (see Ps. 88). At this point, many men run away from their families, as Jesus was tempted to do on the cross. But we must move through this time by *hope*, hope that having lost much, or even all, we shall receive more later on. If we persevere, we shall come to a new birth.

The third crisis, or series of them, is not something we experience directly. But our faith and hope has matured to *love*, and because of our love for others, their trials become our trials. Though our children have no fear when they leave home, we fear for them. And we suffer along with those who experience the other breakings and outpourings of life. Such sufferings lead to the doubling, the multiplication, of our lives.

This sequence is not some "hard and fast" pattern. Some people are more priestly, more faith-full, all their lives. Some are more kingly, more hope-full, all their lives. And some are more prophetic, more love-filled, all their lives. All the same, whether we through our whole life are more like the faith-calling Father, the hope-giving Spirit, or the Bride-loving Son, this process of maturation plays out in all our lives.

10.

Journey to Maturity, Part 1: Leaving Home

Biblical liturgies, and for us this means the Lord's Supper, encapsulate the sequence of biography and of history. Because we have rejected God, we have also rejected the life He has planned for us, both individually and as churches, cultures, and world history. Biblical rites are designed to insert us back into God's guidance of our lives, to plug us back into God's true history so that our lives and cultures can develop properly.

We are moving toward a consideration of Genesis 1 as God's first sevenfold movement in history and the light that this sheds on later history, biography, and ritual. We have been considering the fact that in biography and history we can see three major places of trial and trauma, which form transitional times in our lives. Passing through these trials, these death experiences, leads to new life. We have four lives, separated by three transitions: childhood, priestly/princely life, kingly life, prophetic/imperial life.[65]

In this chapter we begin to go into each of these a bit more, building on the two previous chapters.

Leaving Home

The first transition comes when we leave home and marry. We leave our old home and enter a new one, one of our own. Thus, Adam began as a child with God. Then God put Adam through a transitional death experience, "deep-sleep," during which he was ripped in half (another aspect of death). Then Adam was born again, was doubled, and most importantly gained a wife. Up until this time, Adam has lived with God as both his heavenly Father and as his earthly father. Now, however, since "for this cause a man shall leave his father and his mother and cleave to his wife," Adam separates from God as earthly father. God leaves the garden and does not return until the next day.

Adam's death experience, his passage or transition, was not traumatic. In a world of sin, however, sometimes this transition is very traumatic. It may not be too hard for the child, who may be excited to leave home and get a new job and get married, but it is likely to be hard on parents, and mothers often experience "empty arm syndrome." It's time to adopt a nice, warm, baby-sized kitty cat to hold in your arms.

Let us examine some instances of this transition in the Bible. We have looked at some of these before, but let us now examine them in a bit more depth.

---

[65] I add "imperial" to prophetic to complete the sequence from prince to king to emperor. Yet, in our eldership, as prophets, we are not emperors, but advisors to the "emperors," who are those who come after us, who multiply us. The third stage of biblical history is both prophetic and imperial, characterized by prophets and by the four great empires. Those who come after us should be greater than we, because they should build on what we have accomplished. They, then, are the emperors, where we were only kings.

Journey to Maturity, Part 1: Leaving Home

Abram is called to leave Ur. He moves to Haran, but waits until his father has died before moving to Canaan. At this point, when he arrives in Canaan, he begins his life as a priest, setting up altars everywhere he goes (Gen. 12).

Jacob's story is a bit different. Jacob experiences hardship and difficulty his whole childhood, persecuted one way or another by his brother and his father. His childhood lasted for 77 years, and his suffering climaxed when he followed Rebekah's lead in deceiving his temporarily wicked father and then was sent away to get a wife in Padan Aram. Jacob had to flee from Esau at this point, and he probably did not feel very good about leaving his mother and going out with nothing but the shirt on his back. But he encountered God at Bethel and came to a new birth. Shortly thereafter he married. Thus, Jacob's transition is full of suffering.

So is Joseph's. Joseph is not interested in leaving home at all, but he is put through death (put in a pit) by his wicked brothers and sold into slavery. He finds a new father, Potiphar. He does not marry at this point, breaking the pattern just a bit, but the temptation to lie with Potiphar's wife actually gives us a variant of the pattern. She is the wrong wife for Joseph, and he refuses her advances.

Moses as a baby makes a transition from his old home to the palace of Pharaoh. There is no marriage here, but in that it is the daughter of Pharaoh who takes him in, a new relationship with a new female is at least present. This transition is most traumatic: The Hebrew babies were being killed. It is important to notice that Moses makes this transition through water, which speaks of baptism and correlates to the later transition of Israel out of Egypt through the baptismal waters of the Red Sea.

When Israel came out of Egypt, born again at the first Passover, they were to move to Canaan. But they refused to leave home. Because the transition was traumatic, they wanted to return to Egypt. Just as Abram left Ur and lived in Haran until his father died, so the faithful in Israel had to live in the wilderness until the fathers died. Then they entered the land, and the nation was circumcised at Gilgal. Circumcision is the entry into priesthood and is particularly associated with Abraham, the priest par excellence of the patriarchal era. Israel now enters into their mission as a nation of priests. They are pointedly told *not* to marry with the Canaanites, a command that links with the fact that some kind of marriage accompanies this first transition. They are to keep their marriage to Yahweh instead, the marriage that took place at Sinai.

David, as we have seen, moves from his father's house into Saul's palace and marries, after passing through a struggle with bear, lion, and Goliath.

We can also look at the life of Samuel. Samuel's mother gives him to Eli and his household when he is still a little boy. Samuel becomes a deacon, an acolyte priest, at this point, and is, so to speak, married to Yahweh in the special sense that priests are.

Jesus also leaves home, at the age of about 30, and passes through a death experience in His baptism and in the temptations that immediately follow. This transition is His entry into His priesthood, when He is Crown Prince but not yet King.

Now we can make a very significant application of this transition to the early Church. The Church was baptized at Pentecost and immediately was tested by the devil in persecutions that climaxed with the murder of Stephen. Then the Church scattered from Jerusalem, leaving home in a geographical sense, and their center moved to Antioch, where the believers were first called Christians. But Spiritually, the Church at Pentecost departed from the old household of the Old Creation/Covenant.

This departure was extremely traumatic. First, many of those called to make the transition refused to do so, remaining Jews and rejecting the new world. Indeed, many of those Egypt-loving Jews actively persecuted the new Church during her transition. Second, many who became Christians wanted to bring Egypt with them. These were the party of the Circumcision, against whom Paul had to fight.

Consider a newly married young couple. Suppose the parents of one or the other insist that the new couple live in the parents' home, under the parents' authority. They deny the couple the right to move out and form a new home. Such patriarchalism is a gross and wicked perversion of what God calls us to. We see an example of it in the way the Jews refused to let the Christians move out of the Old Creation into the New, persecuting them for not obeying the older liturgical laws.

Or suppose the parents are willing to let the young couple move out, but the husband won't do so. He won't cut the apron strings. He wants to bring his bride into his parents' home and live there. He wants to have the new world, but he won't leave the old world behind. This is the position taken by the party of the Circumcision. It is a perversion.

REJECTING ALL CHANGE

What is happening here is a rejection of time and history. The Jews and the Circumcision rightly said that God had given the Law and that the old arrangement was good. That's true: It was good as long as we were children. But now we must move on toward adulthood. This movement into the future was what was rejected by the Jews and the Circumcision. For them, all time was the same, and there is no progress in history. They had become philosophers, treating the Law as a timeless Ideal instead of as rules for children in their first home.

This is how all paganism thinks. For them, time and change are evils. The writings of Mircea Eliade explore this hostility to time in depth. The pagan will admit to eternal cycles, but not to any real progress or maturation in history and biography. It is for this reason that pagans never grow up. They never progress beyond childhood and adolescence. Any missionary will tell you this, that the heathen are just like children. Greek philosophy and literature also never progresses beyond adolescence, and Homer's two great poems are about adolescents. Stuck in the time before marriage, the Greeks became homosexuals.

Because this hostility to God's plan is part of our sinful nature, we find that the Church repeatedly falls into the same way of thinking. The Eastern Church maintains that after the so-called Seventh Ecumenical Council, there is really no more progress to be made. One may tinker with things a bit, but no real and radical transition is possible. Thus, the loaf of the Church had to be broken before the Western Church could enter into a new phase. The Western Church, however, eventually decided that everything was settled and no further transitions could be made, so the loaf had to be broken at the Protestant Reformation. Today we find far too many Presbyterians who think that the Westminster Confession of Faith is good for all time, and Episcopalians who think the same way about the Book of Common Prayer—even though both are centuries old by now.

While it is true that a major sin is to cling to the past, to the old way, and not embrace the new birth and the new marriage, it is also possible to move into a new future that is a false future. Think of adolescence. Our very bodies impel us toward a new relationship with a member of the opposite sex. It is possible to enter a sinful future by having sex without marrying first, to seize forbidden fruit. It is possible to leave home in a rebellious way.

We see this phenomenon in a very striking way in the New Testament history. The fact is that what we call the Old Testament was not complete, for the completion awaited the New Testament writings. In the Restoration Era, the Jews became wonderfully enamored with the Bible and studied it constantly. At some deep level of their psyche they became conscious that it was incomplete. But then they jumped the gun and created their own new testament, their own completion of the Bible. This was the demonic Oral Law Tradition that Jesus fought, which was eventually written down as the Mishnah and is commented upon in the Talmuds. Thus, they were impelled forward, but they refused to remain patient.

This false future was really no future at all. The Oral Law is not a new kingdom, but a perversion of the old. The Law of God was taken as timeless truths, as an Ideal, on the model of Greek philosophy, and then turned in upon itself to generate new laws in order to create a perfect, static, timeless order, a Jewish version of Plato's *Republic* and *Laws*. Thus, the Oral Law provided nothing new at all, but rather reflected a complete rejection of time and history. This renunciation of time is highlighted in the second transition trial, to which we shall turn in due time, but it is present here.

The boy who leaves home in rebellion, or who sleeps around with girls and never marries, never grows up. He remains an adolescent forever. His new life is not actually new, but is a perversion of his old life. The fact is that marriage radically changes us, because we are bound by covenant with another person who is radically different from us. Men and women are profoundly different—as different as the Son and the Spirit—and we become quite different people after we have been married for a while. The man who never marries, whether to a woman or to some form of service, as in the Church, never actually leave his old life; he just carries it with him. He does not become new.

Thus, it is possible to sin against God's call to move into a new life either by refusing the new life, or by coming up with a false new life, which is actually just another way of refusing it.

Ritual Applications

With this background in mind, I want to make two ritual applications. The first is to the Trespass and Purification Offerings, which have the same basic law (Lev. 7:7). As we have seen, this is the first of the three groups of offerings, and it speaks of this first transition. Based on what we have seen, the Purification Offering moves the worshiper from childhood to priesthood, from the old house to the new, and into marriage. It is the first bread-breaking event in the sequence.

First, purification is basically the same as cleansing. This correlates with Jesus' baptism, with the baptism of the Church at Pentecost, and with Israel's dual baptisms in the Red Sea and in the Jordan River. Also, since the disposition of blood is highlighted in the Purification Offering, it speaks of circumcision, the rite that makes a man part of the priestly nation.

Thus, second, the Purification Offering moves the worshiper from his old house, whatever that may be (Egypt; his own home; his sinful life), into God's house. The Purification Offering is a sign of adoption by God, the King, and the worshiper becomes a priest (palace servant) of God's house, and a crown prince.

Third, and this will surprise some readers, the display of the blood on the altar, emphasized in the Purification Offering, speaks of marriage.[66] According to Deuteronomy 22, the blood shed on the wedding night is openly displayed as a proof that the bride was a virgin. Similarly, when Zipporah circumcised her son, she called him a "bridegroom of blood" in Exodus 4. What this means is that the blood of the male's circumcision substitutes for the hymenal blood of the virgin on her wedding night. Why? Because we have all played the harlot in Adam and have lost our virginity. Thus, the blood of Jesus covers for us and makes us legally virgins in the eyes of God and of the world. Zipporah smeared the blood on her son's legs. This correlates with the smearing of the Passover blood on the doorposts of the Hebrew houses in Egypt, for legs are posts. It also correlates with the daubing of blood on the horns of the altar, since the altar is a symbol of the human being.

Thus, the Purification Offering speaks not only of our new birth and adoption into God's household, but also of our marriage to Yahweh. But it is more than that. Rituals are not mere symbols, mere teaching lessons. The ritual actually accomplishes, effectuates, this adoption and marriage, renewing our membership in the Father's house as members of the bride of His Son. The worshiper who does the rite in faith receives blessings, while the worshiper who does the rite faithlessly is putting himself into a dangerous position, for new responsibilities are being bestowed upon him as Yahweh's son and wife.

This same transition is seen in the first part of the Lord's Supper. Jesus takes hold of the bread, which is us as children. The bread, and we, are broken. This speaks of leaving our old lives and being adopted and married into God's home. As bread is associated with priesthood, this part of the rite restores us as priests. This part of the rite applies to us anew Jesus' own departure from His home, His baptism, and His successful encounter with the devil.

---

66 I have discussed this at some length in an essay, "Proleptic Passover," contained in my *The Law of the Covenant* (Tyler, TX: Institute for Christian Economics, 1984), 243–260.

11.

Journey to Maturity, Part 2: Midlife Crisis

The second transition comes in the middle of life, when we are tempted to seize authority that God is not ready to bestow on us. God wants us to become kings, to be "born again" as "sons of God," but only when we are ready. We, however, tire of being mere crown princes and want to become kings. As when we were adolescents, we find that we have become too big, so to speak, for our situation. We are impelled to move into something new, and this time the new thing is the assumption of some kind of kingly authority. As the adolescent can sin against a true future by seizing sexual experience before marriage, or by running away from home, so the adult can sin against his true future by seizing authority before it is bestowed on him. Jesus says to take the lowest seat and wait patiently until the King is ready to advance us, but few of us are willing to wait as long as God seems to want us to.

We must fight this temptation, because we shall not be ready to be kings until we have experienced loss and then been restored in a new way. This is because the king, unlike the palace servant (priest) or crown prince, is not under authority any longer. He now exercises the authority. He must learn through experience what it means to be under authority before he will have the wisdom to exercise it. The midlife crisis is the climax of that course of training.

The specific crisis is this: We have grown and developed to the point where we desperately want more than we have, and in particular we want more authority over our lives. But then a crisis comes in which we are morally constrained to take *less* than what we had before. Instead of moving up the corporate ladder, we find that we must leave the company and pump gas for a living. This is typically a moral constraint. We could remain and advance if we were willing to sin or compromise; but if we won't sin, we shall lose everything, or so it appears. Far from becoming a king, we become a pauper instead. And, importantly, this reduction in status is not imposed upon us from above by someone else or by circumstances, but rather is a decision we make ourselves. We *choose* to take less, acting as kings who are willing to die.

I shall use this as a typical pattern, because it is the pattern seen in the Bible. We could look at variants. Some men don't want authority so much as they want peace and quiet to do their work unhindered. With women, the crisis is usually menopause, which arrives about the time children leave and the woman feels that her life is lessening. (This is the time for women to move into an occupation.)

This transition is always traumatic. For Adam, it meant being tempted by the serpent and withstanding that temptation. Adam was sound asleep during his first transition, but he must be wide awake during this one. He must be a warrior and actually fight Satan by rejecting his advice. Adam must struggle. In this struggle he will experience a sense of inner division, of being divided against himself. On the one hand, becoming more like God and becoming a king is a good thing: All the trees were good for food, including the Tree of

Knowledge. On the other hand, it is good to obey God and to wait. Adam must wrestle with this, and in the course of doing so, he will learn wisdom, the wisdom he must have before becoming a king.

The sin of men in the first transition is to cling to the past and refuse to move into the new house and/or to move into a false future through rebellion and sin. The sin in the second transition is the same: to seize the future, which will prove a false future, instead of remaining in the past until God is ready to give us the future. As with sexuality and marriage to the right girl, we must not jump the gun. We must wait for God's future to come to us.

What we learn from this is *timing*. As Solomon writes in Ecclesiastes 3, there is a time for everything, and opposite things, such as weeping and laughing, are appropriate at different times. This is kingly (Solomonic) wisdom. There is a time to seize the future and marry, and there is a time to reject the temptations of the future and wait for God. Timing and patience are seen in the first trial of adolescence, but much more in the second trial at midlife. The adolescent is called upon simply to wait, and in this way he is like Abraham, who is the model of patience. The adult is called upon to wrestle with God over the future, and in this he is like Jacob, whose patience was marked by wrestling: for 77 years with Esau and Isaac and for 20 more with Laban, and all along with God.

This wrestling, these fears and anguish, are much more intense than the distresses of adolescent yearnings. What we learned about patience and timing as adolescents is greatly matured through this experience, either over a longer period of time, or through greater anguish, or both.

The child does not know this. Children have virtually no time sense, and pagans are all children, as we have seen. Moreover, the priest does not start out knowing much of this either. In the Law, all the times for the priest are set out as rules, and all the priest has to do is obey them. He needs to make no hard decisions about what to do when. As the priest matures as crown prince, however, he must begin to learn this, for it is wisdom. The king must decide by wisdom when to make war and when to make peace, because he has no book of Leviticus to tell him.

Thus, the midlife crisis has everything to do with division (loss) and with timing. As we shall see, division and timing are what the Ascension Offering, through which we ascend to become kings, is all about.

Biographies

First, though, let us review our biographies. Abram's whole life is priestly, but still there are these three phases in his life. Consider that as Abram enters the land and becomes a priest, God promises him land and seed, even though he does not possess the land and his wife is barren (Gen. 11–12). Land and seed are good, but Abram must not seize them. He must wait for God. Abram's midlife crisis revolves around these two promises. The land of promise rejects him, for there is a famine and he must move to Egypt (Gen. 12). When he returns, the land still won't produce for him, and so he and Lot must separate in order for each to have enough of this meager land. Notice the separation here: Abram loses his first heir, and also much of the promised land: the best part (Gen. 13). Then there is a war in the land, and though Abram rescues Lot, it is clear that the land is not his (Gen. 14).

Thus, when he speaks to God and God reiterates the land promise to him, Abram asks for proof (Gen. 15). God tells Abram to divide five animals. Abram goes down into death, into deep-sleep. He sees God passing between the animals, bringing them back together symbolically and thereby symbolically marrying Abram to the land, for the two sides of the animals represent Abram and the land. The death experience portrayed here is explained as 400 years of difficulty and separation from the land, after which God will seal Abram's seed to the land.

Now, Abram was in no position to seize the temporarily forbidden fruit of the land, but he was able to have a son prematurely. The temptation comes through his wife, who was probably tired of Abram's moping around all the time—which makes it mainly his fault, I believe. Abram's seizing this forbidden fruit, Hagar, is a sin that causes him to fall out of God's house. He must be restored through a Purification Offering, and in Genesis 17 we find that he is circumcised. He is born again with a new name, Abraham, restored to his marriage with Sarah (also a new name), and now promised a son shortly.

This second crisis was not so much a midlife, king-making crisis, as a repetition of Abram's first transition. He is restored to priesthood. But soon Isaac is born, and then there must be another division, for Ishmael must be sent out. To be sure, Ishmael will be a child of God and doubtless he and Abraham had fellowship from time to time over the years; but first there must be a separation before there can be a new union. Abraham must be willing to undergo division and loss so that something better may come in the future when God is ready.

This extended midlife crisis is all about timing and separations. Abram must learn to wait. He must learn that there is a right time to receive the land and to have a son, and that this time is God's time, not his. Until he learns this, he is not ready to become a king, a lord of times.

We have seen that Isaac failed in his midlife crisis. He intended to seize God's covenant and give it to wicked Esau, instead of obeying God's command that it was to be given to Jacob. He had not learned timing, and he refused to divide his estate, intending to give it all to Esau, though he was tricked (righteously, I believe, by Rebekah, who was obeying God's command) into giving it all to Jacob. Isaac was unwilling to undergo division and loss. He loved Esau and saw Esau as like himself, amazingly. To give it all to Esau was a way of keeping it for himself.

Jacob's midlife crisis is his service to Laban, climaxing with his wrestling with God at Peniel. Jacob knows that God has promised him a kingdom and has promised a tithe of it to God. He makes a deal with Laban, but Laban continually cheats him. Yet Jacob does nothing dishonest and does not seize Laban's property. He lets God give it to him miraculously.

Then comes the focus of the crisis. At Peniel, facing Esau across the river, Jacob must face the fact that God may intend to take it all away from him and give it to Esau. Jacob's prayer during the night that precedes his nighttime wrestling and shows what the wrestling was about demonstrates that he was willing to give up his estate, but that he begged God to spare his wives and children (Gen. 32:13). These two nights are Jacob's "dark nights of the soul." Jacob had learned that the God who had given him much in the past could do so again, if Jacob was willing to let go of his estate. As a result, God approved of Jacob, and Jacob divided his estate with Esau and was able to keep much of it.

Jacob had learned about time. He had come to Laban with nothing and was leaving with a huge estate. This had come to him because he was faithful and patient. But what God had done once, God could do again. Jacob went through a death experience, when it appeared he was going to lose it all. But instead of losing it all, he experienced a division and got to keep much of it and afterward increased more.

Joseph's midlife crisis also had to do with submission and waiting. Joseph was serving Potiphar, captain of the King's bodyguard, as a palace servant. Potiphar's wife came to him with a temptation, the temptation to seize Potiphar's place. His refusal to commit the sin of Adam resulted in Joseph's losing almost everything. Potiphar kept him in his household, but put him over the prison instead of over the palace guard. Joseph's life was divided, but he learned about timing and loss and was able to tell the times to Pharaoh as a result.

Moses' midlife crisis came when he chose to side with the Hebrews against the Egyptians, and in this crisis he had to learn to understand both timing and division, wisdom he had not learned yet as crown prince, as palace servant to Pharaoh. Commentaries are sometimes critical of Moses, but Acts 7:24 and Hebrews 11:24 indicate that he was acting in faith and that Israel should have acknowledged him as their God-appointed deliverer. They failed to do so and remained in bondage. God would deliver Israel, and through Moses, but not at this time.

Moses had to learn this, and his forty years in the wilderness were a time when he learned it in submission to the godly king Jethro. Not only was the wilderness a pleasant death experience, but also, more focally, he had to flee there because Pharaoh intended to kill him. As Jacob fled from Esau to Laban and married Laban's daughter, so Moses fled from Pharaoh to Jethro and married Jethro's daughter. Happily, Jethro was a different kind of man from Laban.

Moreover, Moses had to learn about division. When the Hebrews rejected him after he slew the Egyptian, he began to learn that not all are of Israel who claim to be of Israel. When he returned to Egypt, he had learned about both timing and division. He was ready to wait for God's time and was ready to make divisions between the righteous and the wicked among the Israelites. He was ready to be their judge, their "king," under God.

David's midlife crisis came when Saul rejected him and tried to kill him. David was tempted to kill Saul and seize the throne, but he refused to do so. Over the course of many years as a warrior and crown prince, through distress, David learned to wrestle with God in patience (see the book of Psalms). He almost jumped the gun and killed Nabal (which is Laban spelled backwards, significantly), but learned wisdom from Abigail and waited for God to kill that wicked fool.

Samuel's "midlife crisis" came early. As he approached the age of 20, he saw the wickedness of Eli's sons and Eli's own folly in not restraining them. Doubtless he thought many times that he could have done better, both as a priest and as a judge in Israel. But before long, all three sinners were dead and Samuel became judge, "king."

Israel's midlife crisis is seen in Judges and in the book of Samuel. They were not willing to be patient with only Yahweh as their king. They experienced a degree of societal anarchy and of international threats, and they decided (against all historical experience) that occasional judges/deliverers were not good enough. Instead of wrestling with God, they demanded a king and got Saul. According to Deuteronomy 17, a king is a good thing, but only in God's timing.

Jesus' midlife crisis, of course, is seen at the cross, where He dies at about the age of 33. At His baptism, Jesus had been given everything by the Father, but now He gives it all up. He experiences total loss, the loss of the old creation, so that the new creation may come. Fully submissive through all His trials, Jesus' life is the perfection of timing.

The exemplary midlife crisis of the Church comes during the Apostolic Age and climaxes in the Great Tribulation (which is at the end of that period, just before AD 70), where all seems to be lost as many teachers and apostles are killed. The Church proves faithful, however, under the encouragement of the apostles, particularly Paul in his letters and John in Revelation. She overcomes temptation by being willing to die rather than sin. And thus she is exalted to heaven. Those many who fell away toward the end were those unwilling to undergo loss, to die for the sake of the Kingdom.

Recall that the Jews and the Circumcision were those who refused to embrace the new reality of the New Creation. They refused to leave home and become priests, crown princes. They believed that they already were priests, which was true enough in the Old Creation sense, and they rejected the call to become new priests. Thus, all the controversies between the Circumcision and the Church were over the liturgical, priestly aspects of the Law.

The faithful Church, as priest and crown prince, became a king. This is seen in Revelation 20, when the martyrs ascend to take the seats around Jesus' throne, the seats vacated by the angels who had held them previously.[67]

Ritual Applications

Let us now turn to our two ritual applications. The second pair of offerings in the sequence are the Ascension and Tribute Offerings, the latter being (among other things) a memorial of the former, duplicating it in bread, oil, and wine. The stress is on the flesh, which is cut into pieces. But the name is also important, for ascension has to do with

---

67 See my book *The Vindication of Jesus Christ*.

elevation to kingship. Those who pass through the midlife trial are elevated to kingship, as we can see in the cases of Abram, Jacob, Joseph, Moses, Samuel, David, and Jesus.

The animal is divided into pieces. Two parts, the inner parts and the hind legs (or possibly, all legs), must be washed. The rest, including specifically the head and suet (inner fat around the innards), are not washed. This chopping up of the animal represents, of course, the chopping up of the worshiper in the person of his representative. The life that the animal, the worshiper, has lived up to this point is now killed and cut up, and then put back together glorified in the fire.

Leviticus 1:7 tells the priest to arrange the wood on the fire after the animal has been cut up. This attention to the fire is not found in the other offerings, though all are put into the fire. The fire is that of the Spirit, sent to the altar by the Father, and speaks of glorification. God's Spirit forms His own garment of glory around Him, and this is important for the Ascension Offering: The animal's old skin is removed, and he receives the new skin of glory in the fire.

Thus, what the rite emphases, over against the other offerings, is that the worshiper's life is cut up as he experiences death. Then his life is put back together and glorified, and he ascends on high. I submit that this rite can be seen as focusing mainly on the midlife crisis, for in the midlife crisis a person has grown to a mature point in his life, but then experiences a death and a chopping up of his life. He loses control, it seems. But if he perseveres through hope in God, he will be put back together and will ascend to a position of greater glory.

The chopping up is described in partial detail. Exactly how many pieces the animal was to be cut into is not specified, but we are told of two important clean parts and the two unclean parts are listed. There is an outer clean part (head) and an inner clean part (suet); and there is an outer unclean part (feet) and an inner unclean part (innards). These are two essential divisions that a person comes to understand in the midlife crisis. First, there is a division between his righteous inclinations and his sinful desires. Second, there is a division between his outer life and his inner longings. Redeemed believers experience these two kinds of conflict from time to time throughout their lives, but they come to pointed focus in the crisis.

The promise of the Ascension Offering is that God will save all of us. This offering is unique in that all of it is put into the fire; none of it is given to the priests to eat, or back to the worshiper as a meal. God accepts and transfigures the whole person, cleansing the unclean parts of our lives. Even the ashes are taken to a clean place (Lev. 6:10–11), and here again, while all the offerings left ashes behind, only the ashes of the Ascension are specifically discussed. The ashes, left behind but clean, point to the eventual resurrection of our bodies from the soil at the last day. Thus, even what we have to leave behind in our midlife crisis will someday be returned to us.

The feet are washed because they have been in contact with the soil, just as men washed the curse-prosecuting soil off their feet when they approached God. But more than that, it is the feet that carry us in any ascension toward kingship that we shall make. It is precisely that ascension that is in question in the midlife crisis: Will we ascend when God is ready, and in the way He wants us to be, or will we jump the gun and seize the future, ascending on our own? Will we try to ascend on unclean feet or on clean? The better part of us knows better, and so our head, fat, and the rest go into the fire first. Then, washed and cleansed, the feet follow.

Turning to the Lord's Supper, we can of course once again apply this ritual to the breaking of bread. Jesus personal body was not broken up on the cross, but the ripping in half of the veil signified that rending. Considered as Jesus' crucifixion rather than as His baptism, however, the breaking of the bread points to His transition not to priesthood but to kingship. And kingship is associated with wine. Jesus speaks of the wine as His blood that is shed, and so it is the wine rite that focuses more particularly on the midlife crisis. Jesus produced wine during His sufferings as Crown Prince, and now that wine is given to us, from His side, so that we also may grow to be kings and prophets with Him.

Now, the reader will notice that the Purification Offering, which comes first, focuses on the blood, while the Ascension Offering focuses on the flesh. Thus, first wine and then bread, so to speak. Either our analysis is badly wrong, or else Jesus reverses the order for some reason, or else there is a third explanation. The answer is that there is a third explanation.

The Ascension Offering is not complete until the Tribute Offering is added to it. The Tribute (Lev. 2) consists of bread with oil, which is then broken and put into the fire on top of the Ascension Offering as a memorial. The fact that the part put into the altar (into us, which we eat) is called memorial has everything to do with the Lord's Supper. Jesus said, "Do this as a memorial to Me." This does not mean that the rite is designed to remind us of Jesus (which is the duty of the preceding Word and sermon), but that the Supper is done as a memorial of Jesus' finished work, of His being the first and perfect Ascension Offering. "Do this in memory of me" is a not an accurate translation.

The Lord's Supper is pointedly the new version of the Tribute Offering. The tribute we bring before the Father is nothing less than Jesus. We memorialize Him to the Father.

Now, this memorial starts with bread, but it ends with wine. Numbers 15 says that when the Israelites enter the land, as kings, they are to add wine to the rite. The wine is to be poured out as a libation, as a drink, after the bread is put into the fire. Since it is drunk, the altar is what drinks it.[68] Thus, putting bread into the altar, and then giving wine for the altar to drink, perfectly matches the rite of the Lord's Supper.[69]

---

[68] Remember that wine by itself represents prophetic advice and counsel. The altar drinks the wine, as a king hearkens to a prophet. Thus, eating the bread the altar/worshiper is restored as priest, and drinking the wine the altar/worshiper is made a king and put on the road to becoming a prophet.

[69] Lest the reader think that the wine might put out the fire in the altar, the most that was ever poured out was 1/2 gallon (1/2 a *hin*), and this was upon the entire chopped up carcass of an ox. The altar was large, and the fire was large, and this amount of wine would not have significantly affected the fire.

The wine signifies blood, and the return of blood at the end of the total rite means that the worshiper sheds his blood twice. First, he sheds blood in order to become a king, passing through being cut up and being put back together and then ascending. Then, as king, he gives his blood for others. The crucifixion of Jesus has this same form. First, His head was crowned with thorns (notice the head first), and then His hands and feet were pierced by nails (notice the feet last). This was His first shedding of blood. But then, after He died and gave His spirit to the Father (ascending to become King), blood and water were released from His side.

The first blood of Jesus signifies His suffering apart from us and for us. This blood forms our tokens of virginity, so that we can be His bride. We don't have it, so He provides it. This blood covers our sins and is put not into us, but is splashed upon us and displayed on us. Then His body suffers, and that suffering is also partly given to us as we eat His body. This is His suffering with us, in union with us, as priests. Finally, His blood is given to us to drink, as a libation. This also is His suffering with us, in union with us, as kings.

12.

Journey to Maturity, Part 3: Becoming Prophets

We must now move to the third transition, our passage as kings to being prophets.

Many people do not become priests or crown princes, because they sin in their adolescent passage and never repent of it. Others pass the first test but fail the second and never become real kings, never acquire real wisdom. Now there is a third passage, which again, some never pass successfully because they sin as kings.

As children, we are to be patient and wait until we are ready to marry and enter a new life. As priests (palace servants) or crown princes, we are to obey patiently and wrestle with God, until we are ready to be made kings. As kings, we must rule wisely with the wisdom we have acquired or we shall never acquire the hyperwisdom of prophets and have a good understanding of time and history and of what God is doing in our times.

Ruling well means dealing with our sons properly, guiding them through their twin crises, so that they also become aged prophets, elders. Since Adam and Isaac failed even to become true kings, we cannot look at their lives in order to understand the passage into prophethood.

Biographies

We begin with Abraham. Once again, we remind ourselves that Abraham's life as a whole is priestly, but within that life there are three zones of transition or crisis. The third crisis in Abraham's life comes when he is called upon to offer Isaac as an Ascension Offering to God. Isaac is by this time a young man, able to carry a heavy bundle of wood up a mountain. How will Abraham rule his son? What does kingly wisdom mean? The answer is that Abraham is willing to give his son to God, and that is what kingly wisdom essentially means. We must lead our sons, our subordinates, to God and leave them in His care. This is what a true king does.

Abraham was confident that if he slew Isaac and cut him up into pieces and put him into the fire, God would raise him back up in a transfigured way. This is seen in Genesis 22:5, "*we* will return to you" (compare Heb. 11:19). Isaac was able to perceive Abraham's confidence and learn from it. In this way, Abraham guided his son to an understanding of how God works with human lives.

Also, we recall that the midlife crisis that enabled Abraham to attain to kingly wisdom involved, in part, sending Ishmael away, something that was very painful for him. God promised to be with Ishmael, to be his God, and Abraham could take comfort in that. Moreover, we can imagine that Abraham and Ishmael met occasionally in the intervening years, so that Abraham realized that God had faithfully kept His promise and that Ishmael had become a godly man. We read that Abraham begged God not to take Ishmael away. That was his crisis, but he learned to trust God more fully through it. Contrary to many movies and books and myriads of sermons, we don't read that Abraham begged God not to take Isaac from him. The text records no trauma in the soul of Abraham in Genesis 22.[70] Abraham had learned from his earlier trauma. What he had done once, he could do again, in a more dramatic way, with much greater confidence in God than before.

Abraham's confidence in the future—that God would restore Isaac to life if Abraham slew him—is the crisis that makes him a full prophet. He has learned about the God who controls the future, who brings new life out of death. Abraham was able to communicate this confidence to Isaac. Sadly, Isaac eventually forgot the lesson.

Jacob also ascends to kingship and enters the land. In Genesis 34, however, his sons commit fratricide (brother-murder, repeating the sin of Cain), killing the men of Salem (Shechem) who had become their brothers by circumcision. We find out in Genesis 35 that Jacob had not compelled them to remove the false gods from their tents. Thus, Jacob had failed to lead his sons to God. He had failed to rule them with sufficient wisdom. Earlier, these same sons had sold Joseph into slavery. All of this wickedness stems from their idolatry, which Jacob had not eliminated. Notice that later on, the good kings of Judah are those who destroy the high places and force the people to worship Yahweh alone, and only at His Temple in the way He has prescribed.

Unlike Abraham, Jacob had failed to learn from his king-making midlife crisis. He had encountered Yahweh at Bethel and had vowed a tithe of all that Yahweh would give him. Yahweh had prospered him in Padan Aram, despite all that Laban had tried to steal from him. Thus, through his midlife crisis Jacob had learned who the True God really is. He failed to communicate this knowledge to his sons, however, allowing them to keep false gods in their tents.

---

70 I doubt that Abraham was completely at peace in this situation, but we don't see him pleading with God about it, as he had done earlier when he had to send Ishmael away.

Jacob's failure means that Joseph must become the prophet—though Jacob's repentance means that he does become a prophet in his old age, and this is certainly an encouragement to us. Joseph succeeds where Jacob failed. The third transitional crisis in Joseph's life comes when his brothers arrive in Egypt to buy grain. Joseph is very distressed and weeps apart from them. This is his third "death" transition. He puts them in prison and into trauma, but he experiences the trauma with them. Joseph works out a plan to bring the brothers to repentance. Though they are of his generation, he is Jacob's replacement and thus is functioning as their father; and as Pharaoh's second-in-command, he is surely functioning as their king.

We remind ourselves that the young prophet, exercising that calling simply as a calling, prophesies on the basis of revelations from God. That is what Joseph did in Genesis 37, 40, and 41, and what Daniel does in Daniel 2. The aged prophet, the full prophet, however, prophesies out of his own God-given wisdom. This is what Daniel does in Daniel 5 and what Joseph does in Genesis 50.

Joseph's strategy with his brothers is based on what he learned during his own midlife crisis, when he had to forsake Potiphar's house rather than sin and landed in prison. He learned that God gives and God takes away. In his dealings with his brothers, Joseph repeatedly gives and takes away, alternating blessings with threats. He applies to them what he has learned. Specifically, in Genesis 40, Joseph in prison had appealed to Pharaoh, through the cupbearer. There was no deliverance for him from Pharaoh, however. Three years later, Joseph stands before Pharaoh and makes no appeal to him; instead, Joseph challenges Pharaoh to forsake his older gods of river and sun and to trust Elohim (God). Then, in Genesis 42, the wicked brothers come to get grain from Pharaoh. Joseph accuses them of being spies and, "as Pharaoh lives," Joseph puts them into "death" prison for three days. Then, after the three days, Joseph tells them that his God is Elohim and that Elohim offers them life, if they will obey Him (42:14–20). Thus, Joseph gives the brothers the opportunity to learn what he himself had learned earlier.

Samuel's third transition comes when he sets up his wayward sons as judges in Israel. Samuel has apparently not acted with full wisdom as a "king," because his sons are untrustworthy. This provides the people with an excuse to demand a real king. Frustrated, Samuel warns them that this king will abuse them (1 Sam. 8). I don't know if we should regard Samuel as a full failure or as a partial one, but the transitional test can be seen here either way we look at it.

One thing is for certain: Samuel has failed to learn from his own "midlife crisis," because, though in a much lesser way, he repeats the sin of Eli with his sons. Samuel had seen God remove Eli for just this kind of sin, and now Samuel will also be replaced, by Saul.

David's failure as king is notorious. During his own midlife crisis, David had gone forth to fight Israel's enemies repeatedly, even while being pursued by Saul. Now he forgets what he was taught. At the time kings were to go forth to war, David remains behind at ease in the palace. Arising from bed late in the day, he ravishes Bathsheba, and then turns his sword against one of his own faithful people.[71] In doing so, he set an example for his sons and was never able to rule them afterward. Through his repentance and years of suffering, however, he eventually did become a prophet and prophesied at the end of his life, giving directions to Solomon (1 Kings 2).

Israel's transitional crisis comes during and especially at the end of the Kingdom era. The kings usually ruled badly, and they became especially wicked toward the ends of the kingdoms of Israel and Judah. These kings had learned nothing from the midlife crisis that set up the kingdom, for they oppressed the people in the same ways that Saul and Solomon did. But in the days of Elijah and Elisha, God set up the Remnant Covenant, a new people within the old, gathered around the prophets. These people were faithful. They went into a kind of death experience in Babylon but emerged as a nation of prophets, dispersed throughout the world (as the Levites had been dispersed in Israel earlier) to bring God's ways to the heathen. Before the exile, the kings

---

71 On Bathsheba, see my "Bathsheba: The Real Story," *Biblical Horizons* 93 (March 1997), online at https://theopolisinstitute.com/article/bathsheba-the-real-story.

of Israel had dealt badly with the nations, usually compromising with them and adopting their idolatrous ways. They did not "rule" these "sons" well. The ministry of Daniel to Nebuchadnezzar shows the right way to influence the Gentiles, to bring them to God, and for a time after the Restoration, the Jews were faithful in doing so.

When we come to Jesus' third transition, we move from His earthly life as an individual to His earthly life in His body, the Church. Jesus is our King, and he guides us perfectly, if we are willing to be guided by Him. Jesus is on the road to becoming a full prophet, an elder, but not without us. It is the Church that is to manifest that wisdom, that eldership, as she ministers to all the world after the second great crisis at the end of the Apostolic Age. As a king, Jesus is continually bringing us to God, to the Father, and offering us to Him. He will do so fully at the last, giving all the Kingdom to the Father. He does with us what Abraham did with Isaac. Thus, the entire present age is an age in which the Church is being moved from being kings to being prophets. The entire age is the third great transition. After the final crisis of the Last Judgment, we and Jesus will be full prophets together forever.

Now, what do we learn from the midlife crisis that is to mark our participation with Jesus in the present prophetic age? We learn that the Church overcame by bearing witness and by being martyred. That is the theme of the book of Revelation. As always, the quality of the midlife crisis provides the particular point of wisdom that is to be passed on during the age that follows. We became kings by letting Jesus harvest us as priests (Rev. 14), and if we are going to live as kings, we must continue to be willing to die under His sickle.

We also learn this: that it is through prayer that we become victorious. The desperate times of the second crisis, the midlife crisis, should make us into better people of prayer. Consider how many of David's psalms were written during the time he was being pursued by Saul. The fact is that once our children have left home, we cannot order them around any longer. We can only pray for them, because as Abraham gave Isaac to God, we have given our children away in the fullest sense. We gave them to God when we brought them for baptism, and now God has come to collect them. They have moved out. We see them doing things that make us upset, but there is not much we can say to them. We must pray that God will bring other people into their lives who will be able to say the necessary things. Recall that Isaac sinned for nearly 77 years, preferring Esau to Isaac; but God gave him the saintly Rebekah, who worked out a scheme to bring Isaac to his senses, and Isaac did repent. And recall that it was Abraham who, through his servant, got Rebekah for Isaac. We see in this a picture of a father providing indirectly for his son, and it is parallel to our prayers for our grown children.

Ritual Applications

The mark of this age is the Lord's Supper, which is not only a memorial (like the rainbow or the stones put in the Jordan River), but also a meal. Thus, we come to the third of the offerings, the Peace Offering. The Peace Offering has two distinctive aspects. The first is that it is a full meal, shared between the altar, the priest, and the worshiper. It celebrates that we have arrived to the point of kingship and now sit down with the High King to a meal with Him.

Also highlighted, however, is the disposition of the "fat." The various pieces of fat listed in Leviticus 3:3–4 are the inner parts of the animal. These are what are put into the altar and given to God. Now, these same pieces are listed as set apart in the Purification Offering also, and so they are not unique to the Peace Offering. While we are not taking this matter up in these essays, each of the offerings includes all the rest, but with different emphases. The emphasis on blood in the Purification Offering is not found in the Peace Offering, with the result that the disposition of the "fat" stands out. Moreover, the disposition of the "fat" in the Purification Offering is said to be *like* that of the Peace Offering (Lev. 4:10), so that the "fat" is particularly associated with the Peace Offering.

Since the animal is the worshiper, the fat signifies things that come out of our innermost parts. I suggest that this generally relates to our sons, as Isaac came from Abraham and was given to God. We can become more specific, however: These are the things that we must give to God as we live as kings, moving toward becoming prophets. If we fail to give these things to God, we shall not mature as we should. We shall take these up in the order that will make matters clearest to us.

To begin with, fat: Fat causes the fire to burn brightly. It is, thus, associated with glory. It is, in general, glory that must be given to God and to God alone.

Second, the kidneys with the fat that is on them: The kidneys ("reins" in the AV) in the Bible symbolize the inner emotional life of a person, for it is in this region right below our waist that we feel emotional pain. The fat is the glory around that inner life. This means we must not feel self-satisfaction as kings, but must give God all the glory. It also means, I believe, that we are encouraged to give our inner pain and what in English we call "heartaches" to God.

Third, the fat on the innards: This just means the inner parts. It is more general and covers all the inner life of the person.

Fourth, the lobe of the liver (no mention of fat here): The Hebrew word for "liver" is a variant of the word for "glory, heavy." This means that we must always give all our kingly glory to God, thanking Him for all that we have and do as kings.

Finally, as regards the ram, the fat tail: Since the tail comes behind the sheep, I suggest this points most specifically to our sons, to those under (behind) us. These must be given to God.

As we have seen, those who failed in this third phase of life failed because they compromised with idolatry in the broad sense: prizing something else more than what God had given them. They did not give all their glory to God, but gave part of it to false gods. This has been the difficulty in the Church for nearly 2000 years, as the Church has compromised with philosophy, idolatry, and current trends over and over again. Whenever this happens, the Church fails to be prophetic. She plays with idols and lets her sons do so as well. The results are devastating.

The Lord's Supper carries forward the Peace Offering in that it is a meal. The Supper applies to us all that Jesus has already done for us, and we eat His work as we eat Him before the Father's watching eyes. The Supper as a whole tells us to focus all our attention, as kings, on Jesus, and to give Him all the glory.

Conclusion: The Three Crises

We can associate these three transitions, these three crises, with our earlier paradigm of faith, hope, and love as these manifest the Father, Spirit, and Son.

The Purification Offering is adoption (justification), as we have seen, and thus speaks most of the Father. The blood covers our sins, restores our virginity as Daughter and Bride, and provides us a new birth, a transition into priesthood. The Father gives Himself to us. This is a time of faith, as we move happily into our new life full of expectations.

The Ascension Offering is glorification and speaks most of the Spirit. The Spirit carries us through this transition in hope, as we trust God to bring us to the future exaltation that is particularly right for us. We don't know what kind of "king" we should become. Left to our own, we would make the wrong choice and seize a false kingship. Only God knows, and so we wait for Him, in hope. The chopping up of the parts, and their transfiguring reunification in the fire provides us a new birth as kings, as "sons of God."

The Peace Offering speaks of the fullness of righteousness, of the life of covenant loyalty, of love, where we give all our kingly glory to God, and since we do it as kings, it speaks most of the Son. We love others because Jesus loves us, and in our love for them, we seek what is right for them. Our midlife crisis has taught us the particular and peculiar thing that we must pass on. We seek to bring them to God and to cause them to forsake all idols.

From Bread To Wine

13.

Genesis 1: History and Biography

The sevenfold progress of human life and history that we have been considering finds its first expression in the seven sequential days of Genesis 1, and it is to that matter that we must now turn our attention. It is not readily apparent that the events of the second, fourth, and sixth days correlate with transitions to priesthood, kingship, and prophethood respectively. Only as we get into the deeper meanings of Genesis 1 will we be able to see that, indeed, the correlations are there, for the same Spirit who worked with the creation is now within us and works in our lives, and He does it the same way because He is the same Spirit. We can also see the parallel when we consider that in Genesis 1 the Spirit is working with the earth and that man is made of soil that is being worked by the Spirit.

A consideration of the sequence of creation week as it corresponds to the course of human life and to the course of human history is going to look like "allegorizing" to some readers, and because modern evangelical Christians have been taught to be very afraid of allegory, some readers will balk at what follows. What I must say in defense of this essay is that the objectionable kind of allegorization involves taking ideas from philosophy and trying to fit the Bible into them. This was the kind of allegorizing that cropped up in the early church, multiplied in the middle ages, and was rejected by the Protestant Reformers. It was usually very simplistic, very stupid, and usually wrong in that it tried to wed biblical revelation with pagan philosophical concepts.

But we must understand and insist upon the fact that everything God does reveals Himself and His life, and thus there are analogies between all the things God does. God created the world in seven days. God superintends all of human history, manipulating it toward His glorious end. And God superintends our individual lives also. We should not be surprised to find that the sequence of things God did in creation week corresponds roughly to the sequence of events in history and in biography. The proper word for such an investigation is "typology,"[72] the study of how God is impressing His life on, or better, into the life of His creation.

In my book Through New Eyes,[73] I take up many of the fundamental symbols in the Bible, showing how biblical symbols are related not only to the cosmos, but also to human life. The same symbols are used in both areas, because man is a microcosm of the macrocosmos. These symbols start in Genesis 1. Genesis 1 describes the actual creation and initial development of the cosmos, but the features of that cosmos, such as sea, heaven, land, trees, birds, fish, are all used in the rest of the Bible as symbols of human beings in various capacities, relations, and aspects. Thus, it is appropriate to take a symbolic interpretation of Genesis 1, provided that we understand that a "literal" interpretation is also true and in fact foundational for the symbolic interpretation.

---

72   Greek: *typos*, a stamp or die.

73   James B. Jordan, *Through New Eyes: Developing a Biblical View of the World* (Eugene, OR: Wipf and Stock, [1988] 1999).

Genesis 1: History and Biography

Genesis 1 is the work of the Spirit as He labors with the world. The Spirit's attribute is glory, as the Father's is holiness (personal integrity) and the Son's is righteousness (covenantal unity). Thus, the Spirit's work is revealed not in propositional sentences, but in art and music. If we are going to consider the flow of human life from the perspective of the Spirit (sevenfold rather than threefold or fivefold), then we are going to have to pay attention to the flow of symbols and images on the Spirit's canvas of human life.

Genesis 1 passes from symbol to symbol as the days progress. If we are going to allow Genesis 1 to speak to us about the sequence of human biography, we shall have to allow the symbols to switch out from day to day, while sustaining the same general anthropological meaning throughout the whole week of human life. Thus, I shall argue, from one perspective, children are plants on the third day, stars on the fourth, fish and birds on the fifth, and land animals under the first human couple on the sixth. At the same time, such children are being spoken of in slightly different ways on each day: springing from the soil of their parents, elevated with their parents in the heavenlies, multiplying new generations as fish and birds, serving their parents as animals under human beings.

The Spirit moves the world, and believers, "from glory to glory." At the end of each of His works, God sees that things are "good," yet things can be better, so that at the end of the next work things are also "good." Our lives also move through phases from glory to glory, and we have seen that it is profitable to consider human life in seven such phases, each phase more mature than the preceding. Symbolically, each phase is associated with a set of symbols in Genesis 1. Thus, to anticipate our discussion, we are

1. a dark world under God's light, and then
2. a sea under God's firmament mediator, then
3. land that springs forth plants, then
4. firmament lights elevated to some degree of honor, then
5. multiplying through children, then
6. elevated to full rule over the world, and finally
7. join God in His rest at the end.

A final preliminary observation: As the images and symbols in the seven days of Genesis 1 are used in more than one way with regard to human life in the rest of the Bible, the sequence of these images and symbols can have more than one application. The lifespan covered by that flow of images is the same—from birth to death, from the beginning of history to the end—but we can see Genesis 1 applying in more than one correct and useful way. To anticipate: Is the elevation of the lights on the fourth day to be associated with the glories of Solomon and the Kingdom Era or with the coming of Yahweh as King of Israel at Sinai and thus with the Sinaitic Era? It is possible to do it either way, as we shall eventually see, and I think both are valid. The symbols are general enough that they can provide hints, types, adumbrations, of the future course of history in more than one way.

What follows cannot be a full development of these themes. That would require a book much larger than Through New Eyes. My purpose is to work toward a better understanding of liturgy and worship as they relate to life and history, and so I shall discuss enough to make that relationship clear, without going into every possible implication and application.

The proof of the pudding is in the eating, as the saying goes, and so I invite the reader to consider whether what follows makes sense. If you find it helpful, as I have, then I shall be glad. If it makes no sense to you, then discard it.

We have already seen how human life moves from faith to hope to love and how it moves in a fivefold way that replicates the movement of the Spirit from the Father to the Son and back again. We have also already laid out a sevenfold sequence of human life, expanding the first two models in significant ways. With this in mind, we can consider how human life might also replicate the work of the Spirit in Genesis 1, as the Spirit also guides our lives.

The womb of the mother is empty, dark, and has no form. Then God says, "let there be light," and the baby is conceived. The Spirit (the Source of the original light) enters the womb along with the fertilized ovum, and the baby comes to life. During the nine months of gestation, the baby acquires form, and then he comes forth, adding to (multiplying) the number of humans who already exist. The child enters into the light: "Let there be light" again. On the first day, the light of God shone directly on the earth. This is, in human life, the time of childhood, when the child is directly under his parents, when it is their faces who shine upon him. And, from a different but correlative perspective, since "the lamp of the body is the eye," when the baby is born and opens his eyes, this is another form of "let there be light."

The firmament puts a barrier between God and the world, between father (God) and son/daughter (world). Thus, as children grow, they become more independent. "Terrible twos" is the first phase of this growth into independency. This links to the second day. The firmament is called "heaven," and what the child is going through are times of separation from his parents and into fuller and more direct relationships with God. The firmament that is being inserted between parent and child is God Himself, so that when the child leaves home, he is face to face with God apart from his parents as mediators of God's presence.

The point in time when this firmament is put between the child and his parents, between God and the child, is baptism. Baptism showers down on us the waters above the firmament, the heavenly waters, establishing a new link between the child and God. That new link is a barrier between the child and his parents, for now he must begin to grow into having God as his Father, instead of his earthly parents. Baptism begins our growth into maturity under God and destroys all patriarchalism, all tendencies for parents to keep their children as their own.

But the divisions are not finished, and God does not say that this work is good until the middle of the third day. There is a second division, between dry ground and sea. This we can link to the separation of boys and girls. This second division or separation is essential for human growth and for God's plans for history, for there can be no marriage without this prior separation. The ground and sea are in a new relationship once the separation is completed, and this speaks of marriage. Thus, the events of the second day and of the first part of the third day carry us through the first "death and resurrection" trauma of life: separation from parents, adolescence, and marriage.

Now, applying the whole third day to human life involves taking more than one perspective. The day can be viewed in more than one way, though all the various ways speak of boys and girls, marriage, and in some cases, children. Viewing the third day from more than one perspective arises, as discussed above, from the fact that the symbols here are very general and are employed by the Spirit later on in more than one way.

To begin with, the word for sea in Hebrew is masculine and the word for "dry ground" is feminine. This fact provides one perspective, for if we continue to let Genesis 2 fill in the anthropomorphic implications of Genesis 1, we can see the following progression. Genesis 2:4ff. concern the generations, the offspring, of the heavens and the earth, and that offspring is humanity. First, we have the dust of the ground, which is 'adamah, the mother. From this first mother (earth), the man is taken as life is put into him by the Spirit (heaven). If we look closer at Genesis 2, we find that a river arises in the land of Eden, flows down through the Garden, and from there to the rest of the world as four streams. This corresponds to the waters above in Genesis 1. Now, this stream initially is said to flow over and impregnate the land so that plants grow from her. Then the Spirit, not earthly water, impregnates the land and makes the man, so that man is offspring of heaven and earth. Since plants grow up as a result of the impregnation of the land with heavenly waters, the overall picture here is that the waters above are husband, the land is wife, and the plants are children. The femininity of the land corresponds later on in human history to the emergence of men from their mothers.

From this perspective, the land is the bride, surrounded by her husband. But the symbolism can also be just the opposite. The sea below the land is feminine, and we see over and over again that men meet their wives at wells in the Bible (think of Jacob, of Moses, and of Jesus with the Samaritan woman). The land, from which the plants break forth, is the man. As we have seen, water also comes forth from the land, from above the sea, and this is also a masculine image, for the "water" of reproduction comes from the body of the man. In this perspective, we can think of the plants springing from the male land as Eve coming from the side of Adam, as he lay supine and asleep while the Spirit worked on him.

Thus, in general, the plants on the soil speak again of the formation of a bride for the man. Yet, in that there are two kinds of plants, we can also see in this compact imagery a contrast and relationship between the two kinds of plants. This provides yet a third perspective on the marital implications of the third day.

It takes little imagination to see the emergence of plants as corresponding to the growth of hair at adolescence. Indeed, since man is made of earth, the hairs on the human body do indeed correspond to the vegetation that grows on the earth.

I hope that no one will take offense if I suggest that the upward pointing trees are more masculine and the grains are more feminine. All the Hebrew words are masculine, but the grains are said to be "seeding seeds" (Gen. 1:11–12), and it is the "seed" of the woman who is brought before us in Genesis 3. She is considered a fruitful plant. The thought that upward pointing trees are a male image may be shocking to some readers, but we must not avoid the facts of human life as God has designed them. These things are good, even if we usually avoid speaking of them. Now, in Creation in Six Days[74] I pointed out that the fruit trees of day 3 include the olive, while the grasses are the grain plants. Flour is ground up seed, while oil is made after the seed is removed from the olive.

Notice that in the bread of the sacrifices, oil is always put with the flour to make the bread (Lev. 2). The "salt of the covenant" is also added, covenantally joining the oil and the flour. We can see the woman as flour, as bread, and the man as carrying the oil, the fluid, that goes into her when the salty covenant of marriage is formed. (Compare

---

74 Jordan, *Creation in Six Days*, 14–15, 184-185.

the liquid river and the dry ground of Gen. 2.) This is how God has designed us, and our design is good. Thus, to see the trees as adolescent boys and the grains as adolescent girls is not a strange suggestion.[75]

The trees and grains may be seen either as the children of the marriage of water and land or as another adumbration of the marriage of boy and girl.

To summarize: The separation of the second day speaks of the separation of children from their parents, and the separations and multiplications of the third day speak of boys and girls and of marriage and children, in several ways.

On the fourth day we find the sun and moon, which speak of the exaltation of the married couple to a kind of kingship over the starry children that are associated with them (see Gen. 37:9–10). This move from priestly to kingly associations, from bread and oil to sun and moon, hints at the second great trial of our lives, and thus of the cross, where Jesus as priest became Jesus as King.

I suggest that the multiplication of fish and birds on the fifth day also speaks of children, and of our influence in the worlds of both sea and land after our midlife crises. We have seen that from one perspective children also grow up from the watered earth and fully join the firmament when they marry, and along these lines fish and birds can speak of children as they start on their upward journey. As creatures of sea and land respectively (Gen. 1:22), fish and birds carry overtones of boys and girls, with the "great sea creatures" as parents.

As I continue this application of Genesis 1 to the course of human life, I notice that first fish and birds are mentioned and then, on the sixth day, land animals. I suggest that this sequence provides us another picture of children growing up and then becoming land animals, sons and daughters who are useful in the household of their parents.

---

[75] The grape vine, which is not a tree of course, seems to have been among the "shrubs of the field" created after the creation of Adam (Gen. 2:5–6). In the Bible, bread is first and is priestly, while wine is later and is kingly. It is when Noah is given kingly rule after the Flood that we first see the grape in evidence, while the olive sprang up immediately after the Flood.

The creation of man and woman on the sixth day may be seen to relate to the third set of trials in our lives, our trials as kings. Human beings do not wrestle much with fish and birds, at least in the Bible, but they do wrestle with the various land animals in various ways. Swarming and creeping things can get into your house and defile it (Lev. 11). Wild animals can attack your flocks, as David fought bear and lion. Domestic animals, like sheep and oxen, have to be wrestled with in various ways also.

Then, at the climax of our lives, we enter into sabbath rest with God, corresponding to the seventh day. When we are old, we become elders, with wisdom to pass on to others, wisdom that we have learned, wisdom consisting of how to rule the world properly. Elders rule in the fullest sense, and the narrative of Genesis 1 moves to that point. Our own lives are a course of maturation that results in our becoming elders, prophets.

SEVENFOLD COVENANT HISTORY

Now, while we might reflect on all this, and expand on it and defend it at length, I want to proceed from the sequence of Genesis 1 to the sequence of human history, the large contour of human life. Human history is the biography of Adam, as restored and completed by the New Adam, written large.

In terms of what we have seen thus far, I suggest that the days of Genesis 1 apply to the whole course of history in a double way, first as the history of the covenant people recounted in the Bible, and then also as the whole course of human history. At the center of human history would be the fourth day, with Jesus elevated as the Sun of Righteousness and the Church as the moon. At the center of Bible history can be seen either the Sinaitic or the Kingdom covenants, as we shall see, corresponding to the fourth day.

First, the covenant history in the Bible. As we begin, it will be well to list the covenant eras of the Bible, before we link them (in more than one way) to the days of creation:

    Adamic Covenant Era

Noahic Covenant Era
Patriarchal Covenant Era
Sinaitic Covenant Era
Kingdom Covenant Era
Remnant Covenant Era (beginning within the Kingdom at the time of Elijah and continuing until the Restoration from Babylon)
Restoration Covenant Era
Apostolic New Covenant Era (AD 30–70)
Present New Covenant Era
Final New Covenant Era (the eternal sabbath)

These ten eras have to be "fit" into the seven days of Genesis 1. We can do it either of two ways, both of which are profitable, and both of which have some biblical support. The first is this, arising from the ten statements "and God said":

Day 1: Adamic Era (light)
Day 2: Noahic Era (firmament; rainbow)
Day 3a: Patriarchal Era (land and sea; Hebrews and Gentiles)
Day 3b: Sinaitic Era (grains and olives: priesthood)
Day 4: Kingdom Era (sun, moon, stars: kingship)
Day 5: Remnant Era (fish and birds: blessing; prophethood)
Day 6a: Restoration Era (land animals)
Day 6b: Apostolic Era (humanity)
Day 6c: Present Era (command to eat)
Day 7: Final Era (sabbath)

The second is this:

Day 1: Adamic Era (light)
Day 2: Noahic Era (firmament; rainbow)
Day 3: Patriarchal Era (land and sea; Hebrews and Gentiles)
Day 4: Sinaitic Era (sun, moon, stars: Yahweh as king)
Day 5: Kingdom Era (fish and birds)
Day 6: Remnant Era (humanity)
Day 7: New Covenant Eras (moving into sabbath)

In the first sequence, the fourth day is linked to the establishment of human kingship, while in the second it is linked to the establishment of Yahweh's kingship at Sinai. Let us now look at these in more detail.

Day 1: Heaven and earth are face to face, each illuminated by the Spirit's light. The Spirit's establishment of light corresponds to His entering Adam and making him a "light" in Genesis 2. Adam is the human light over the world. Thus, the first day anticipates the Creation Era, the first week of the world.[76]

Additionally, there is a move from darkness to light on the first day. The establishment of formal worship at the time of the birth of Adam's grandson Enosh might be seen as a new "creation" of light (Gen. 4:26), a light carried by the Sethites in the world until they sinned by intermarrying with the Cainite women.

Day 2: The firmament mediatorial-barrier is set between heaven and earth. This period of time, when men live under the sky, anticipates the Noahic Covenant. Notice that the sign of the Noahic Covenant is a rainbow in the firmament. In a real sense, Noah as "king" is the new firmament over all the humanity that follows him, for Noah does not die until two years before Abram is born, as a careful study of the chronology shows.

Day 3a: Land and sea are separated, and this corresponds to the separation of the priestly people (land) from all the other nations (sea) at the call of Abram. Notice that the sign of the Patriarchal Covenant is circumcision, which is an act of division that signifies, in part, the separation of the priestly nation from the other nations.

Day 3b: Men and women (trees and grains) begin to multiply in the "land" when Jacob has twelve sons and at least one daughter. This process continues in the Egyptian Sojourn, when the people greatly multiply. Then the people multiply to a host, signified by the plants.

---

[76] On Adam as the light of the world, see my *Creation in Six Days*, 153–154, where I show that the seven acts of "Yahweh God" in Genesis 2–3 correspond to the seven days of "God's" actions in Genesis 1, and the creation of light on the first day of Genesis 1 corresponds to the creation of Adam as the first act of Yahweh God in Genesis 2.

This way of looking at the whole of the third day takes it all as adumbrating the Patriarchal Era. But if we allow the grain and oil plants to be priestly (as wine is kingly and prophetic), we can also take the second half of the third day as pointing to the Sinaitic Era, when Israel was a nation of priests.

Day 4: The Kingdom comes, as Yahweh is enthroned King over Israel at Sinai. This begins the Sinaitic era. This is a time of trials, as Israel is tempted to seize the prerogatives of the Tree of Knowledge and have an earthly king for themselves. We can also, as noted above, see the fourth day as a day of "kingly" glorification of the previously "priestly" marriage of the third day, in which case it speaks of the Kingdom Era.

Day 5: We now have earthly kings, the "great sea monsters," who symbolically rule the fish and birds. From one perspective this is the Kingdom era. It is the time when Israel fills the land, not as priestly plants, but as kingly creatures, with world influence (as Solomon had). Or we can associate the fifth day with the Remnant Era. During the Remnant, for the first time the prophets begin to speak to the Gentile nations (the fish, ruled by great monster-kings) as well as to the Israelites (the birds, associated with the heavens and the land).

Day 6: There are three paragraphs or events in the sixth day. First the land animals are created. Then the mature man is created. Third, the man and his wife are told of the food God has given them.

Day 6a: Following the Remnant, this would be the Restoration Era. The Restoration is the beginning of the New Covenant (see for instance Jer. 31:27, 31, and 38), its first phase. Now the prophets are glorified, in the sense that Israel moves from being a nation of kings to a nation of prophets, ministering to the world. The land animals can speak of this, especially when we consider that the perverse Jews of the book of Revelation are associated with a Land Beast.[77]

Day 6b: The creation of man and his wife should be linked to the coming of Jesus and His exaltation and the call of His bride, all of which happen in the Apostolic Era. Though the gospel goes forth, it only goes

---

77 See my *The Vindication of Jesus Christ*.

(in Acts and the Epistles) to the oikumene set up in the book of Daniel, and not to the whole world. Full "fruitfulness and multiplication" do not happen until the death and resurrection of the Bride, following her Groom, in the great tribulation and the following resurrection of the Church (Rev. 14–20).

Day 6c: Here the provision of food is found, which I submit can speak of eating all the world into the life of the Husband and His bride.[78] This really begins in earnest once the Bride has died and been resurrected, after ad 70. Thus, it links to the Present Era.

Day 6: Or we can associate the sixth day with the Remnant Era. The elevation of the prophets over the Kingdom (of the fifth day) provides the picture here, but for a full discussion of this association we shall have to wait until we link the whole sequence to the seven feasts and fasts of Leviticus 23.

Day 7: The Final Era of the eternal sabbath finishes the sequence. Or, we can consider the seventh day as in focus in the Restoration Era, when Israel is permitted and encouraged to enter into rest as a priestly people and build a new temple as a house of worship for all nations. As the beginning of the New Covenant, this Restoration sabbath time extends into the Apostolic, Present, and Final Eras.

SEVENFOLD WORLD HISTORY

Now to the whole course of human history: As the first three days culminate in a preliminary sabbath on the fourth and then move to the seventh, so human history moves to the completion of Jesus' work and from there to the end.

Day 1: The Father sends the Spirit, creating Adam and humanity.

---

78   Eating is a symbol of incorporation in the Bible. To "in-corpor-ate" literally means to eat, to take into one's body. In the Lord's Supper, we eat Jesus. In Revelation 3:16 we see Jesus eating us. For a full study of eating in the Bible, with particular attention to what is to be eaten (incorporated) and what is not to be eaten in the Levitical dietary laws, see James B. Jordan, *Studies in Food and Faith* (Niceville, FL: Biblical Horizons, 1989–1990).

Day 2: The firmament is set up. As before, I believe we should associate this with the elevation of Noah to kingly status. The Noahic Covenant continues in force among the Gentiles until Jesus comes, until the fourth day when He is established in the firmament as the Sun of Righteousness.

Day 3: Land and sea are separated, and the land flourishes. This is the whole history of Israel, separated from the Gentile sea.

Day 4: Sun and moon are married, and new celestial children (stars) are added to them. This corresponds to the coming of Jesus and His marriage to the Church.

Day 5: God's creatures multiply on land and sea. I suggest that this corresponds to the period of the Apostolic Church, down to ad 70, when many converts were made from both Gentile and Jew.

Day 6: The end of the Apostolic Era is the end of any God-appointed Jew-Gentile distinction. All animals are land animals on this day. Jesus stands clear as the Husband of humanity, with full dominion over all the world, and His bride stands with Him. This is the ascension of the saints to rule at the beginning of the millennium (ad 70) and the resurrection of the Church on earth at that point.[79] The "creation of the world" is finished, and now True Humanity is manifest as the ruler of the world.

Day 7: The final judgment at the end of history, the eternal sabbath of man with God.

God and Genesis One

Before moving farther into ritual considerations, we must at this point consider the revelation of the Trinity in the days of creation, as it keys us further into the wider meaning of the events of the first week of history.

---

[79] For details, see my *The Vindication of Jesus Christ* and the other material listed in the appendix of that book.

Genesis 1: History and Biography

As I discussed in my book Creation in Six Days,[80] the seven days of Genesis 1 form a chiasm, and the activities of the Persons of God are highlighted in the various days. To understand this we must let the imagery of Genesis 1 work on us in terms of everything else the Bible and human life teaches us, seeing Genesis 1 in terms of the motions of the three Persons of God and seeing that first week as a prophetic microchron of the whole Week of history:

Day 1: The Father sends the Spirit, who is already hovering over the world before any Word is spoken, establishing the preliminary Day.

Day 2: The Son is established as Firmament-Mediator between heaven and earth. The Firmament is revealed by the light of the Spirit. We have linked this above with the elevation of Noah as a preliminary "king of the world" (king-son), and with the fact that children begin to become independent of their parents and to relate more directly to God, as the God of the "highest heavens" (Father) is revealed in the "firmament heavens" (Son).

Day 3: The bride (humanity, both men and women) grows as bread and oil plants on the earth, through the life-giving power of the Spirit.

Day 4: The Son and His bride are enthroned in the firmament heavens together as sun and moon, with the stars also. Gen. 37:9–10 speaks of the sun, moon, and stars as a family.

Day 5: By the Spirit, the bride multiplies as birds and fish on land and sea.

Day 6: The Son and His bride are revealed as mediators between God and the world, corresponding to the firmament.

Day 7: All returns to the Father in the fullness of Day-time.

Thus, the sequence can be fleshed out again as follows:

Day 1. The Father sends the Spirit.

Day 2. The Son is revealed by the Spirit.

Day 3. The Spirit draws the bride from within the creation.

Day 4. The Son and His bride are exalted in preliminary marital rest.

---

80   Jordan, *Creation in Six Days*, 60–61, 43, 195, 211ff.

Day 5. The Spirit moves from Son and bride to fill the world.

Day 6. The Son comes into fuller focus and the marriage to the bride is brought to fullness.

Day 7. The Father is glorified as God over all.

Or more simply, condensing the sevenfold sequence into the fivefold sequence of Father – Spirit – Son – Spirit – Father:

1. The Spirit proceeds from the Father to reveal the Son (Days 1–2).

2. The Spirit proceeds from the Father to bring the bride to the Son (Day 3). Procession from Father to Son is now complete, and a preliminary sabbath ensues (Day 4).

3. The Spirit proceeds from the Son, through the Bride, to make the world teem with life (Days 5–6a).

4. The Son and His Bride are revealed (Day 6).

5. All returns to the Father (Day 7).

14.

GENESIS ONE AND RITUAL

The progression of history and biography is also the sequence of ritual, for God's rituals are designed to reinsert His people into His true history and kingdom. As before, we shall use the ritual of the Ascension Offering as the basis of our considerations.[81] I want now to probe into this matter a bit more fully and make some revisions to what I suggested in that earlier discussion.

To begin with, let us lay out again the full sequence of the Ascension Offering:

1. Yahweh enthroned in the Tabernacle (Exod. 40; 2 Chron. 5)
2. Spirit-fire sent into the Altar (Lev. 9:24; 2 Chron. 7:1)

---

[81] In "Re-creation in the Ascension Offering," *Biblical Horizons* 107 (July 1998), I explored the ritual of the Ascension Offering in Leviticus 1 as it seems to duplicate, at a symbolic level, the events of Genesis 1. What follows is a more fully developed essay into the same consideration.

3. Son-of-the-herd (Lev. 1:5) brought near
4. Hand laid on animal-son
5. Animal-son slain
6. Blood displayed
7. Animal-son skinned
8. Animal-son cut up
9. Fire stoked up
10. Clean pieces put into fire
11. Unclean pieces washed
12. Cleansed pieces put into fire
13. Ascension in smoke
14. Sweet savor to God
15. Worshiper departs

History and Ritual

If we apply Genesis 1 to this sequence, we can see this ritual application in Leviticus 1 and its connection to the three courses of history that we have set out in the previous chapter:

Day 1. The *Father* sends the Spirit. Here is the fire coming onto the altar from the throne of God after the building the Tabernacle, the creation of the world, steps 1–2 of the ritual.

Day 2. The *Son* is revealed by the Spirit. The animal is brought near, revealed, as the place of mediation between God and man, the living firmament between the twain, step 3. Link this with Noah's establishment as king-son.

Day 3a. Hands are laid on the animal and it is slain, steps 4–5. The blood (liquid) is divided from the body. The blood is splashed against the altar and runs down its earthly sides into the gutter at its base, step 6, which recapitulates the elevation of the land over the sea. God puts His hand on Abram, calling him, and then Abram is circumcised, which is the token of the Patriarchal era.

Circumcision links to the skinning of the animal, step 7. Circumcision means that Abram and his seed are called to die for the rest of humanity, to suffer being cut in half and to have their blood poured out. Ultimately, of course, this comes to pass in Jesus' crucifixion. In Genesis, however, we repeatedly see the patriarchs' dying to their hopes and dreams, dying so that the Gentiles may hear. This is the outworking of circumcision.

Let me briefly summarize before we move forward, for it is this dying that is recapitulated and symbolized in the slaying of the animal:

After the circumcision of Abram, and his name-change to Abraham, some of the wicked Gentiles are destroyed, and the patriarch goes to Gerar and has a ministry among the Gentiles there (Gen. 17–20).

After the trauma of offering Isaac (Gen. 22), we find Isaac marrying (Gen. 24) and then having a new ministry in Gerar (Gen. 26).

After Jacob is sent out from his mother and father and dies to his old life, he goes to the Gentiles and marries Gentile women (Gen. 28–30).

After Jacob wrestles with God and prevails, he receives a "death" wound in his thigh and is elevated and allowed to take the land. As a result, he is able to minister to Esau (Gen. 32–33), and he has a witness among the men of Salem (Shechem), though that ministry is destroyed by his murderous sons (Gen. 34).

After Joseph is cast into a pit, another symbol of death, he sustains a ministry in Egypt; and then after being put into prison, he is elevated and ministers to the whole Gentile world (Gen. 37, 36–41).

The circumcision of Moses' son in Exodus 4 prefigures the first Passover. In both cases, the blood was displayed and the Angel of Death departed. Passover brings to a climax the theme of the shedding of blood as we have been considering it here.

Day 3b. The *Spirit* draws the bride from the creation (as plants). The animal is divided into parts, some of which are clean and some of which are unclean (step 8). We see here the multiplication of the land (the animal) into many forms of grain and fruit trees. Compare this to the Egyptian Sojourn.

Day 3b can also be linked to the Sinaitic Era, as we have seen. During this time, Israel was a priestly but not yet a kingly nation, and thus the grains and (olive) trees, priestly things, are tokens of the period.

And as we have seen, this period of division also corresponds to the entire history of Israel up to the coming of the New Covenant, when all will be brought back together in Christ as the various dividing walls are cast down in Him (Eph. 2:14).

Day 4. The *Son* and His bride are exalted in preliminary marital rest, becoming the fiery sun and the reflective moon. Compare this to the stoking up of the fire, the revelation of that fire, on the altar (step 9), and with the Sinaitic era. The placement of the clean parts into the altar-fire first (step 10) speaks of the elevation of Israel into the first form of the Kingdom of God at this time in history. This is Israel considered not as a community of sinners, but as God's son.

Day 4 can also be linked with the Kingdom Era, in that the elevation not only of the sun but also of the moon and the stars can be seen as the exaltation not only of King Yahweh but also of His bride, Israel.

This type is fulfilled in the death and fiery ascension of Jesus, which is what corresponds to this ritual event in the larger history of the whole world.

Day 5. The *Spirit* moves from Son and bride to fill the world. The unclean parts are washed (step 11). Washing is with the Word, and there is now a king in Israel who can speak such a word (Psalms, Proverbs, Ecclesiastes, Song), so this is the Kingdom era.

Day 5 can also be linked to the Remnant Era. The prophets pick up the duty of the kings to speak God's washing Word to the people and to the nations. The prophetic words of these men is even closer to the act of cleansing than the wisdom words of the kings.

In world history the fifth day corresponds to the rite of baptism, which cleanses humanity in a definite way during the Apostolic Age, as both former Jew and former Gentile are baptized into "one new man" in Christ. While we still baptize today, joining this union, that union was definitively created during the Apostolic Age, and thus the whole age was a time of washing, of baptism.

Day 6. The *Son* comes into fuller focus and the marriage to the bride is brought to fullness. The worshiper lives in obedience to the Son, Yahweh, king of Israel and of humanity. In Israel's history, this can speak of the Remnant Covenant, initiated by Elijah and Elisha, which continues through the Babylonian Sojourn. The Remnant, while they suffer, are the protected bride of Yahweh. A study of this period will show that however much the rest of Israel suffered, the Remnant as a whole were spared. Moving into Babylon spared them going through the destruction of Jerusalem. Thus, the cleansed parts of the animal joining the clean parts in the Spirit's fire (step 12) squares nicely with this period of history.

In the other sequence, the sixth day corresponds to the Restoration, Apostolic, and Present periods of the New Covenant Era. These can be seen as stages in the presentation of the cleansed pieces of the animal into the fire.

In world history, here is the Present Age of the New Covenant era, wherein our marriage to Jesus is revealed much more fully.

Day 7. The *Father* is glorified as God over all. Here is the eternal kingdom after the Last Judgment, as God fully accepts all of us together, Son and Bride (steps 13–15). In Israel's history, this can be the three New Covenant Eras, which began when Israel returned to God's land, ascending from Babylon, and rested with God while they ministered to the world. Indeed, we can break down the last three steps of the ritual this way:

A. Ascension to God: Restoration Era (Temple rebuilt).

B. Sweet Savor to God: Apostolic Era (the suffering Church).

C. Worshiper goes out to the world: Present Era.

Calendar

Before we turn finally to Christian worship, we will find it useful to apply this sequence also to the seven feasts of the Levitical calendar as we find it in Leviticus 23. The cycle of feasts and fasts corresponds to the shorter sequence of Bible history, the second sequence laid out in our previous studies.

1. *Sabbath Day.* This links with the first day, in that in under the Law it was forbidden to stoke up one's own hearthfire on the sabbath, on pain of death.[82] That is, on the first day, to begin life anew each week, the Light of God, His hearthfire at the central altar, burned brightly because of the extra sacrifices offered there, and our subordinate lights were to be left burning low so that His Light would be the Light for all Israel. Link this with steps 1–4 of the sacrificial sequence, where God takes His throne, lights His light on the altar, and we draw near in the commanded weekly convocation so He can lay His hands on us. Consider this with the Adamic Era.

2. *Passover.* This links with the second day in that it is the Passover animal who mediates between God and man, between heaven and earth, and its displayed blood provides a firmament covering (atonement, which means covering) for us in our sins. Link this with steps 5–7, the slaying of the animal, the display of its blood, and its skinning. Consider this with the Noahic Era, which began with the slaying of the human race and the skinning (circumcision) of the physical earth by the Flood, and then with the new covering of the earth by the rainbow.

3. *First-fruits.* This links with the third day in that a sheaf of grain is waved toward God and back again. While the Passover lamb or kid (it could be either) was not to be divided up, at First-fruits a male lamb is offered in the usual way. We can connect this, once again, with the divisions of the earth on the third day, and thus with cutting the animal up into pieces (step 8). Consider this with the Patriarchal Era.

---

82   See my *Sabbath-Breaking and the Death Penalty: A Theological Investigation* (Tyler, TX: Geneva Ministries, 1986).

4. *Pentecost.* The Law was given on the first Pentecost and Yahweh was enthroned as King of Israel, marrying Israel, so consider this with the Sinaitic Era. The offerings of this day speak of this. The bull and the he-goat speak of the rulers of Israel (Lev. 4), and the other animals offered must be male (husbands). The bread that is offered represents Israel, the bride. This elevation into semi-heavenly (firmamental) rule links this feast with the fourth day.

The unleavened bread of Passover and First-fruits has now matured into leavened bread as a result of the new leavening work of the Spirit after the cutting off of the leaven of the old year, the old Egyptian leaven. The bride has made herself ready, so to speak. Thus, Pentecost links to the stoking up of the fire and the placement of the two clean pieces of the offering into it, steps 9–10.

5. *Trumpets.* The trumpets summon Israel to the convocations of the seventh month. The host is gathered in, and this links with the hosts of fish and birds of the fifth day. Israelites are the birds, but the Gentile fish are also invited to the Feast of Clouds (Booths) which is at the center of this month. I suggest we link this event with the baptism of the unclean pieces, in preparation for their placement into the fire, step 11. As the kings summon Israel for war and worship, consider this with the Kingdom Era.

6. *Day of Covering.*[83] While the Passover offering suffers and dies alone, apart from the people, the stress at Covering is that the people suffer and die along with the kid of the Covering offering, ascend in union with it, and in the person of their high priest receive new clothing. Now the people, considered as a cleansed bride, enter into the fire of the Spirit along with their Lord. Of course, this links with the creation of Eve to join with Adam on the sixth day, and with step 12, the presentation of the cleansed pieces into the altar. Consider this

---

83 Usually translated "day of atonement." Atonement, however, is associated usually with reconciliation, at-one-ment. The Hebrew verb, however, means "cover," and covering is the main idea. The high priest removes his old garments, performs the ritual, and receives his garments back as a new covering. The blood put on all the altars is a covering for them.

with the Remnant Era, when God's faithful were separated from the unfaithful and joined with God in a new way under the ministry of the prophets.

7. *Clouds (Booths; Tabernacles)*.[84] This is the great feast of wine, the prophetic symbol, as the people gather for not seven but eight days with God, and when the Gentiles are included. The people enjoy sabbath rest in this seventh month, in leafy "clouds" around God's palace, itself being a symbolic replica of God's glory-cloud. This links with the completion of the sacrificial offering, steps 13–15.

This sequence applied year after year the first year of Israel's life as she emerged from Egypt; to wit:

1. *Sabbath*. God manifested in plagues, especially the ninth, when there was darkness over Egypt and light over Israel in Goshen.

2. *Passover*.

3. *First-fruits*. The gathering of the people initially at Sinai.

4. *Pentecost*. The giving of the Law.

5. *Trumpets*. Moses' ascension into the Cloud of God on Sinai to receive instructions for the Tabernacle. Moses represents all Israel gathered to God.

6. *Covering*. The restoration of Israel after the sin at the golden calf.

7. *Clouds*. The rest of the year, when the people rested at Sinai and built the Tabernacle.

The sequence also displays, once again, the Bible history of the Old Creation, and also moves into the New:

1. *Sabbath*. The Adamic era, when God was at rest but mankind had not rest (Gen. 5:29), yet God's light shone through the ministry of Enoch and the other Sethites.

---

84 On the translation of *sukkoth* as "clouds" rather than as "booths," see my essay, "The Oddness of the Feast of Booths," *Biblical Horizons* 90 (December 1996).

2. *Passover*. Moses is presented as a new Noah in Exodus 2:3. The destruction of Egypt is a new flood on a corrupt "world," the world around Israel. The Passover alludes, thus, back to the sacrifices Noah offered as the new world began after the Flood.

3. *First-fruits*. This is the Patriarchal era, when there were only a few sheaves of grain before God.

4. *Pentecost*. We arrive at Sinai, at the giving of the Law, and at the Sinaitic era.

5. *Trumpets*. Once Israel receives a king, it is the king's duty to blow the trumpets, so to speak, and gather Israel for holy war and for worship. This is the Kingdom era.

6. *Covering*. The affliction of their souls that the people are to do on this day links with the Remnant era, when the righteous remnant formed a suffering servant for Yahweh.

7. *Clouds*. The inclusion of Gentiles at this feast points to the Restoration era and the worldwide (or at least oikumene-wide) witness of the Jews.

8. There is a second paragraph devoted to the Feast of Clouds in Leviticus 23, focusing on the people's rest with God around His palace. This points to the New Covenant era.

Thus, once again the sequence of ritual, this time of the calendar year, is the same as the sequence of history. We could apply this sequence to the sevenfold sequence of world history, as we have laid it out, but I shall leave it to the reader to compare what we have written here with what we have set out previously.

BIOGRAPHY

We notice that the three great feasts, Passover, Pentecost, and Clouds, come in connection with the second, fourth, and sixth days. These are to be linked with the three times of passage, trial, and transition in our personal lives. Feasts with trials? Well, consider the theology of the book of Ecclesiastes. Solomon repeatedly says that in the midst of the suffering and confusion of life, we can "eat, drink, and be merry," for this is the free gift God has given us in the midst of our difficulties. It is when we experience trials that we need festival the most.

Thus, the entire calendar year can also be seen as a sketch of human biography; to wit:

1. *Sabbath*. Childhood rest and freedom under the authority of our parents.

2. *Passover*. The transitions of adolescence, culminating in marriage.

3. *First-fruits*. The beginning of the new life as a new person after marriage, entering into a new occupation.

4. *Pentecost*. The coming of the law in a fuller way, as a chopping up of our former life in midlife crises.

5. *Trumpets*. The summons into the final phase of life.

6. *Covering*. We struggle as prophets, as elders, with those under us, suffering in union with them.

7. *Clouds*. The peace that we should experience at the end of life and the joys of heaven and eternity.

CHRISTIAN LITURGY

We have considered Christian worship as a movement through three and five covenant-renewing steps. We can now add in two more steps, which were only implied before:

    Entrance:
        God calls us
        God cleanses us (confession)
        We praise God
    Word:
        God instructs us (Word and sermon)
        We offer ourselves to God (offertory)
    Sacrament:
        God feeds us
        God commissions us and sends us forth

The season of praise and the offertory are what come into new focus in this display of the ritual.

We have seen how in the threefold sequence we move from Father (faith) to Spirit (hope) to Son (love). In the fivefold sequence we move from Father to Spirit to Son to Spirit to Father. While the seven days of creation are all the work of the inworking Spirit, we have seen that there is a focus on the Persons of God on the days as follows:

1. Father as Alpha.
2. Son revealed as firmament.
3. Spirit prepares bride for Son.
4. Son and bride enthroned.
5. Spirit multiplies children.
6. Son and bride fully manifested.
7. Father as Omega.

As we apply this sequence to worship, I shall add in some comments from my book Theses on Worship,[85] where some aspects of this sevenfold sequence of worship were first set out; to wit:

1. *The Father calls us.* In Leviticus 1, this is the enthronement of God, the sending of fire to us as altars (calling us), the animal brought near (our gathering for worship), and the hand put on the animal (God's laying hold of us). Day One. Focus on God's initiation of all things. Here is the call to worship. In Leviticus 23, this is the Sabbath.

2. *The Son is manifest to us as our Redeemer.* In Leviticus 1, this is the slaying of the animal, the display of its blood, and its skinning. The skin is given to the priests. Jesus' skin is given to us as our covering, as the skin of the slain animal was given to Adam and Eve in Genesis 3. Day Two. Focus on transition and separation of heavenly things from earthly (waters above, waters below). Here is the confession of sins and the transition into the Kingdom. In Leviticus 23, this is Passover, the transition from the old to the new. In worship, this cleansing (blood put on us, who are the altars) restores us as priests.

---

[85] James B. Jordan, *Theses on Worship: Notes Toward the Reformation of Worship*, 2nd ed. (Niceville, FL: Transfiguration Press, [1994] 1998).

3. *The Spirit reveals and multiplies the bride.* In Leviticus 1, the animal is cut up. Day Three. Focus on deposition, the covenant-grant of the gift of the Kingdom. Throughout the Old Creation, that grant is seen as land, and on the third day the land with its fruitful blessings is made. Here is the absolution from sins and the praise of God for His bounty. In Leviticus 23, this is First-fruits, the celebration of God's bounty. As priests, like the Levites at the Temple, we enter into a season of prayer and praise, and in traditional worship, this is where we sing the Kyrie, the Te Deum, the Gloria in Excelsis, and various psalms. All of these hymns celebrate the gift that God has given us.

4. *The Son is manifest to us as our King.* In Leviticus 1, the fire is stoked up and the clean parts of the animal are put into it. Day Four. Focus on stipulation, for the heavenly lights are set up into the firmament to regulate times and seasons. Here is the law of God, the reading of Scripture, and the main sermon. In Leviticus 23, this is Pentecost, which celebrates the giving of the law. In worship, the Law (Word) of God comes to us to make us kings.

5. *The Spirit comes to call us as kings to the great feast.* In Leviticus 1, the unclean pieces are washed in preparation for their ascension. Day Five. Focus on convocation, for the creatures of the fifth day are said to swarm in groups, analogous to the host gathered around God's throne. Here is the offertory, where we offer ourselves and our gifts to God, and the prayers of cloudy incense offered to God. In Leviticus 23, this is Trumpets, which summons the kingly people to God.

6. *The Son is fully manifested as our Husband.* In Leviticus 1, the cleansed pieces join their husband in the fire. Day Six. Focus on affirmation, for on the sixth day man was made. This is communion, as we participate in the new humanity by feeding on the body and blood of Christ. In Leviticus 23, this is the Day of Atonement. As we have seen, the Supper gives us again the priestly and kingly deaths of Jesus, so that we can become prophets, brides of Jesus as Prophet.

The Supper recapitulates the first five parts of the worship liturgy and then applies it afresh to us; to wit:

A. Call. Jesus takes His seat, and we gather to Him.

B. Cleansing. Jesus takes the bread into His hands.

C. Praise. Jesus gives thanks, and we join Him.

D. Word. Jesus takes the wine of the prophetically-governed kingdom into His hands.

E. Offertory. Jesus gives thanks, and we join Him.

F. Communion. Now all these elements are repeated, but the bread is broken and given to us, and the wine given also.

7. *The Father is manifested as the One to whom the Son has returned us by His Spirit.* In Leviticus 1, the animal ascends to the Father. Day Seven. Focus on rule, for on the seventh day God rested enthroned in His creation, and now in Christ so do we. In worship, this is the benediction. But we press beyond:

8. *Day Eight.* Focus on mission, for after resting on man's first day (God's seventh), we are sent forth. This is the charge and commissioning. In Leviticus 23, there are two sections devoted to the Feast of Clouds; the first emphasizes rest (vv. 33–36), and the second emphasizes mission into the future (vv. 39–44; future generations, v. 43). Clouds, interestingly, was the feast that lasted eight days, during which seventy bulls were offered for the seventy nations of the world, a missionary emphasis.

Appendix A: Christian Piety: Deformed and Reformed

The term "piety" is rather vague in meaning, and that is as it should be, for it refers to something that is rather vague in nature. There is nothing wrong or unsatisfactory about this. It is important that languages have both vague and precise ways of speaking. It is not, for instance, false to say that the sun rose about 6:00 this morning, but such a statement is relatively vague when compared with "The earth's horizon dropped to reveal the sun at 5:58:16 a.m., Central Standard Time, as observed from the west side of Tyler, Texas." Thus, the fact that "piety" is a vague term in no way impairs its usefulness for analysis.

---

86 Revised slightly from original publication as *Geneva Papers* 2.1 (September 1985).

What, generally speaking then, do we mean by "piety"? Piety can be described as the whole mental outlook or religious "sense" that pervades the activities of believers in all areas of life. For the purposes of this paper, we shall limit the discussion to two zones of life: the liturgical and the practical.

(We might use a threefold division: liturgical, domestic, and practical. This would correspond to the division of the world into sanctuary [garden of Eden], home [land of Eden], and the outlying world where labor takes place [Havilah and the other downstream lands of Genesis 2:10–14]. Man leaves his home in one direction for the exercise of special worship, and in the other direction to carry out his cultural mandate task of glorifying the world. At the same time, the Bible presents a Divinely ordained ambiguity between "two" and "three." Thus, it is at the mouth of two or three witnesses that any matter is confirmed. Also, sometimes Scripture speaks of two special offices [priest and king] and sometimes of three [adding prophet]. Sensitive theologians have debated whether the essential "marks" of the Church are two [Word and sacrament] or three [adding discipline]. The Bible presents us with an alternation between special and general time [sabbath and ordinary time], but with "middle" times of quasi-sabbatical festivals. The approach to the question of piety being used in this paper most readily lends itself to discussion in terms of a twofold division of liturgical and practical, and thus we shall not be making continual application specifically to the domestic sphere.)

In this paper we shall attempt to cover three areas, however briefly. The first is the original structure of piety, its ruin in the fall, and its restoration in Christ Jesus. The second is the corruption of Christian piety under the influence of paganism in the early and later Middle Ages. The third is a brief discussion of the piety of John Calvin, as an example pointing us to reformation today.

PRIMEVAL PIETY: ITS CORRUPTION AND RESTORATION

Genesis 1:26–27 states that man is made the image of God. This assertion does not come in a vacuum, because Genesis 1:1–25 has already shown us a great deal about God, in whose image man is now made. Thus, while "righteousness and holiness" definitely have to do with man's imaging of God (as traditional creeds state), in biblical context the imaging of God pertains to the things God has been shown doing in Genesis 1.

God could have made the world instantaneously or He could have done it over the course of six billion years. He could have taken six seconds or six millennia. The fact that He chose to take six days is significant, for His sole revealed purpose in doing so was to set a pattern for His image. This is stated in Exodus 20:10–11, where man is told to work six days and rest on the seventh, because that is what God did. The world was designed for man, and God's actions in building up the world are prototypes of human actions in continuing to build up and glorify the world, transforming the raw materials of Eden and Havilah into the perfected beauty of New Jerusalem, from glory to glory.

God's original creation of the heavens and the earth out of nothing is inimitable. From that point on, however, God acts in ways that man can copy. He brings light to darkness, gives form to the shapeless, names the unnamed, apportions the restructured world to various kingdoms, etc. Man copies these acts of illuminating, restructuring, naming, distributing, etc. For reasons that will become clear as we proceed, let us synthesize the material in Genesis 1:2–2:4 into a fivefold sequence of actions.

1. *God takes hold of the creation.* This is expressed by the phrase "And God said." The Word of God is the Member of the Divine Trinity who acts in the world to restructure it according to the plan of the Father and under the hovering guidance of the Spirit (see Prov. 8:30; John 1:3, 10; Heb. 1:2, 3). The Father plans; the Son executes. The Son comes to do the will of the Father. Thus, the Word of God is the "hand"

of God, and so the glorified Son is seated at the right hand of the Father. Man images this aspect of the Divine work when he lays hold on any created thing, to begin to work with it.

2. *God restructures the creation.* This is particularly in focus in the first three days of the creation, wherein God separates light from darkness, waters above from waters below, and land from sea. The world, which was already glorious in that it reflected God's glorious Person, is rendered even more glorious in the course of time by being broken down and restructured. Men continually and inescapably image this action of God. If I remove a book from my shelf, I have broken down the original form of my room and restructured it. If I dig up ore from the ground and heat it so as to separate gold from dross, I am restructuring. This act of restructuring is what we generally think of as work in the strict or narrow sense.

3. *God distributes His work.* This is particularly in view in the last three days, during which God gives the firmament to the sun, moon, stars, and birds, the sea to fishes, and the land to animals and men. This act of distribution follows naturally upon work in the strict sense. After I have made something I can do one of three things with it. I can keep it for myself (as God kept the sabbath time for Himself, and as He temporarily reserved the fruit of the Tree of Knowledge of Good and Evil), I can give it away, or I can trade it for the work of someone else (barter or sale).

4. *God evaluates His work.* This is noted in the text where it says, "God saw what He had made and it was good," and in 1:31, "God saw all that He had made and it was very good." Initial evaluation is preliminary to consumption or full enjoyment. Before eating there is tasting. Thus, when mother makes a soup and distributes a bowl to each member of the family, the first taste elicits an evaluation. "Well, how do you like it?" That question comes not at the end of the meal, but after the first taste or so.

5. *God enjoys His work.* God's sabbath rest on the seventh day was not apart from the creation, but in it. God's temple is always set up in the world; for instance, in the midst of the Israelite camp, or in the

center of the land. Having tasted His work and found it good, God relaxed and enjoyed it. Similarly, if the soup is good, we enjoy a whole bowl of it, and maybe a second.

These five simple actions are very ordinary, and are inescapable. It is, or should be, encouraging and invigorating to realize that the imaging of God is not focally the performance of great, heroic acts, but the carrying out of very ordinary activities. For instance, for me to give you a glass of water means:

1. *I take hold of a glass in the cabinet, and take hold of the faucet.*

2. *I restructure the cabinet by removing the glass.* Just as God separated the waters from the waters by putting "firmament" between them, so I separate one glass from the rest, putting space between them. Also, I separate water from the pipe into the glass, dividing water from water.

3. *I distribute the glass of water to you.*

4. *You evaluate the water.* It might taste bad if the faucet has not been used for a week and I failed to run the water out of the pipe first. Or it might taste fine.

5. *Assuming your judgment is that the water is good, you enjoy it by drinking more of it.*

Such simple, mundane actions constantly and unavoidably imitate God's actions in the building of the world. Every calling in life, indeed every action in life, thus has immeasurable dignity.

Because all men, Christian and apostate, thus constantly imitate God in their work, it cannot be in the area of works that the final distinction between the righteous and the wicked is found. Rather, it is the attitude or faith that accompanies these works that makes the difference. This requirement of right faith is set out in Genesis 2 and 3 and is seen in that God required an additional step in the performance by man of this sequence of actions. That additional step is the giving of thanks, a conscious act of self-submission to God, affirming that He is the One who set up the conditions for human labor and affirming that He does all things well. The placement of this act of thanksgiving is immediately after the first step of "taking hold," before the act of "restructuring." While all our actions are to be pervaded by a spirit of thanks, an act of thanks is at least sometimes to be performed at this point in the sequence.

What is thanksgiving? It is a rendering of praise and an affirmation of dependence upon someone else. A person does not thank himself; thus, God did not thank Himself when He made the world. That would be absurd. When, however, I thank you for something, I am acknowledging that you have done something for me (acknowledging dependence) and expressing gratitude (not resentment).

Romans 1:21, speaking of all men and thus pointedly of Adam and Eve, says "for even though they knew God, they did not glorify Him as God, or give thanks." Man was created on the sixth day of creation week. He was made in the middle of the day, after the animals. Before that first day was over, God brought various animals to Adam for Adam to name. The next day was the sabbath, the time when Adam was to come before God and give thanks, glorifying God as God.

It is important to reflect on what it meant for Adam to name the animals. This was not a work of restructuring. To put a name on something is a way of laying hold on it. We cannot deal with things we cannot name. Thus, it was not labor in the strict sense for Adam to name the animals. Rather, Adam was simply taking hold of the creation.

Before beginning to work with the creation, Adam was to give thanks to God, affirming His sovereignty. Conceptually, Adam was not to give thanks to God empty-handed. Rather, it was with God's creation in his hands that Adam was to render thanks to God. This involved the dedication of his future works to God. Thus, Adam's future works would involve moving the creation from glory to glory by restructuring and redistributing it.

Adam's sixfold rite for life, thus, was as follows:

1. Adam was to lay hold on the cosmos

2. Before working with it, Adam was to give thanks to God for His gift of the cosmos. This is an act of primordial oblation, offering God's world to Him, apart from human works. It is, thus, an act of faith apart from works. (This corresponds to the sabbath as the first day of man's week.)

3. Adam would then break down and restructure that portion of the cosmos within his grasp.

4. Adam would then distribute his works to others. Ten percent would be given to God, on the sabbath day of judgment, for God's evaluation. The rest Adam would keep for himself and/or distribute to others through giving or trading.

5. Adam's works would then be evaluated. Adam would evaluate his own works, and so would other people. That portion given to God would be evaluated by Him, the part for the whole. This is an act of eschatological oblation, offering God's world to Him as transformed by human works. It is, then, an act of faith that embraces human works. (This corresponds to the sabbath as the last day of the week.)

6. The works of the unfallen Adam would be enjoyed by all, particularly by God, for whom they would be a savor of sweet incense.

There are two aspects of this I should like to call attention to. The first is that this process takes place in time. Thus, what is "good" at an early stage of history may not still be "good" later. A drawing by a child may be evaluated "very good" by adults, but the same crudities from the hand of an adult would not be given the same evaluation. It is important to affirm the eschatological character of the good, because it helps to explain the fact that the products of human work do not endure.

The second aspect of this, which also pertains to the fact that human works do not in themselves endure, is that man's sixfold action is an act of glorification. Man is God's agent for the glorification of the world. The world was created glorious but is to become more glorious progressively under the hand of man.

"Glory" is a difficult concept to describe, but clearly it has to do with the revelation of God. We know that God is fully revealed, and thus fully glorified, in all that He has made. Yet, the work of man is to reveal God even more and bring Him even more glory. This is a theological paradox, called sometimes the "full bucket difficulty." If God is fully glorious, how can the creation add to His glory? If God is fully revealed in creation (Rom. 1:19–20), how can He become more fully revealed? This is a mystery, but it is also clearly the truth.

The progressive revelation and glorification of God in history does not take place by a process of unveiling what is hidden but by transforming what is already revealed. This is the mystery of time, of growth, of history. It means something amazing, however, that even in the simplest of human actions, God's glory can be enhanced and His Person revealed more fully.

This second aspect also gives perspective to the transitory nature of human works. The great paintings of the Reformation era are darkening and cracking with age. Many have been destroyed in wars. Of Bach's five great Passions, only two are extant. All our works are like castles of sand.

Thus, it is sometimes argued that human work in the creation has meaning only in that it trains men: Adam himself is progressively transformed and glorified through the sixfold action.

While this touches an important truth, the problem is with the word "only." By itself, the notion that human labor exists only to train men reduces the value of work to the subjective dimension only. The objective foundation needed is the confession that human labor, if it is eschatologically worthwhile, progressively reveals and glorifies God. Even if the artifact does not itself endure, like the crude sketches of a child, yet the revelation of God and glorification of the creation is cumulative.

Unfortunately, this process of glorification was corrupted. The sin of Adam lay precisely at the second step of his rite. He refused to give thanks to God, because he could not do so. With the forbidden fruit in his hand, intending to eat it (an act of restructuring), Adam could not give thanks to God. Thus, Adam's original sin entailed (among other dimensions) the failure to glorify God as God (by restructuring the creation along His desired lines) and the failure to give thanks (by expressing dependence upon God and gratitude for what God had given him). Thus, the sixfold action designed for man's good was corrupted.

In Cain we see this fleshed out:

1. Cain laid hold of the creation, to restructure it into the city of man (Enoch).

2. Cain did not give thanks, or express dependence and gratitude, to God or to anyone else.

3. Cain restructured part of the land of Nod into the wicked city of Enoch.

4. Cain distributed his work to his son, Enoch, and to his heirs.

5. God came down to evaluate the works of men, and found them evil.

6. God "enjoyed" man's works by "delighting" to destroy them.

Thus, instead of progressively glorifying the world, man's labors progressively degraded it, Instead of a process of glorification, we have a process of debasement (though restrained by "common grace," the crumbs that fall to the dogs from the Lord's Table). Instead of a paradoxical increase in the revelation of God, we have an equally paradoxical obscuring of that revelation (yet God continues to be fully revealed!).

Unless arrested, this process of debasement would lead to the destruction of the world. God's promise after the Flood, however, was that never again would He permit the process to go that far. Rather, in man's youth God would intervene to set things right. That restoration, of course, entailed the whole work of Jesus Christ, especially His death under God's wrath as a substitute for our sins and His resurrection as the inauguration of the transfigured Kingdom of God.

In practical terms, Jesus set at the center of His Kingdom a rite designed to restructure our thinking and reset our course along the true lines of our calling. He did this by establishing the ritual of the Lord's Supper, which ritual restores us to the holy sixfold action:[87]

1. Jesus took bread; and took the cup after He Himself had supped from it.

2. Jesus gave thanks for the bread, and for the wine.

3. Jesus restructured the bread by (a) breaking it and (b) renaming it His body. He restructured wine by renaming it His blood.

4. Jesus distributed it to all present.

5. They all tasted of it. "O taste and see that the Lord is good" (Ps. 34:8). All but one evaluated it as good. Judas evaluated it as bad—assuming for the sake of argument that Judas was still present when the Lord's Supper was instituted, a disputed point.

6. (After Judas left) The godly disciples remained with Jesus, enjoying His fellowship and teaching for a time (John 14–17).

The performance of this weekly rite in worship is the heart of liturgical piety, and this is seen in both major sections of the worship service. Its performance in the Eucharist is obvious, but it is also performed in the Synaxis. In virtually every kind of Church, regardless how non-liturgical it may seek to be, during the time of proclamation the Word is first read, then thanks is offered, and then the Word is preached. Thus, the rite as applied to proclamation is:

1. The reader lays hold of the Word, reading a portion or portions of it without comment.

2. Thanks is offered for the Word and the Spirit is requested to bless the exposition of it.

3. The Word is broken down and restructured in the preaching of it, and in that preaching...

4. The Word is distributed to the people listening.

---

87 I am obviously building on the discussion of the "fourfold" action found in Dom Gregory Dix, *The Shape of the Liturgy* (London: Dacre Press, 1945).

5. The people evaluate what they hear. By that I do not mean to imply that the people are obligated to pass some kind of professional judgment on the sermon but that inevitably they will evaluate what they hear.

6. Assuming they find it good and profitable, the people will take the message and inspiration with them as they leave and integrate it into their lives, finding enjoyment therein.

Not only is the performance of the rite in worship the heart of liturgical piety but it also restores us to true practical piety. Jesus gives us the pattern we are to follow in all of life. Because of His work we can, in Him, lay hold on the fallen creation, no matter how perverse it has become, give thanks for it, and go to work on it, restoring and transforming it progressively to the glory of God.

By transforming (in a mystery) bread into His body, Jesus provides a paradigm for the entire nature of the Kingdom. The Church is also called Christ's body, which means that as men are brought into the Church, this is parallel to the transformation of bread into Christ's flesh. Men are broken, cut in half by the covenant Word (Heb. 4:12), and restructured into the body of Christ.[88] Eve (the Bride) is cut off from her one-flesh relationship with Adam and restructured into one-flesh (by the Spirit) with the New Adam. The fallen first creation, whether bread or people, is transfigured by death and resurrection into union with Christ. Indeed, since all things are in Christ, not only men but also the entire cosmos is progressively transformed by being restructured (repositioned) into the "cosmic body" of Christ (Col. 1:17–23).

---

88 Covenant-making in the Bible always entails the act of dividing and restructuring. Thus, Eve was divided from Adam, and then rejoined to him in the one-flesh relationship. Similarly, when covenant was made with Abraham, the animals were divided in half (Gen. 15). I have discussed this briefly in my essay, "Rebellion, Tyranny, and Dominion in the Book of Genesis," in Gary North, ed., *Tactics of Christian Resistance*, Christianity & Civilization 3 (Tyler, TX: Geneva Ministries, 1983), especially 63–64. See also O. Palmer Robertson, *The Christ of the Covenants* (Grand Rapids: Baker, 1980), especially 127ff.

Thus, the structure of liturgical piety and of practical piety is the same: the sixfold action. The redemptive key to both is thanksgiving in Christ. Liturgical piety serves practical piety by (a) setting the basic pattern in the Lord's Supper and (b) transferring men into union with Christ and then sending them out to transform the world after that same image.

The distinction between the Christian and the apostate thus lies at the point of thanksgiving. It is not possible to take hold of the world with the intention of sinning and still give thanks to God for it. A man cannot visit a prostitute, take hold of her, and then give thanks before having his way with her.

The Eucharistic liturgy that grew up rapidly and organically around the basic sixfold rite of the Supper (and "eucharist" means "thanksgiving") stressed thanksgiving. This is still seen in any liturgical church today. The following, or something like it, is found in the worship of all the historic Churches that have preserved the old catholic liturgical forms.

In the Preface the officiant, after the sursum corda ("lift up your hearts," an ascent into heaven for worship), says, "Let us give thanks unto the Lord our God," to which the people reply, "It is fitting and right to do so."

Continuing, the officiant prays, "It is truly fitting, right, and salutary that we should at all times and in all places give thanks unto You," affirming that thanksgiving must characterize all that we do and not just the central act of worship. "Therefore, with angels and archangels, and all the company of heaven, we laud and magnify Your glorious name," he says, whereupon follows the sanctus, ascribing praise to God for His holiness.

The eucharistic prayer that follows includes thanksgiving as well, with such words as "Remembering therefore His salutary precept, His life-giving suffering and death, His glorious resurrection, ascension, and enthronement, and the promise of His coming again, we give thanks to You, Almighty God, not as we ought but as we are able."

After the Lord's Supper, the officiant exhorts the congregation, "O give thanks to the Lord, for He is good," to which the people reply, "And His mercy endures forever." There follows another prayer of thanksgiving: "We give thanks to You, Almighty God, that You have refreshed us with this salutary gift...." The service closes with the benedicamus, the officiant saying, "Bless we the Lord!" and the congregation replying, "Thanks be to God."

In this way, worship keys the believer into the proper frame of mind for all of life. Since men continually and unceasingly are engaged in acts of restructuring, distributing, and evaluating, it would be impossible to try to sort out every action in life and engage in a particular act of thanksgiving at the appropriate spot in the sequence. We do not ordinarily stop to give thanks, for instance, when we get a glass from the cabinet, to return to the example used above. All the same, there are certain specific times in the day when, according to the consensus of Christian wisdom of all ages, it is appropriate to stop and give thanks. The most obvious of these is mealtime. After the food has been set on the table (so that we visually "take hold" of it), we offer thanks and then get to work eating it (restructuring, appreciating, etc.). Similarly, first thing in the morning, as we lay hold on the day's chores and events, we give thanks. Public meetings used to begin with prayer before getting down to work. In this way, the simple sixfold rite is applied constantly in daily life, and in this way the Kingdom comes.

The stress on thanksgiving in liturgical piety is thus the key to practical or laborial piety. In the early Church, all life was thus worship, either the special worship of the rite or the general worship of thanksgiving in all of life (1Thess. 5:18). This worship-centered piety was the characteristic of the earliest Church. It is to the deformation of that piety in the ensuing centuries that we must now turn our attention.

The Deformation of Piety

What we have seen is that practical, daily piety ("religious sense") flows from liturgical piety. The sense of how man approaches God in formal public worship before His throne determines the sense of how man serves God in daily life. It follows from this that changes in practical piety are largely a reflection of changes in liturgical piety. At the same time, as we shall see, misunderstandings of practical piety feed back into liturgical piety. A practical piety that focuses on negation of the world rather than on its transformation will work to destroy the spirit of thanksgiving in the liturgy and will also give rise to wrong understandings of what is happening during the Lord's Supper.

The important shift in piety in the early Church was from biblical piety to "mysteriological" piety. Because his discussion is so valuable, I shall lean very heavily upon Alexander Schmemann in this section of the essay.[89]

A change in liturgical piety is not the same thing as a change in liturgy. The same acts may be performed, but with a different meaning.

Let us take as an example the elevation of the sacraments. The act of holding up the bread and wine can have several meanings. It may mean a "heave offering," in which the gifts are given to God and then received back from His hand—and nothing more. It may be seen as an act of consecration by which the bread and wine are physically transformed into something else. It may be seen as a ritual affirmation of the ascension of Christ and His return to earth in the Person of the Spirit on Pentecost. Or, it may just be something done because it has always been done and because it is prescribed to be done. Each of these "mentalities" reflects a different piety. The first is a biblical liturgical piety. The second is superstitious. The third is sentimental. The fourth is legalistic. Schmemann writes of the ability to accept and experience

---

[89] Alexander Schmemann, *Introduction to Liturgical Theology*, trans. by Asheleigh E. Moorhouse (Crestwood, NY: St. Vladimir's Seminary Press, 1966), especially chapters 3 and 4. This book is the most valuable study of this subject I have found. One point of criticism I should like to make, however, is that Schmemann fails to see that the sabbath was both Adam's first and his last day, and as a result Schmemann drives too great a wedge between the New Covenant Lord's Day (first day) and the Old Covenant sabbath (which he sees only as last day). The result of this, I find, is that Schmemann does not fully appreciate the contribution that the Old Covenant scriptures can make to our understanding of worship.

traditional forms "in new ways and to 'project' into them psychological and religious experiences stemming often from completely alien sources—such are the characteristics of liturgical piety."[90]

At the same time, a shift in piety will naturally feed back into liturgical practice, changing not only how the rites are perceived, but the rites themselves. A shift in liturgical piety becomes "the occasion for a whole series of additions and accretions in the ritual of the liturgy that have tended to destroy its original structure."[91]

Schmemann begins by noting for historians of the "Protestant" persuasion the luxurious growth and complication of the cult after Constantine ... is nothing but a tarnishing of the original Christian worship, a process of corruption.... For historians of the "Catholic" party this whole liturgical growth was only a manifestation of what was contained in the Church's worship from the very beginning.[92]

Clearly both sides have a case, and the issue cannot be simplistically reduced exclusively to either alternative. Seeking to sort out what actually happened, Schmemann suggests that the history of worship, beginning with the conversion of the Emperor Constantine, can be reduced to the following basic processes: (1) the development and complication of the external ceremonial of worship, related at first to the building of churches; (2) the increasing complication of liturgical "cycles"—the Church Year, the week, etc. ...; (3) the rapid growth of hymnody, which gradually became the main element of worship [replacing psalmody – JBJ]; and finally (4) the extraordinary development of the Sanctoral—the reverencing of the tombs of the saints, relics, etc.[93]

These developments were partially outgrowths of biblical piety, and partially changes in it.

---

90   Ibid., 78.

91   Ibid., 77.

92   Ibid., 72.

93   Ibid., 73.

The tragedy of early Christianity, as its apologists knew and keenly experienced, was that as a result of this poisoning of everything by paganism the early Church was really unable to "put into practice" her positive attitude toward the world, the whole force of her power to make the world—and in it, human life—intelligible, the whole of her cosmic inspiration. She was unable to manifest them fully and was therefore compelled to proclaim them schematically, so to speak, within her cult. Liturgical historians have taken insufficient notice of the fact that the persecutions, conflicts, sufferings, and isolation of Christians are almost completely unmentioned in the prayers and liturgical texts of early Christianity. The worship of the early Church was not only more "majestic" and triumphal than later Byzantine worship, it was in some sense even broader in its "scope" and inspiration. It resounds with cosmic thanksgiving and embraces in its vision the whole of creation, the whole of history.... Thus the freedom of cult bestowed by Constantine was, first of all, an opportunity for her to express at last what she had hitherto been unable to express fully.[94]

Unfortunately, however, this was not the only factor operating. The Church's worship did not develop in isolation from her whole life in the world. While the Church clearly set herself against the piety of the mystery cults of the Hellenistic world, even so, the change that began gradually to come into being in Christian worship as a result of the changed position of the Church in the world may be seen in the assimilation by the Christian cult of a mysteriological character, in the adoption of that understanding and experience of the cult that we have called mysteriological.[95]

What is mysteriological piety?

In the broadest terms mystery or mysteriological piety can be defined as a faith in cult, in its saving and sanctifying power. If the idea of mediation was the unifying principle in Old Testament, then the idea

---

94   Ibid., 75–76.

95   Ibid., 86.

of sanctification stands in the foreground of the religion of mystery. Through participation in the mystery man is sanctified, initiated into higher secrets, receives salvation, acquires "sanctity."[96]

For mystery religions, faith was in the cultic act itself, but

Christianity was preached as a saving faith and not as a saving cult. In it the cult was not an object of faith but its result. Historians have not sufficiently emphasized the fact that cult had no place in the preaching of Christianity, that it is not even mentioned in its kerygma. This is so because at the center of the Christian kerygma there is a proclamation of the fact of the coming of the Messiah and a call to believe in this fact as having saving significance. A New Aeon is entering into the world as a result of this fact, is being revealed in the world; faith is what brings man into this New Aeon. The cult is only the realization, the actualization of what the believer has already attained by faith, and its whole significance is in the fact that it leads into the Church, the new people of God, created and brought into being by faith.[97]

In other words, the truth (preaching, proclamation) calls men, and men come together to give thanks to God. Worship does not save men; rather, it is the reflex of saved men.

In the pages that follow, Schmemann illustrates the Church's shift into a more and more mysteriological mentality. He points out regarding church architecture that "as with all things in the experience of early Christianity, the idea of the temple or church building was subordinated to the idea of the Church, and was expressed in the categories of Eucharistic ecclesiology."[98] That is, the building was the place where the Church met to give thanks and was special for that reason only. Gradually, however, the church building was "freed from subordination to its ecclesiological meaning, [and] acquired its own independent significance."[99] Buildings were "sanctified" by rite and

---

96   Ibid., 83.

97   Ibid., 83–84.

98   Ibid., 89.

99   Ibid.

became "holy places." The important thing here is that this "setting apart" did not result as an outflow of the sixfold rite of thanksgiving but was an act of piety next to it, different from it.

The same thing happened to the liturgy as a whole. Instead of the act of worship being a remembrance of the saving character of the whole work of Christ, it came more and more to be seen as a "repetition" of the historical details of that life, in symbolic form. The repetition of these events was seen as having a power, a "sanctifying" significance.

Schmemann next turns to a discussion of monasticism. While in part a reaction against compromise, the primary motivation in monasticism was "a hunger for moral perfection."[100] This involved a subtle denial of the completed work of Christ. The rules of monasticism were "developed not as an ordo of worship, but within what might be called a 'pedagogical' system. They were needed to guide the monk on his way toward 'spiritual freedom.'"[101]

Within monasticism there was a twofold shift away from the original faith. First, there was a shift from the corporate to the individual. Instead of the Church and her worship being seen as a calling together of believers to be united in the praise of God by the one bread of the Eucharist, what came to matter was the individual and his ascent to moral perfection. This is the wellspring of schism. Indeed,

without being noticed the receiving of Communion was subordinated to individual piety, so that piety was no longer determined by the Eucharist (as in the early Church). Instead the Eucharist became an "instrument" of piety, an element of asceticism, an aid in the struggle against demons, etc.[102]

Second, monasticism brought with it a lessening of consciousness that the Kingdom has come and is the present possession of believers.

---

100   Ibid., 104.

101   Ibid., 107.

102   Ibid., 109–110.

There is no better evidence of this change than the gradual extinction in the Christian community of the eschatological doctrine of the Church, the replacement of the early Christian eschatology by a new, individualistic and futuristic eschatology. "The Kingdom of God," salvation, and perdition came to be experienced as primarily individual reward or punishment depending on one's fulfillment of the law in this world. The "Kingdom of God" or eternal life, having become "ours" in Christ, paled in the experience of believers (not dogmatically, of course, but psychologically), and no longer appeared as the fulfillment of all hopes, as the joyous end of all desires and interests, but simply as a reward.[103]

In other words, a "postmillennial" confidence in the present possession of the Kingdom was being replaced with an "amillennial / premillennial" belief that the Kingdom is still future and something to be earned. In this context, thanksgiving must naturally decline, because the "givenness" of the Kingdom is no longer affirmed.

The significance of this for the Church was that the monastic ideal became the ideal for every Christian. Not all could be monks, but all could emulate the ideal as much as possible.

Schmemann concludes his book with several illustrations of the shift in piety. He discusses the change in how fasting was viewed, from a solemn celebration of the coming of the Kingdom (in that the fast was shortly broken by feasting) to fasting as an ascetic discipline.[104] He discusses the multiplication of special days, separated from organic connection with the Lord's Day, the day of the Eucharistic thanksgiving. He points out that these days came to be regarded mysteriologically as sacred time as opposed to profane time.[105] Instead of worship flowing into life, by means of the sixfold rite as we have seen, worship came to be something "wholly other" than worldly life.

---

103 Ibid., 106.

104 Properly, fasting is a way of dramatizing to oneself the separation from the old world with a view to entrance into, or joining with, the new creation.

105 Elsewhere Schmemann has analyzed the distinction of sacred and profane as

At this point, let us summarize the shift in piety and its effects. The loss of biblical piety involved two basic elements. One was the progressive separation of liturgy from life, of worship from work. Work in the world was seen as inferior, especially when compared with ascetic and mystical religious devotions. The biblical view saw the world taken into the Kingdom, by the sixfold action, and renewed thereby. The new piety saw the world as something to flee. The piety of the Church came to be focused on a series of legalistic negations. Fasting overwhelmed feasting, and the Love Feast of the early Church disappeared.

The other was the progressive additional of all kinds of ceremonial and other religious features to the worship of the Church, features that had no organic relationship to the sixfold rite and the act of thanksgiving. Legalistic technique replaced joyous worship. Individualistic perfection replaced corporate celebration.

We could expand this paper at length discussing the details of this, but those who want further details are directed to Schmemann's invaluable study. In a similar, though briefer account, Louis Bouyer, in Liturgical Piety, points out that in the Middle Ages of the West

> the practice of the liturgy [in the monasteries, and then influencing the Church at large] ... [was] invaded by a strange overgrowth that soon developed independently, on its own.... [This] obscured the meaning of the liturgy itself; and its original primitive pattern began to be immersed in a formless ocean of inorganic prayer.[106]

What is of interest is that the same kind of problem exists in evangelical and Reformed Christianity today, and for the same kinds of reasons. There is a separation of liturgy and life.

It is not understood that the work of Christ renews the world, and this is not celebrated in weekly communion. The Lord's Supper is something done occasionally because Jesus said to, but is seen to

---

the foundation of magic and of magical piety in the Church. See "Worship in a Secular Age," included in Schmemann, *For the Life of the World* (Crestwood, NY: St. Vladimir's Seminary Press, 1973).

[106] Louis Bouyer, *Liturgical Piety*, Liturgical Studies 1 (Notre Dame, Indiana: University of Notre Dame Press, 1955), 247.

have no organic connection to weekly worship, let alone life at large. The performance of the Supper itself is usually not suffused with thanksgiving but with morbid and mournful sentimental reflections on Calvary.

Legalistic "dos and don'ts" abound, generally drawn from the grotesque heritage of American Unitarianism (anti-alcohol, anti-tobacco, etc.)—note the parallel to the influence of mysteriological thinking on the early Church. The religious work of pastoring is seen as a "higher" calling than the mundane sixfold action of laboring in the world to manifest God's glory. Religious exercises are performed as a means of acquiring strength and perfection, not as an expression of gratitude.

The fragmentary separatism of the American ecclesiastical situation directly parallels the separatism of the monks, for whom no Church was good enough. The loss of true ritual (the sixfold Eucharist) in the Church has meant (a) no organic growth and flowering into more elaborate, biblical public worship and (b) the multiplication of religious events and symbols unconnected to the one God-ordained rite (such as the altar call, Thanksgiving Day,[107] the religious trinkets for sale everywhere, etc.). Indeed, the loss of liturgical piety has frequently resulted in a belief that the performance of liturgy will work in some strange way against the interests of preaching![108]

Finally, though this list is by no means exhaustive, we may call attention to the obvious fact that all second-blessing and pentecostal groups are steeped in the errors of mysteriological piety, with their emphasis on ascent through stages of sanctification by means of initiatory experiences and their denial that the Kingdom fully comes to the believer through faith in Christ.

---

107 One of the most curious facets of Thanksgiving Day is the way in which the American mass media speak of "things we can give thanks for," without ever saying to whom we are to give thanks!

108 Which means that preaching itself has been distorted, either into the mere communication of information, or into legalistic exhortations to "do good" in a context devoid of Kingdom consciousness and Eucharistic piety.

The Reformation of Piety

The Protestant Reformers were faced with this problem at an advanced stage of corruption. Their twofold solution was to affirm the worth of every calling under God and to strip away the unorganic ceremonial accretions of worship so as to lay bare the foundation stones of Scripture and the basic sacramental ritual.

The sounder aspect, for instance, of the Puritan objection to the ceremonial of the Anglican Church lay just here: that it involved a collection of things that had no organic relationship with biblical prescriptions. The Puritan solution, in the main, was to cut away everything not precisely prescribed by the Bible (and of course, this led to many internal debates) and to forbid any organic flowering of biblical principles along true lines in worship. While that Puritan solution entailed an unbiblical rejection of maturation and an unbiblical rejection of the creation at some points, the motive for it was fundamentally sound.[109] It is also useful to note that the Puritans seem to have been quite hostile to the "mere Spiritual presence" Zwinglianism of the Anglican party, insisting with Calvin (and the historic Church) that there is communion with Christ's humanity,

---

109 On the Puritan debates over sacrament and ritual and the attempt of some Puritan divines to rebuild ritual on a firm foundation, see E. Brooks Holifield, *The Covenant Sealed: The Development of Puritan Sacramental Theology in Old and New England, 1570–1720* (New Haven: Yale University Press, 1974). The development of worship from simple to more glorious and elaborate forms is a biblical principle, seen from a study of the history of worship in the Old Covenant. This developmental aspect was not considered, generally speaking, by the Puritans. Similarly, the Puritans believed in developing the world *outside* the Church, but believed that culture should not be brought into the worship of the Church. Ultimately this entails a failure to understand the meaning of the sixfold action. The result of all this is that Puritanism can best be regarded as a movement advocating liturgical *minimalism* as a principle.

though in a mystery, in the Supper.[110] The high sacramental view of the early Puritans might have led to a re-flowering of liturgy, organically related to the Eucharist, had the historical situation permitted it.[111]

During the later Middle Ages in the West, the Devotio Moderna arose to stress the performance of monastic spirituality among the laity. In a study of the relationship between the Devotio Moderna and the thought of John Calvin, Roman Catholic scholar Lucien Joseph Richard has called attention to the depreciation of the sacraments among the adherents of the modern devotion.

Spiritualistic stress on religious and almost stoical ethical standards led the Devotio Moderna to minimize the effectiveness of the sacraments.... Because of its insistence on direct communion and unity of the soul with God, it tended to become individualistic and divorce itself from common liturgical worship and the sacramental life of the Church.[112]

Over against this, Richard points out the difference between Calvin and the Devotio Moderna. The primacy of worship so characteristic of Calvin's spirituality was not strongly defended in the Devotio Moderna. Calvin's stance on the centrality of worship reinforced his absolute opposition to idolatry in all of its different forms. The uprooting of idolatry became a real mission for him.... For Calvin worship was the sharpest weapon in his struggle against superstition.[113]

While Calvin did advocate a kind of "contempt for the world," his advocacy differed greatly, in its setting and import, from that of the Devotio Moderna. As we previously described, there seem to have been

---

110 Louis Bouyer, *Orthodox Spirituality and Protestant and Anglican Spirituality*, A History of Christian Spirituality III, trans. Barbara Wall (New York: Seabury, [1965] 1982), 135.

111 For a discussion on the abortive rebirth of liturgical elements among the Puritans, see Holifield, *Covenant Sealed*, 126–138.

112 Lucien Joseph Richard, *The Spirituality of John Calvin* (Atlanta: John Knox Press, 1974), 33.

113 Ibid., 123.

two contrary tendencies in the spirituality of the Devotio Moderna: on the one hand, a call to withdrawal from the world, to perfection in solitude, and on the other, a summons to involvement in the world that is in need of reform. We saw that the De Imitatione Christi was essentially a monastic spirituality. There was no more effective way in its thinking of preparing for the coming of the kingdom of God than through contempt for the world and renunciation of it. The monastic way of life, with its strict discipline, became even outside the monastery, a model to be followed. The Third Orders were originally intended as a substitute for real monastic life, a second opportunity for all those who for some reason had to remain in the world. This was an attempt to pattern life in the world on life in the cloister.

The spirituality of Calvin represents a complete break from the monastic type and so differs radically from the spirituality of the Devotio Moderna. Like Erasmus's, Calvin's spirituality is essentially apostolic in nature: a spirituality of the service of God in the world. Calvin's contemptus mundi is based on very different reasoning from that of the De Imitatione Christi. For Calvin, contempt of this world was achieved through comparison with the future life. Meditation on the future life makes us understand the vanity of the present. But such a contempt must not "be of a kind to beget hatred of it or ingratitude" [Institutes 3:9:3], since everything created is the work of God. This life is but a pilgrimage; we are to use its blessings only insofar as they assist us in our progress. To use them without danger, one must be truly free, indifferent. The things of this world are good in themselves, but if our lordship of this world is to be true lordship, we must refuse to be enslaved to anything.[114]

Richard goes on to point out that "for Calvin the fulfillment of the Kingdom included within it the renovation of the world, the restoration of the created order. At the very core of Calvin's eschatology

---

114 Ibid., 125–126.

was the belief that the coming of God's Kingdom transforms the created world."[115] "In a real sense the Christian must become an agent of the restoration of order throughout the world."[116]

What we can see from this is Calvin's desire to integrate life and worship, work and liturgy. Calvin desired greatly that the rite of the Lord's Supper be present each week in worship and that the thankfulness highlighted in worship be extended into all labor. In this way, the principles of the Kingdom would flow from worship into the highways and byways of all of life. For this reason also, Calvin produced liturgies that involved the people greatly in the performance of worship, for the performance of public worship was training for the performance of work.

If there is a deficiency in Calvin's program it lies in an insufficient appreciation of the ritual sequence, the sixfold action, itself. At the time, sacramental discussion was focused almost exclusively on questions of what happens to the bread and wine, how Christ is really present (if He is at all), and the like. Thus, the importance of the actual rite or sequence was little appreciated, as we have tried to set it forth in the first part of this paper. All the same, the principles set forth by Calvin (and Bucer and the rest) were eminently biblical and catholic, and we suffer today because they were unable to persuade men to follow them.

As a result, the same labor of reconstruction lies before us today.

---

115 Ibid., 175.

116 Ibid., 177.

Appendix B: Twelve Fundamental Avenues of Revelation[117]

Theologians often speak of "special" and "general" revelation, or of "natural" and "supernatural" revelation, or of "word" and "deed" revelation. While there are many worthwhile insights in these discussions, particularly in the discussions in Cornelius Van Til's Introduction to Systematic Theology, I have not found any that satisfied my quest for a full picture of revelation grounded in the doctrine of God and creation—by which I mean that I have my own concerns and agendas as a theologian and what I have read from others has not supplied what I have needed, or at least has not supplied it in the form in which I needed it.

By no means do I intend the present essay to say all that should be said about the subject of God's self-revelation to and through the creation. My purposes, as stated, are (a) to provide for myself and others a useful general conceptual grid and (b) to provide a framework that is useful in discussing the unfolding of God's plan and glory in human and cosmic history.

---

117 Revised from original publication in *Open Book* 30–34 (December 1996–August 1997).

That said, let me begin by pointing out that almost without exception, discussions of this topic seek to divide revelation into two kinds, such as "general" and "special" or "verbal" and "non-verbal." As a trinitarian schooled at the feet of such men as John M. Frame and Vern S. Poythress (who should be credited for much that is worthwhile in this essay, but who should not be held accountable for such infelicities as are doubtless present), I am disinclined to follow. God has revealed Himself in three ways, in three Persons, and we should expect there to be three irreducable avenues of revelation from Him.

The tendency to reduce everything in theology to pairs, or dyads, such as two kinds of revelation, or two testaments, or "body and soul," is, I submit, a holdover from Greek philosophical ways of thinking. For the Greek philosophers, the universe is not created by a living God, but is self-creating, an emergent manifestation of "being." Accordingly, the universe consists of two things: "being" and "non-being," or "form" and "matter," as it is also put. Since the universe is god, or somehow embraces god, then the "good high stuff" is divine while the "bad low stuff" is non divine or even anti-divine. In Christian thought, this dyad played strongly into the division between "nature" and "grace" as these developed in the history of theology.

If, however, we start strictly from the genius of biblical revelation, the very Word of God, we come up with a different scheme. The only true duality is that of the creature and the Creator. It is this duality that the various Greek and Greek-modified schemes point to, though without sufficient clarity. God Himself, however, exists in three Persons, each with unique properties. The creation adds a fourth "person" to this community, so that the creation exists in four directions or aspects, as revealed symbolically in the four faces of the cherubim. That is, creation displays the three Persons/aspects/properties of God as well as her own unique non-divine aspect/property. History is structured in such a way that the three Persons of God are revealed in order, and such that any fourth period of creation history is also the first of a new cycle of three.

For the Christian, unlike the Greek philosopher, God unfolds Himself to us in history, progressively, from glory to glory, from Father to Son to Spirit in a repeating spiral, each of which takes His Daughter-Bride to a new level of maturity. For the Christian, unlike the Greek philosopher, God is a person, and so He communicates by language. Hearing rather than sight is the primary mode of revelation, as one person speaks with another.

Trinitarian Revelation

God reveals Himself as Person, Word, and Energy (Power, Movement). In another sense, each of these is a Person (Father, Son, and Holy Spirit), but the particular property of each is different. Thus the Father is the Ultimate Person and the Archetype of personhood. The Son, as a divine Person, is the Image of the Father, and the Spirit is the Image of Father and Son.

The Son's property is language, for He is the Word. He is "spoken" by the Father as well as "begotten" by Him.

The Son also speaks back to the Father, and this requires not just "thought" but "breath" (motion, energy) so that the Holy Spirit enables the Son to speak back to the Father. The Spirit is the Energy that enables the Word to leave the mind of God and to go forth. Thus, the Spirit energizes the Word in the first place, from the Father, acting almost as a mother to the Son; and the Spirit energizes the Word back to the Father, acting almost as a bride to the Son.

There is, however, no true feminine in God, for God is creator over against the creation. The creation is the feminine. Accordingly, it is the Spirit who comes into the creation at the beginning and continually moves alongside the creation, alongside creation's apex, humanity, to enable humanity, and through us the creation, to converse back with God.

This triune communication of intra-trinitarian revelation is the ground of revelation to the creation. Thus, we have revelation through three modes: persons, language, and movement. It is an error to speak of only two kinds of revelation, such as word and deed, for there is also revelation through persons. It is an error to speak of only two aspects of the Church, word and sacrament, for the community of persons is a third. It is wrong to speak of only two "means of grace," word and sacrament, for persons are means of grace to one another (John 7:38–39; cf. 3:8).[118]

The replication of this triune revelation is seen at the level of human persons, in that we are priests, kings, and prophets. We must correct Calvin and the Reformed/evangelical theological tradition at this point, because the modes of revelation that the Bible sets forth for these three are not quite those we find in the standard literature. The priest primarily reveals personhood, so that his dress and position are most important. The king primarily reveals language, for he speaks laws and rulings and gives direction to society. The prophet is primarily the man of action, for he goes places and performs dramatic actions, blown by the Spirit. Of course, all three aspects are found in all three persons, as we shall discuss in due course.

For now, in summary:
- Father – Personal revelation
- Son – Language revelation
- Spirit – Action revelation

Three Modes in Four Spheres

When theologians speak of "special" and "general" revelation, they usually mean something like, on the one hand, the particular revelation of God directly through the Word, together with the special history recounted in the Bible, and, on the other hand, the general revelation of God through the created world, which cannot help but reveal its

---

118 John Frame, in class lectures on the doctrine of the Word of God, has shown that each of these forms of revelation is also a form of the Word of God, which is self-expressive (person-revealing), meaningful (linguistic in itself), and powerful (energetic). Thus, the Son (Word) reveals the essence of the Father and the essence of the Spirit, while the Father and the Spirit also reveal themselves directly.

Appendix B: Twelve Fundamental Avenues of Revelation

Maker and Sustainer. Yet any theologian will have to distinguish between "general" revelation through human life and history on the one hand, and through the lower creation on the other.

From what we have seen thus far, this vague distinction between "special" and "general" does not flow from the nature of God and the creation. In addition to a triad of what is being revealed, we also need a triad of spheres through which it is being revealed, and that gives us nine avenues of revelation. When we add God Himself to the three created spheres of revelation in which He discloses Himself, we come up with twelve avenues of revelation. For reasons that will be explained in due course, one of these must be divided, for a full total of fifteen avenues.

"Special" revelation is usually considered the redemptive revelation God provides to man after our fall into alienation, while "general" revelation is said not to contain redemptive content. This bifurcation is open to serious question, since the order of redemption follows the order of creation. The present essay will not, however, address this distinction. We are at this point concerned only with avenues of revelation, and we shall set aside the question of redemptive versus non-redemptive content.

The best way for us to proceed is to set this out in a scheme (see page 217) and then discuss it. In that way, the proof of the pudding will be in its eating, so to speak. I believe that these twelve categories, being a (threefold) revelation of the Trinity in the (four-aspect) creation, can summarize all the various avenues of revelation, exposing to view several that are extremely important and generally overlooked.

Immediately we must make an extremely important point, which is this: In the opera ad extra of God (i.e., God's works outside of Himself, in the creation) each Person of God is involved, yet so that one Person is more prominent than the other two. To use the popular phraseology: All of God does all that God does. Thus, theophany is not a revelation of the Father apart from the Son and the Spirit, but in theophany the Personhood, and therefore the Fatherhood, of God is preeminent, while Word and Glory (energy) are also present. We shall explore these revelational relationships as we proceed.

1. Revelation Through Persons.

God comes into creation Himself. He comes through various other things, but He also comes directly, in the Divine Person, Word, and Power (Energy). That is, we can distinguish (if not always separate) between God's Person, Word, and Power over the creation and God's Person, Word, and Power through the creation. Here we are concerned with the former.

A1. Theophanous Revelation. A theophany is an appearance of God. The various times God appeared in the time before the incarnation of the Son anticipate His final and full theophany in Jesus Christ. John 1:18 says that no one has seen God (the Father) at any time, so that with a few exceptions all visible appearances of God in history are appearances of the Son. The Spirit occasionally becomes visible, as when He gave forth light on the first day of creation and when He appeared as a dove at Jesus' baptism. Note that the Spirit never appears in a humaniform shape.

Theophanies are always accompanied by words and actions of power (miracles), so that the linguistic and energetic aspects of God's self-revelation are also present, but the aspect of theophany as such is personal. Thus, it is preeminently associated with the Father, even though it is the Father's Image (the Son) that is the particular Person present in the theophany. In a theophany, the Father is revealed by the appearance of His Divine Image (the Son) via the energy of the Spirit.

Theophanic revelation is historically progressive, or eschatological, in character. First of all, in Genesis 1:2, the Spirit appeared inside the creation, sent by the Father.[119] After the creation of man, the Spirit

---

[119] The act of creation is simultaneously the act of sending the energizing Spirit into the creation. The Spirit has traveled with the creation ever since. He has never departed. God has chosen to travel with the cosmos and with humanity in the temporal flow of the unfolding and maturation of the creation. By being with sinful humanity, God allows Himself to suffer and be grieved by human rebellion. Passages of the Bible that speak this way are not figures of speech that are needed because God is actually outside the world and beyond emotional reach. Rather, they reveal that God has chosen to be with us in this world and to put Himself within emotional reach. God Himself is not without emotion; He is rather the fullness of emotion, and of mind, will, etc.

Appendix B: Twelve Fundamental Avenues of Revelation

worked and works with humanity to bring us to maturity, from Daughter to Bride to fruitful Mother. He used angels for this purpose under the Old Creation.

The Bible speaks of angels as winds and fire (Heb. 1:7), associating them with the Spirit in the way that humanity is associated with the Son. In the Old Creation, the theophanic appearances of the Son were as the Angel of Yahweh, often as enthroned in the Pillar of Cloud (wind) and Fire. In this way, the Spirit progressively brought the Son into the world, revealing the Son. At the incarnation, the Spirit (the Power of the Most High) overshadowed the virgin Mary and brought the Son into the world as man. At Jesus' baptism, the Spirit came upon Him in full measure to guide Him.

	A. Father	B. Son	C. Spirit
GOD	Person	Language	Act
From outside the creation:			
1. Divine Scripture	Theophany	Speech	History
CREATION	Particle	Field	Wave
	Matter	Space	Time
Through the creation:			
2. Human (Father)	People	Language	Deeds
3. Covenantal (Son)	Church	Preaching	Sacrament
	Rulers	Direction	Interaction
4. Cosmic (Spirit)	Angels	Relations	Activity
	Things		

A1 Theophanous Revelation
A2 Personal Revelation
A3 Personal Covenantal Revelation:
    A3a Through Church
    A3b Through Rulers
A4 Object Revelation

B1 Word Revelation
B2 Linguistic Revelation
B3 Linguistic Covenantal Revelation:
    B3a Through Preaching
    B3b Through Judgments
B4 Relational Revelation

C1 Special Historical Revelation
C2 General Historical Revelation
C3 Dynamic Covenantal Revelation:
    C3a Sacraments
    C3b Acts of Power
C4 Dynamic Cosmic Revelation

In Jesus, humanity comes to maturity and no longer needs angelic tutors (Acts 7:53; Gal. 4:23–5:6; Heb. 1:14 & 2:2; Rev. 1–22).[120] In the New Creation, human beings are tutors in Christ. The servant priesthood of ecclesiastical ministers is provided to bring the entire Bride to maturity (Eph. 4:11–13). These overseers are to be elders, older men whose maturity then sets an example for all. In the same way, the older women are to guide the younger.

---

120   The appearance of the Son as the Angel of Yahweh in the time before the incarnation is, thus, appropriate for the age. In fact, the Angel of Yahweh is a replacement for the fallen Lucifer, who was originally created as humanity's chief tutor. Thus, before the Son came as the new Adam, He had to come as the new Lucifer (light-bearer).

Appendix B: Twelve Fundamental Avenues of Revelation

As the Spirit revealed Jesus, so Jesus reveals the Father. The Son is revealed throughout the Old Creation, at Mount Sinai dictating the law and through the prophets dictating their prophecies. The Father is little revealed in the Old Creation. What is new in the New Creation is the revelation of the Father through Jesus. Jesus, the now-incarnate Yahweh of the Old Creation, continually points up to the Father. Yet, even in the New Creation the Father remains somewhat hidden behind the Son, so that Philip could yearn to see the Father (John 14:8). Jesus said that He reveals the Father, and in Revelation we do begin to see the Father on His throne (Rev. 4:2–3). Yet, until the removal of the firmament-sky at the end of history, we shall not see the Father revealed in the cosmos.

This historical revelation can be summarized as follows:

1. The Father sends the Spirit into the cosmos coordinate with the act of creation (Gen. 1:1–2).

2. The Spirit reveals the Son, who comes into the cosmos as Angel, and the Spirit causes us to fear Him (Rom. 8:15; Prov. 1:7).

3. The Son comes into the cosmos, incarnate, and men fear (Mark 4:41; 9:32; 10:32; 16:8).

4. The Son sends the Spirit into our hearts, crying "Abba, Father!," revealing the Father (Rom. 8:15; Gal. 5:6).

5. At the end, we are brought to the Father (1 Cor. 15:24).

Since God is not a creature, visibility is not an attribute of God. In Himself, He is invisible. He chooses to make Himself visible. For now we "see" Jesus, but at the end, the Father will also choose to make Himself visible to our resurrected and transfigured sight.

A4. Object Revelation. There are three fundamental forms of Personal revelation in the cosmos, in addition to the Person of God Himself. The first, historically, consists of the angels and the created objects of the cosmos. Each of these objects, considered in and of itself, is a revelation of the Creator. Objects in the world reveal God's person by their "thereness and thatness," not by their words or actions (though such are inseparable from them).

This cosmic furniture was brought about through the labors of the Spirit during the week of creation and serves His purposes, as guided by Him and by the angels. To wit: All these things exist to train humanity for maturity. As I demonstrated in Through New Eyes,[121] these various things in the universe teach mankind about God and about humanity. Men are like birds, animals, fish, trees, thorns, grasses, air, water, stars, stones, etc. All of these, and all the rest of creation, symbolize human beings and human life.

During the first phase of human existence, which we call the Old Creation and also "childhood" (Gal. 4–5), these objects were used through the Spirit to teach us. We were "under" them in that sense. In the second phase of human existence, which we call the New Creation and also "maturity," these objects are used through the Son by us in the exercise of dominion and in our work of transforming the world from glory to glory. Thus, in a real sense, the world comes to us first as a revelation of God, as something we have no control over. This is the truth that is warped in all childish religions, such as "animism," which view created things as possessing divine fearfulness. Only as we have matured in Christ, and as we have grown from childhood into the abilities of adult maturity, does the world become something "under" us that we use and manipulate. Then the world ceases to be such a strong avenue of revelation, and God's self-revelation shifts "upward" to other avenues; that is, revelation becomes more concentrated in persons and less in objects.

God's personal self-revelation through worldly objects, coming to us as children and producing awe, embraces such things as the following:

a. Angels (spirits), or demons (fallen angels).
b. Stars, rocks, plants, lower animals, earth, air, water, etc.
c. Higher animals, which are considered semi-personal, and not static objects (Exod. 21:28ff.; Num. 22:22ff.).

---

[121] James B. Jordan, *Through New Eyes: Developing a Biblical View of the World* (Eugene, OR: Wipf and Stock, [1988] 1999).

Appendix B: Twelve Fundamental Avenues of Revelation

Additionally, human beings can use the furniture of the world as symbols of God and of His image, man. This is possible because these things already are symbols of God, avenues of revelation. When man takes the things of the world and makes them into symbols, he acts creatively, with maturity, instead of merely receptively, as a child.

For this reason, the various articles of furniture, tools, curtains, etc., of the Tabernacle and Temple are each symbolic of human beings. They are all "fabricated persons," whose construction, whose placement in relation to other objects, and whose use portray aspects of human personhood, which is itself a copy of the Divine person. God Himself dictated the form of these objects, but they were made by Spirit-led men (Exod. 31:1ff.), so they stand in the middle between God's original creation and man's symbolic creations.

A few other comments are necessary at this point. The cosmos consists of substance (matter), space, and time; and things in the universe can be considered in terms of their peculiar particle aspects, their relationships with other particles in the field of existence, and their movement through the wave of time, as they alter and change in themselves and in their relationships. These aspects of the cosmos, considered as a whole, reveal the three Persons of the Trinity; to wit:

1. The distinctive quality of any given substantial object, its particularity, reveals the unique particularity of each Person of God, and thus primarily of the Father.

2. The relationships of objects in the spatial field of the cosmos reveal the linguistic connections between the Persons of God, and thus primarily of the Son-Word. (We shall take up the relationship of language to spatial fields below.)

3. The movements and changes of objects in the wave of time reveal the movement and transforming energy of the Persons of God, as they relate to one another actively, and thus particularly reveal the Spirit.

Reflect for a moment on how we as particular human beings relate to space and time. The relationship of things in space is seen with the eye and determined by and understood by language. A sense of proper timing, and a sense of the times in which one lives, is not something that can be taught so much as it is something that is caught. The mode of spatial, relational understanding is that of the Word primarily, while the mode of temporal understanding is that of the Spirit primarily. We shall return to these matters as we proceed.

A3. Personal Covenantal Revelation. A second class of particles consists of human beings who have status as leaders among other human beings: parents, husbands, masters, overseers, elders, older siblings (especially firstborn sons), rulers, governors, etc. Such rulers have a covenantal relationship with those they rule. That rule will be exercised through words and deeds, but here we are considering the rulers as such, as symbols or revealers of God's lordship.

As angels yield their oversight of the world to humanity, so the Spirit yields to the Son. The Spirit is no longer bringing the (preincarnate and then infant) Son into the world; rather, the (now mature) Son sends the Spirit at Pentecost. This is not an absolute change in history, but a relative one, for in one sense the Spirit is always bringing the Son and the Son is always sending the Spirit, in all times.

The first Spirit-made ruler was Noah, after the flood, and this is a picture of the New Creation when humanity ascends in Christ to full rule over the cosmos (in principle, at least).[122]

Rulers are representatives of the Son, brought by and moved by the Spirit, whose job it is to bring all humanity to maturity through sacrifice. As Jesus died for His Bride, so the husband must be ready to die for his wife, the parent for his or her child, and the ruler for his people (by defending them in combat, as David was willing to fight Goliath when Saul would not).

It might seem that rulers should preeminently picture the Father rather than the Son. From one perspective, that is doubtless the case; and since all three Persons are involved in all of these avenues of revelation, it is certainly a legitimate perspective.

---

[122] On Noah's ascension, see my "The Sin of Ham and the Curse of Canaan," *Biblical Horizons* 96–98 (June–August 1997).

Appendix B: Twelve Fundamental Avenues of Revelation

My reason for not associating rulers with the Father directly is fivefold. First, I submit that it is preferable to associate the Father with human persons as such (see below), not with human persons as rulers. Second, rule is exercised primarily by speaking words and directing other people by means of words. Thus, rule is linguistic, which associates it more closely with the Son. Third, rule always involves fear of some kind, and fear is associated with the Son rather than with the Father: At the last judgment it will be Jesus, not the Father, who passes judgment. Fourth, as we have seen, true rule is also associated with sacrifice and death. Finally, the Bible associates sonship with rule and authority (e.g., Ps. 2; 2 Sam. 7). The father is not so much ruler as elder-advisor to the mature son, who actually rules.

In addition to specific rulers, the Church is also, as a body, the ruler of this world. All authority has been given to Jesus Christ, and the Church is in union with Him. As the book of Revelation shows, through her prayers and faithfulness the Church actually determines the course of history. Thus, as a special body of people, the Church must be placed here as a particular avenue of revelation from God, for the Church (to the extent she fulfills her calling) reveals God to the world.

The many different kinds of superior-inferior relationships in humanity provide many avenues and aspects to this category of "authority revelation."

Now, the avenues of Personal Covenantal Revelation, which I originally thought to term Authority Revelation, must be grouped under two main heads. Rulers are over other people, while the Church is in a sense "under" other people, "ruling" through prayer and service and sacrifice. The history of the Kingdom begins with the work of the Church, and climaxes in the production of mature godly rulers in every sphere of life. The goal of the Church is the discipleship of nations into theocracies, where Jesus is recognized as king.

In terms of Personal Covenantal Revelation, the Church reveals the glory of Christ's lordship by serving and suffering and teaching, all the things that initiate history over and over again. The Church manifests the glory of the cross. The other spheres of life reveal the glory of

Christ's lordship primarily by ruling and passing judgments, the things that maintain history and bring it to places of relative consummation. These other spheres manifest the glory of the ascension.

In all the forms of Covenantal Revelation, as we shall see, there is a mutual relationship between above and below, server and served, lord and servant, etc., which point to the relationship between God and man. Such covenantal relationships are at the opposite pole from casual relationships. Such strong relationships form larger "particles" of their own, such as families, nations, and churches. Each of these is an avenue of revelation about man and God.

A2. Personal Revelation. Preeminently, of course, human beings are the images and likenesses of God the Father. This is true of all people, of people as people. The goal of history is for all people, or at least all the elect, to grow into the fullness of God-likeness.

The concept of "image" is static. Human beings simply are the images of God, whether in heaven, earth, or hell. So, apparently are angels, though in a different way. The image of God is not something in man, or an aspect of man, that may be lost or diminished or increased; rather, man simply is the image of God. The concept of "likeness" is dynamic. Human beings grow in the likeness of God, or else depart from it (Gen. 3:22). Angels apparently do not grow in this sense.

The many different kinds of human beings—races, cultures, individuals, the two sexes, etc.—provide many aspects to this avenue of "personal revelation."

This brings me to a comment on what I consider to be an error in Reformation theology, which is that the sacraments are considered "visible words." That is, they make Christ visible. In fact, visibility has nothing to do with the sacraments. Baptism is tangible, while the Supper is edible; neither is to be gazed at. Moreover, they are primarily not "words," for the Word in worship is the Scripture and its proclamation. They are, rather, works of the Spirit: miracles. The closest thing to a "visible word" would be the human person, especially the human face.

Appendix B: Twelve Fundamental Avenues of Revelation

Several implications flow from this first group of considerations. First (A4), nature and natural objects reveal God to the eye of faith. The study of nature is the study of the design of the Spirit, and from it we learn how God designs things and how we as His images can design things, thinking His thoughts after Him.

Second (A3), rule and authority reveal God to the eye of faith. The study of government, in church, state, family, business, etc., is the study of the Son, and from it we learn how God governs things and how we as His images can govern things. We learn positive and negative things, because we live in a world held captive under sin. Yet, the Christian must learn to see the face of Christ in all rulers, even in evil ones to the extent that they actually rule and govern.

Finally (A2), the study of persons and of human life and of how human beings are constituted is a study of God. The human body-soul-spirit complex is the image of God the Father, the Person, and a faith-full examination of the human person is a revelation of the nature of God. For instance, what does it mean that the human person, unlike any animal, has the ability to fall prostrate before a ruler, to kneel in submission, to stand to receive orders, to sit forward to pay attention, to sit back to judge and evaluate, to recline to eat, to dance and leap in ecstatic worship, to engage in sexual relations face-to-face, etc.? All of this is revelatory.

Thus, in summary, we have found four/five avenues of revelation in the area of Personhood. First, we have found that God reveals Himself as a Person through theophanies. Second, we have found that God reveals Himself as a Personal object ("particle") in each and every one of the lower parts of creation. Third/fourth, we have found that God reveals Himself as a Ruler in the human rulers of this world, and as a Servant in the Church. And finally, we have found that God reveals Himself as a full Person in the personality and total constitution of each and every human being.

We have thus far considered revelation apart from language and activity, and to these we now turn.

2. Revelation Through Language.

By revealing Himself as Word, God reveals Himself as Language. We are not speaking here of the Bible in particular, but of language as such. Language, its various forms and aspects, is a revelation of God. This is one of the most important avenues of revelation that is generally overlooked in discussions of "special" and "general" revelation.

B1. Word Revelation. God states that He is Word, and this is associated with the Son, the second Person of the Trinity. God is Alpha and Omega, the first and last letters of the Greek alphabet, and thus also Aleph and Tav, the first and last letters of the Hebrew alphabet.[123] A number of the psalms, four chapters of Lamentations, and some other Bible passages are structured as a list of 22 items each beginning with a successive letter of the Hebrew alphabet. God is not only Alpha and Omega but Alpha through Omega; not only Word, but Alphabet!

It is important to see that God comes to us, as Word, first as Speech and then as Scripture. Hearing involves submission, while reading involves much less. I cannot close my ears, but I can close my eyes. I cannot go back and listen again to something I hear (before modern audio recording technology), but I can go back and re-read and meditate on what I read. The first hearing of something comes as a new thing, as an authority that I must either accept, reject, or set aside for future reflection.

For this reason, there is a great stress in the Bible on hearing the Word of God. We are to listen to it in Church, submitting to the words of the reader, and hearkening to its amplification in the sermon. If all we do is study the Bible, without hearing it, we have dominion over it. The goal, of course, is for it to have dominion over us.

Once we have heard something, we can "write it down" in our memory and meditate on it. Memory, however, is notoriously selective, and that is nowhere more true than in moral matters and in matters

---

[123] The oracle kept in the pouch of the high priest's ephod was called Urim (beginning with Aleph) and Thummim (beginning with Tav).

relating to God. Sin means that we shy away from God and readily forget what He says. "Oral tradition" is no trustworthy safeguard of memory, despite what many early twentieth century scholars maintained.

Thus, writing has been with humanity from the beginning. It has always been necessary to write down things that have to be remembered, especially contracts and covenants. Long before he died, we can be sure that Adam was writing things down in some fashion. It is no surprise, then, that the God who speaks is also a God who writes down what He has already said. He spoke the Ten Words and then wrote them down Himself. He dictated laws to Moses and sermons to Isaiah, who then proclaimed them. They were written down, to be a memorial for all time. Note in this regard especially Jeremiah 36:2, where Jeremiah was told to write down all the messages God had been giving him to proclaim over the years. Speech comes first, and then the creation of a memorial through writing.

Once again, then, we see an eschatological dimension to linguistic communication. First God speaks, exercising direct authority over us in our childhood. Then God causes things to be written down, giving us more authority over His words so that we reflect on them, compare them, and expand upon them by making applications. In fact, the four fundamental periods of biblical history reveal this sequence twice:

1. The Law period (Genesis-Joshua) is primarily a time of dictation.

2. The Kingdom period (Judges, Ruth, Samuel, the five wisdom books) is a time of revelation by inspiration.

3. The Prophetic period (the rest of the "Old Testament") is primarily a time of dictation, when God dictated to the prophets.

4. The Gospel period (the "New Testament") is, except for Revelation, a time of revelation by inspiration.

Books of vision, like Daniel, Zechariah, Ezekiel, and Revelation, lie in between dictation and inspiration, for God shows things to the prophets, and the prophets write up the matter under inspiration.

I should add that whether dictated, inspired, or revealed through vision, the Word of God is equally inerrant and infallible. I might also add this:

Dictation – Son (words from God)
Inspiration – Father (out of the personal reflections of the writer)
Visionary Revelation – Spirit (visible mode)

B2. Linguistic Revelation. Linguistic revelation is different from revelation through things because while God is not visible and is not material (not a creature), God is language. He is Word. We must, of course, maintain the distinction between Creator and creature in the area of language, but the analogy between the two is "closer" and more pregnant than the analogy in the area of visible objects. We see this in that God in Himself is a linguistic being, while in Himself He is not visible. Thus, God demands that His worship must be through language, and in no way through images and icons.

Since language is an attribute of God, the study of language is a study of a revelation of God, and perhaps more particularly, a study of human beings, the images of God. Human languages are a revelation of human existence; linguistics is correlative to anthropology. The study of language is the study of the medium between one person and another, including between God and human beings. Throughout his writings and lectures, Eugen Rosenstock-Huessy provides valuable insights into the revelatory character of language as such, calling for a complete reevaluation of grammar and linguistics on a Christian base.[124]

Because language is an attribute of God, linguistic aptitude is a characteristic of God's people, while linguistic ineptitude is a characteristic of rebels. In a society under the influence of the Bible, languages improve in precision and populations become better speakers and readers. When Christianity declines in a society, as it has in Western civilization, the result is a decline in literacy and in

---

124 See especially his *Speech and Reality* (Norwich, VT: Argo Books, 1970).

linguistic precision. When the Spirit comes tongues are loosed, as at Pentecost. In hell all is silent: No one desires to communicate with anyone else, for each is turned in upon himself. For a fine picture of this, see C. S. Lewis's novel The Great Divorce.

The original language that God taught Adam was almost certainly Hebrew. Some language was spoken before Babel, and it was either Hebrew or something else. Why would it be some other language? Moreover, the names in the early chapters of Genesis are Hebrew words, and the words spoken by God have some double entendres and puns in Hebrew. All of this strongly implies that Hebrew was the language of that primordial revelation.[125]

In such a line of thought, Hebrew was the primordial language, perfectly fitted to man's first stage of life; and it will always be the language to which we corporately must return as we repeatedly re-start our lives in the covenant. At Babel, however, Hebrew expands to become the germ of many languages, with different configurations, which then multiply further. This is the glorification, the maturation, of language in history. The verb system in Hebrew, for instance, is built up largely of voices, with tenses only implied; certain other languages are built up largely of tenses, with only a few voices. This diversification, affirmed and sealed at Pentecost, is not to be undone; rather, each language has its own perspective on God, humanity, and the cosmos. In the world to come, we will be learning all these languages, and enjoying all these millions of perspectives on God.

Someday someone will have to study Hebrew with a view to how it is fitted to be the primordial language and the language of God's Word in its first three installments (with a little Aramaic in the third). What does it mean that the primordial language is so largely built up of voices (modes, stems)?

Now, each language implies all the others, and so all truth can be expressed in each language, though some languages are more felicitous for one purpose than another. It is hard to translate some things from

---

[125] For a fuller discussion, see my review of Isaac E. Mozeson, *The Word: The Dictionary that Reveals the Hebrew Sources of English* in Open Book 27 (June 1996).

Dutch to English, but if you use enough words, you can do it. Once we know them all, however, we can use the right language for the right purpose.

What language do we speak in heaven? All languages, not some other language. Learning languages in heaven will be learning new appreciations for the Word. It will be a neverending delight.

The vast number of languages and dialects, with their "body language" and tonal sing-song, provide a tremendous variety of avenues of "linguistic revelation." The dances and musics of various peoples are related to their body language and the tones of their speech.

B3. Linguistic Covenantal Revelation. There is a middle kind of linguistic communication that stands between general language and the Word of God as spoken into the creation from God Himself, and that is the proclamation of the Word, preaching, and with that, the kind of language that initiates and maintains covenants in history among men and between men and God.

The Bible maintains an authority over all languages, for when the Bible is translated into a language, that language is "Hebraized" to some extent and is reformed to become a more fit vehicle for the Word of God. This does not mean every language is to be Hebraized as a whole, but rather that every language receives a special "priestly" form for use in its relationship with God, which form is a Hebraized version of that language. Worship and our engagement directly with God continue to be the first aspect of human life, setting the course for all else, and thus it is appropriate that the first language be used (in translated form) at that point in human life and culture. The involvement of certain human beings in this work of translation—those who have the abiding form of the gift of tongues—places this work in the middle between the original Word of God and ordinary human language.

Similarly, the preaching of the Word in the context of official worship, where the community is officially gathered under her leaders and in the context of the Lord's Supper, has a certain power and authority not present at other times. And, flowing from this occasion, and then flowing back into it, are the times when the Bible is taught and studied and applied more generally by anyone able to teach and apply it, as when one person encourages another by quoting and applying specific passages or teachings of the Bible.

The Spirit-led proclamation of the Word of God mediates the Word into human life and thus is a special linguistic event, different from ordinary language. Preaching, thus, is a distinct avenue of Divine revelation.

Preaching is biblical study and teaching that takes place in worship, in a setting of covenant renewal. We must make a distinction between language that is merely descriptive or conversational and language that initiates future states of affairs or maintains those states of affairs. Preaching and evangelism are one form of such language. Evangelism initiates people into God's family covenant and preaching maintains it, renewing the covenant. Similarly, law codes and national constitutions and covenants consist of language that creates societies, and the decisions and proclamations of judges and rulers maintain such societies.

As above, we must distinguish between two kinds of Linguistic Covenantal Revelation. The covenantal language in the Church is fundamentally protological; that is, it creates a new world. (Thus, it is "Hebraized.") Preaching continually calls us out of "Egypt" and into God's Kingdom. We start over again in the Church, week by week, as worship on the first day of the week ushers us forward.

By way of contrast, the covenantal language in other spheres of life is fundamentally eschatological. A marriage comes about after a time of courtship. A nation is formed out of a crisis in history, as at the Exodus from Egypt or as with the Constitution of the United States. Law codes are formed based on prior experience, though they also determine the future (since the law is also a teacher). The words of judges conclude cases at law.

Of course, all covenantal spheres of life employ both protological and eschatological language, both teaching and testing, both rules and judgments, etc. I hope it is clear enough, however, that there is a fundamental temporal difference between the most powerful forms of covenantal language: the language that creates a new world and the language that develops into history and eventually closes an old one. The Church is primarily oriented to the former, while the other spheres of life are primarily oriented to the latter.

Thus, for 430 years the Hebrews possessed the constitutive, prophetic words given through Abraham, Isaac, Jacob, and Joseph—words of genesis, beginnings. They had these kinds of covenant words, but not the covenant words of the Law that constituted Israel as a nation. That came later. Even then, God constituted Israel as a nation with priests but not with kings. The kings came later still, when God decided the people were ready to be given David. At two levels, then, Church preceded nation, Church-covenant words preceded national-covenant words. In both cases, the nation-constituting covenant words came after periods of crisis (the sojourn in Egypt and the period from Eli to Saul), as did the covenant-initiating words to Abram after the Babel crisis. To see a purely initiatory covenant we have to go back to Adam.

So, Linguistic Covenantal Revelation is a particular kind of language. This is the kind of language that gives direction to people. We can call it directive, but I prefer to call it covenantal. The Bible itself is this kind of language, as it comes from God. Man as the image of God also utters this kind of language.

This kind of language is revelatory in a particular way, different from ordinary language. It reveals man as the image of God, as the ruler of creation, as having authority over other persons in various ways, etc. It is the particular kind of language used by rulers as they rule and the particular kind of language used by the Church as she acts as the hidden servant-government of the world.

Such constitutive or covenantal language has many aspects or dimensions, all of which are avenues of revelation about God, such as:

Constituting covenantal documents.
Law codes.
Legislation.
Decrees.
Songs for use in directing life (like the Psalms).

Appendix B: Twelve Fundamental Avenues of Revelation

Pointed questions designed to elicit reflection.
Prayer.

B4. Relational Revelation. There is a kind of communication that takes place between the various semi-persons (higher animals) and objects in the lower creation. Our general scheme requires us to regard this as another avenue of revelation, which I am calling Relational Revelation. To start with, consider the way animals communicate with each other, the way your cat and dog tell you things, and the way angels and God communicate with the lower aspects of creation.

In a sense, the linguistic ability of human beings counts for and represents the whole creation, for humanity is the leader and acme of revelation. Plants convert earth, air, water, and fire (light) into food, which animals and human beings eat, and humans also eat animals. In this way, humanity eats into itself the cosmos and transforms the cosmos into full personhood, and through human speech the cosmos speaks.

Yet we know that some kinds of speaking occur in the higher animals, and this will have to be considered as another dimension of linguistic revelation. Indeed, there may be a great deal more going on in this area than we are presently aware of.

Let us stop thinking about language for a moment and consider instead that all the objects in the cosmos exist in relationships with one another. This is true of human beings as well and of all things as they relate to God. This is the spatial or field aspect of created existence, and it is a manifestation of the Son, who is Word.

Now let us return to language. Language sets things in relationship with one another. For instance, certain words are used to create the relationship of marriage, or to create a new nation, or to baptize a person into the Church. Laws and judgments set persons into relationships with one another: taxpayer and bureaucrat, guilty and innocent, etc.

All language expresses relationships. Performative language, as we have just indicated, creates relationships. Declarative sentences express relationships ("That house is white"; "John went to the store"). Commands express relationships between persons ("Bring me my slippers!"). Interrogations call relationships into question ("Where is my book?" "Adam, where are you?"). General patter either lubricates human relationships ceremoniously, or wrecks it through gossip.

Thus, language is relational, spatial. Sentences can be diagrammed, laid out in relationships in space, visible to the eye.

Now, what I must write next may baffle some readers, but please bear with me. There is evidence to suggest that something like language exists as a field in the universe as a whole and moves between objects of the same kind. We can start with the Bible. Colossians 1:17 says that all things are connected together in and through the Second Person of God, the Word. Similarly, Hebrews 1:3 says that the Son upholds all things by His powerful word.

Moving from such hints in the Bible, let me call attention to the work of Rupert Sheldrake.[126] Sheldrake presents experimental evidence to show that communities of the same kinds of creatures are linked throughout space by fields of "morphic resonance." For instance, if a group of mice is trained over a period of time to perform certain acts in New York, another group of mice trained in Sydney six months later will learn the same acts in a shorter period of time. Clearly, there is no biological explanation for this, and Sheldrake argues that the explanation lies in a kind of communication among all mice.

Sheldrake's work explains the seemingly impossible links between certain animals and the world itself: the way fish find their way back to spawning grounds, or the way an abandoned cat will travel a thousand miles to come home.

The evidence presented to back up this theory is not limited to animals, but also extends to non-living things and plants as well. One experiment involved crystals. A new kind of crystal was precipitated out of a solution, a process involving a certain amount of time. Later on, the same crystal precipitated faster and more easily.

---

[126] *A New Science of Life: The Hypothesis of Formative Causation* (London: Blond & Briggs, 1981); *The Presence of the Past: Morphic Resonance and the Habits of Nature* (New York: Vintage, 1989); and *Seven Experiments That Could Change the World* (New York: Berkeley-Riverhead, 1995).

Sheldrake's interpretation of this phenomena smacks far too much of pantheism, but his evidence is what is of interest to us. This is not the place to go farther with this. I only want to show that there may be good reason to believe that something like language operates in every aspect of the cosmos to create relationships. This linkage of communication is itself a revelation of God.

One final point along these lines. We saw above that angels were particularly involved in revealing God's truth to us when we were children in the Old Creation. Angels used animals, stars, plants, etc., for this purpose. It may be that angels maintain the lines of communication between the parts of creation.

3. Revelation Through Event.

Thirdly, God reveals Himself through actions, His own and those of His creatures.

C1. Special Historical Revelation. By this we mean the actions of God Himself in the sphere of cosmos and history, particularly as focused in the special covenantal history of the Old Creation (from creation through the apostolic age).

We can distinguish several kinds of special actions by God. The first is the act of direct creation, bringing into being something that did not previously exist. One example, obviously, is the creation of the cosmos itself. Another is Jesus' changing water into wine at the wedding feast at Cana, for the grape molecules, as well as such sediment as might have been found at the bottom of the jars, were created out of nothing. Another is the turning of the Nile river and all the waters of Egypt into blood. Both of these creative miracles were the first God performed as part of a larger series during the two exceptionally important periods of covenant-making. It is likely that the provision of manna from the sky during the wilderness wanderings is another example of creation out of nothing.

A second kind of direct action by God consists of acts of transformation, whereby God transforms something that already exists by using powers that do not exist within the cosmos itself. The various resurrections performed by God in the Bible fit into this category, as doubtless do some of the healings.

A third kind of direct action by God consists of works of extraordinary providence that are timed to coincide with prophetic predictions. I have in mind bringing millions of frogs over the Egyptians all at once, or bringing vast swarms of lice and flies. Some of the healings might fit here also.

Yet another kind of direct action involves symbolic demonstrations of Divine power, such as walking on water (which recalls the hovering of God over the creation in Gen. 1:2).

We could probably come up with other categories as well, but these suffice for our purposes.

In the main, God's special miraculous acts are part of the Old Creation history, and these miracles are particularly grouped around times of covenant making: the original creation, the Flood, the Exodus from Egypt, the formation of the Remnant Covenant under Elijah and Elisha, and the coming of the New Covenant. Miraculous events done by God have occurred also in the history of the Church from time to time.

Also here we must consider God's special guidance "behind the scenes." God generally guides all of human history "behind the scenes," but the history recorded in the Bible involved special guidance as God brought His original covenant with Adam to maturity in Christ. This special history involved the fulfillment of previously-revealed prophecies, and that is what distinguishes it from the more general providential guidance of God in history.

C2. General Historical Revelation. Since man is the image of God, human life at all levels reveals God. The biographies of individuals reveal God, as do the histories of families, churches, businesses, schools, nations, civilizations, and human history as a whole. Because man is sinful, much of what is found in such histories reveals God by way of contrast, but it still is inescapably revelatory.

In contrast to Special Historical Revelation, General Historical Revelation is directed by human beings rather than by God. Human beings are the actors in history, and so history tells us "more" about the images of God than about God Himself.

Thus, human history is not just "one thing after another," as the saying goes. Rather, it reveals the nature of man and the nature of God.

As miracles pointedly reveal God by forcing our attention, so crisis times in history are "more" revelatory than ordinary times. In crisis, people act according to their basic natures, for good or ill. The various works of Eugen Rosenstock-Huessy and of René Girard are particularly valuable in exposing some of the revelatory aspects of social upheavals, revolutions, and crises.

Yet, the ordinary day-to-day actions of human beings also teach us about God. Human beings like to dress well, because God is robed in glory. Human beings eat, incorporating other things into themselves, and God "eats" us into His fellowship (see Rev. 3:16, as well as the whole sacrificial system). Human beings study and investigate the world. Human beings rework and transform the world. All the things that human beings do reflect the things that God does.

C3. Dynamic Covenantal Revelation. As there are certain special persons and groups of persons (i.e., rulers and the Church), and special covenantal words spoken by such persons, so there are special covenantal deeds done by them. All such special deeds are revelatory.

First of all, the general ruler-ruled relationships. The particular deed that the state does is to bear the sword. The magistrate may go to war and he may put people to death. Such events are crises in society or in the lives of individuals. The ruler may also command taxes, maintain roads, and do other things that are less of a crisis nature, but all of which display his position as covenant head of a certain society in a certain aspect. All of these things are things that God also does, and so the covenantal deeds of the ruler reveal things about God.

The particular deed that the husband and wife do is sex. In sex, the husband takes the wife to himself. He is fundamentally active and she is fundamentally passive: He penetrates her. This interaction is pleasurable and non-threatening in a good marriage. It reveals how the Persons of God fully enjoy being one with each other, and also how the creation is passive under the penetrating and life-giving actions of God.

When covenants and contracts are engaged, they are normally sealed with a meal. The covenant meal is revelatory, since both parties eat the same food at the same time in the same place. Thus, the two parties become one by taking the same food into themselves, which food is transformed into each of them. This is a form of union and communion that is the opposite of sex in certain ways, but like sex it is pleasurable and reveals how the Persons of God enjoy being one with each other and with Their friends.[127]

Let us now turn to Dynamic Covenantal Revelation in the Church. Here we are concerned with the revelatory character of the sacraments, which like the other actions we have studied spring from the energy of the Spirit. The sacraments are primarily the dynamic work of the Spirit. As the Spirit is sent by the Son, certain words are spoken first, and then the action is performed. "Do this," said Jesus, not "Contemplate this."

The word "sacrament" is not found in the Bible, and there is always discussion as to what makes something a "sacrament." We shall bypass that discussion. There are four special "miraculous" works of the Spirit that the Church performs as special covenant rites. They are Holy Baptism, the Lord's Supper, Unction, and Ordination.

Baptism makes us new persons, and so in this work of the Spirit, the Fatherly aspect of our existence comes to the fore. Unction for the sick is a kind of extension of baptism to those who need it.

Ordination sets aside certain persons as special representatives of the Son, to oversee the congregation, the preaching, and the rites. This work of the Spirit has a special relationship to the ruling/serving aspect of our existence, that of the Son.

Finally, the Lord's Supper is the act of the whole congregation, and so in this rite, action comes to the fore. What we do in the Supper is a memorial presented to God the Father, and what we eat is in a miracle the Theoanthropos, but the energy of the Spirit is paramount in the rite.

---

127 Sex is private and involves only one other person; meals are public and involve many people. In sexual union, one new thing is potentially created (a child), while in culinary union, one old thing is shared (food).

Appendix B: Twelve Fundamental Avenues of Revelation

In the order of worship, we first confess sins and are restored as persons. Then we hear the Word and pledge renewed allegiance to Him. Finally, we receive the power of the Spirit. The Spirit first binds us together as one loaf in union with Christ, as we all eat the same Bread. Then the Spirit imparts to all of us collectively the death of Christ through His blood, so that we are enabled to live sacrificially as martyrs, dying more and more to sin and rising more and more to righteousness.

Since the "sacraments" are generally understood to be avenues of revelation, I need go no further at this point.

As we move toward a consideration of Dynamic Cosmic Revelation, there is a further aspect of revelation through action that should be discussed here, and that is this: God is particularly revealed to us in times of crisis and distress. When things are going well, we forget God. When distress comes, we cry out to Him. We see His hand in the distress. All human beings do this, because all human beings know (a) that they are guilty and (b) that God is behind everything that happens.

Eugen Rosenstock-Huessy has pointed out, in class lectures on "Comparative Religion," that if we look at the heathen and their gods, we can see the kinds of things that overwhelm men and that are accordingly considered divine. Let us briefly discuss a few of these.

War and oppression overwhelm human beings. They are "gods" in a very general sense, for they are radically "over" man. Thus, the heathen identified war as a god. The Greeks called him Ares; the Romans called him Mars. Gods of oppressive and capricious government can be seen in Zeus and Jupiter. Such personifications are long gone, but the psychology remains. In the foxholes, men believe that they will not die until their number comes up, until a bullet with their name on it is fired. War pressures men into superstition or faith, or some combination thereof. War thus reveals God as a fearful threat who operates through other men. The fearfulness of war as a revelation of God is, I suggest, particularly related to the Son, the Judge, the "Man of War."

Love overwhelms human beings. We discussed sex above, as a special kind of covenantal action. Love impels people to marry. A man or woman in love can think of little else. Jealousy and unrequited love are intensely powerful emotions. Thus, every heathen society has a god and/or a goddess of love: Aphrodite, Cupid, Venus, Eros, etc. The power of love reveals to us that intensity with which the members of the Trinity love each other, and the intensity with which the Son loves His bride.

Enthusiasm overwhelms human beings. When a person is very excited, he is "beside himself." Thus, there are gods of dance and movement and enthusiasm, like Mercury. Enthusiasm makes people dance. Enthusiasm as a revelation of God is particularly to be associated with the Spirit.

Mobs overwhelm human beings. I suspect that "mob psychology" is related to the kinds of "morphic resonance" that Sheldrake discusses. In any event, a person will be "swept along" with a mob, and in the process may do things he or she would never ordinarily do. Positively, the music and liturgy in worship can form a bond among people and make them better than they usually are. Being influenced by a group is, I suggest, a revelation of the unity of the triune God.

C4. Dynamic Cosmic Revelation. The "thereness and thatness" of the world and its contents reveals God to us, and that fact is widely recognized by those who write on "general revelation" or "natural revelation." What is not generally recognized or discussed is that we are usually blind to such revelation because it does not come to us in a crisis, in such a way as to force our attention.

It is actually when nature becomes catastrophic that God is pointedly revealed. God is seen in the storm, in the whirlwind, in the volcano, in the earthquake. Such events as these cause man to realize his weakness and smallness before the God behind these events. Thus, the gods of the untaught always include gods of storm and fury, the powers that overwhelm man. As a revelation of the true God, catastrophe reveals God's power.

Appendix B: Twelve Fundamental Avenues of Revelation

Of course, we should perceive God in the ordinary activities and events in the cosmos. We should perceive Him and learn about Him from the processes of change and development and transformation in the day-to-day cosmos. But as sinners we find it easy to tune all that out. A meteoric strike from outer space is harder to ignore. A flood is harder to ignore.

Another aspect of the creation that overwhelms human being, and thus is godlike, is wine; and so every people has a god of wine, such as Bacchus or Dionysus. For the Christian, the overwhelming nature of wine reveals the sabbath of God, His eternal peaceful rest, which He shares with us.

The more ordinary activities in the creation are also revelatory. Angels used created things to train human beings, by means of their angelically-stimulated activities. Animals multiplied in the world first and discovered which plants are good to eat, formed trails to watering places, and generally prepared the way for humanity. Some animals serve man, while others punish him for his sin. The same is true of plants, with their thorns, and of the sun, with its burning rays, etc. Thus, the actions of created objects reveal much about God, about man, and about the relationship of man and God.

www.ingramcontent.com/pod-product-compliance
Lightning Source LLC
Chambersburg PA
CBHW052020070526
44584CB00016B/1839